Rave reviews for
MAN'S RISE TO CIVILIZATION

"Peter Farb has three qualities: ability to describe, see, narrate; a very interesting mind; and a grace or eloquence of feeling."

—Robert Lowell

"This is a mind-stretching book. It leaves us with a clearer picture of the developments of man . . . Crammed with information that will surely surprise—no less crammed with exciting ideas about the past, present, and future of mankind."

—Clifton Fadiman,
Book-of-the-Month Club News

"An original, challenging and insightful work . . . This book is not only a learned but a moving one."

—*The New York Times*

"Farb is an original thinker as well as a graceful and lucid writer."

—Alvin M. Josephy, Jr.

"He holds his many-stranded theme together, half by a scientist's discipline, half by a moralist's passion."

—*Time*

"It is the season's most original, challenging, literate anthropological study."

—*San Francisco Chronicle*

Bantam Books by Peter Farb

MAN'S RISE TO CIVILIZATION
WORD PLAY

Man's Rise to Civilization: The Cultural Ascent of the Indians of North America

Peter Farb

Revised Second Edition

BANTAM BOOKS
TORONTO · NEW YORK · LONDON

*This low-priced Bantam Book
has been completely reset in a type face
designed for easy reading, and was printed
from new plates. It contains the complete
text of the original hard-cover edition.*
NOT ONE WORD HAS BEEN OMITTED.

MAN'S RISE TO CIVILIZATION:
THE CULTURAL ASCENT OF THE INDIANS
OF NORTH AMERICA

*A Bantam Book / published by arrangement with
E. P. Dutton*

PRINTING HISTORY

First Dutton edition published in 1968 under the title: Man's
Rise to Civilization as Shown by the Indians of North America
from Primeval Times to the Coming of the Industrial State
Revised 2nd Dutton edition published March 1978
Bantam edition / September 1978

The four lines on page xvi are from Rudyard Kipling's Verse,
Definitive Edition, *reprinted by permission of Mrs. George
Bambridge, Doubleday & Company, Inc., Macmillan Company
of Canada, Inc., and Methuen Ltd.*

*All maps and charts were originally prepared
by William Sayles.*

Portions of this book previously appeared in SATURDAY REVIEW,
AUDUBON MAGAZINE, NATURAL HISTORY MAGAZINE, HORIZON,
AMERICAN HERITAGE, *and* AMERICAN WEST.

*Bantam Books are published by Bantam Books, Inc. Its trade-
mark, consisting of the words "Bantam Books" and the por-
trayal of a bantam, is registered in the United States Patent
Office and in other countries. Marca Registrada. Bantam
Books, Inc., 666 Fifth Avenue, New York, New York 10019.*

PRINTED IN THE UNITED STATES OF AMERICA

For Oriole

Contents

PART THREE: Societies Under Stress

Illustrations

Photographs in the inserts of this book were provided by the following:

PF   Peter Farb

RMC   Riverside Museum Collection, Brandeis University

SI   Smithsonian Institution

Preface and Acknowledgments

More than a decade has passed since the original edition of this book was completed. Some controversial ideas contained in it have subsequently been shown to be in error, while others have been vindicated; most of the material has remained valid. I have nevertheless rewritten to the extent that scarcely a paragraph remains exactly the same, not only to reflect new knowledge and interpretations, but also in response to the changing times and my own changing views. Certain ideas seemed truly important a decade ago; some of them now seem only contentious and have been modified or eliminated. Others—such as the early date for the arrival of the ancestors of the Indians in the New World —have been stubbornly adhered to because the weight of evidence increasingly is in that direction.

This book has an evolutionary bias, which I have made no effort to conceal. That bias has been tempered to some degree, I hope, by an eclectic willingness to look at the same information from more than one point of view. Some oversimplification must inevitably occur, simply because it is impossible to cover all the major topics and at the same time make room for every minor caveat and exception. As Walter Bagehot, the nineteenth-century British social scientist, put it, "To illustrate a principle you must exaggerate much and you must omit much." I have tried to keep both sins to a minimum.

No book can be written without the collaboration, both direct and indirect, of many people. Rudyard Kipling wrote:

When 'Omer smote 'is bloomin' lyre,
He'd 'eard men sing by land an' sea;
An' what he thought 'e might require,
'E went an' took—the same as me!

It is a pleasant duty to enumerate here the debts I have accumulated, both intellectual and personal. I am conscious of having appropriated freely the thoughts of three modern anthropologists: Elman R. Service, Julian H. Steward, and Leslie A. White. I realize that in some ways this book departs from or takes exception to specific points in their writings, and that occasionally some of my inferences go beyond their original intentions; but their pervasive influence nevertheless will be apparent.

Elman Service, Betty Meggers, and Clifford Evans did me the great kindness of reading the manuscript of the original edition in its entirety, submitting both my facts and my interpretations to conscientious scrutiny. Beth Dillingham has kindly granted the same courtesy for this edition.

Personal encouragement, advice, and stimulation were received from the following during the years of work on the original edition and I wish to reiterate my debt to them here: George Agogino, Director, Paleo-Indian Institute, Eastern New Mexico University; Ignacio Bernal, Director, Museo Nacional de Antropología, Mexico; Lewis Binford, Department of Anthropology, University of New Mexico; George F. Carter, Department of Geography, Texas A&M University; John Corbett, National Park Service; Clifford Evans, Office of Anthropology, Smithsonian Institution; the late J. Louis Giddings, Department of Anthropology, Brown University; Esther S. Goldfrank; Shirley Gorenstein, Department of Anthropology, Rensselaer Polytechnic Institute; Marvin Harris, Department of Anthropology, Columbia University; the late Paul S. Martin, Chief Curator of Anthropology, Field Museum of Natural History; Betty Meggers, Office of Anthropology, Smithsonian Institution; James Officer, University of Arizona; Harry L. Shapiro, former Chairman, Department of Anthropology, The American Museum of Natural History; Albert H. Schroeder, National Park Service.

I am acutely conscious of the tremendous debt I owe those field workers on whose findings I have drawn so heavily. Rather than attempt to list them here by name, I have called attention to their most enduring monuments, their publications, in my Notes and Sources. I also profited greatly from the numerous reviews of the first edition, in particular those that took exception to specific facts or points of view. In almost every instance where a proposed change seemed justified or reasonable, I have made that change. Those instances where suggested changes could not be made involved points so heatedly in dispute as to call for an attempt to adjudicate intramural squabbles in anthropology, something of little interest to the nonspecialist reader for whom this book was written.

My acknowledgments would be incomplete without mention of John Macrae III, my editor, whose wise and helpful suggestions were of great aid in both editions of this book. Amy Clampitt was, as always, of great assistance in the final preparation of the manuscript and Marjorie Weinstein once again has been of splendid aid in checking proofs; Sharon Fretwell assisted cheerfully in research and typing. The facilities of the University of Massachusetts Libraries at Amherst have been extremely valuable. I would also like to thank Nettie and Louis Horch for their unwavering faith and encouragement over many years.

P. F.

Foreword to the Second Edition

This new and completely revised edition of *Man's Rise to Civilization* is a good and hopeful moment in American publishing history. I say this for several reasons, the major one being that it brings to public attention once again a trend-setting work that has strongly and gracefully withstood the passage of that very trend it did so much to create and which indeed has kept pace with subsequent developments. Then too this new edition manifests the continued faith of the publisher both in the inherent worth of this work and in a public still receptive to words about the American Indians. Demonstrations of such faith are truly hopeful signs for us all, and here at least they are justified, for Peter Farb's words are hope-bringers. Through his writing the general reader may derive a clear, uncluttered, holistic view of the Indians, one not hedged and qualified by sentiment and special pleading. The presentation of such a view constitutes an important social service, as much now that the Indian trend has crested as before it had begun. Then as now it is obvious that we are yet much in need of the insights, judgments, and information provided here in these pages on our continent's original possessors.

For many years Indians had been dead letters as far as our publishing world was concerned, and the mere mention of the topic was usually enough to kill any writer's project. But then came *Man's Rise to Civilization*, a book so wise, factual, and dispassionate that it showed us all that the Indians were worth writing and reading about. It also showed that they had been very much misunderstood. The book's success, I believe, rests here: it forces the general public to confront and reassess its knowledge of American Indians, past and present.

For one thing, the book pushed back the chronology of humans in the New World to more realistic distances and in doing so forced us to reconsider our own position in an archaic habitat. Also, it significantly revised upward the population estimate of the pre-Columbian Americas, and this had the effect of forcing a reconsideration of the subsequent scale of destruction as well as of our fond old canard that the Americas had been nothing more than huge game preserves roamed by a handful of hunters. Both of Farb's positions have received further support within the past decade, and readers of this new edition will find that he is up to date on the recent archeological evidence such as the important new digs in California and Texas.

The other signal contribution Farb made was through his intelligent application of the once-discredited theory of cultural evolution. Darwin's impact on Western civilization was so profound that for a half century after *Origin of Species* virtually every aspect of life was tinged by some application of evolutionary theory—everything from newspaper cartoons to social legislation. Now we can see that many of these applications were either spurious or crude, and from such the infant science of anthropology was not exempt. Now in these last twenty years we have relearned the application of evolutionary theory to the understanding of specific cultures, and Farb's study of the aborigines of these continents shows us the slow drama of native cultures at work on the possibilities of their habitats, moving toward some point at which further elaboration or development is either impossible or else unthinkable. In impressive detail he shows us both the environmental challenges they faced as well as their distinctive adaptations and achievements. His vision has the additional merit of revealing to us our own exhausting of this same habitat we now call ours, and this perspective is indeed a sobering one.

Much has happened in Indian affairs since 1968: heightened public interest; the rise of Indian militancy, culminating in Wounded Knee II; and the current struggles of the tribes to regain through our courts some portion of what they have been swindled out of. The Indians have their own spokesmen now, and one or two or them have felt compelled to criticize this book. Any work so ambitious is, of course, vulnerable at various places, yet Farb's achievement remains a high one, and it is one from which Americans of all colors may derive real benefits. After almost five hundred years we have still not really understood the people who first greeted the strange boats that cut through the surf to native shores. No book can rectify such a long history of neglect, but a few can help us to understand the Indians of North America. This is one of those.

Frederick Turner
Editor, *Geronimo* and
The Viking Portable *North
American Indian Reader*

Foreword to the First Edition

This book has two great virtues. It is the best general book about North American Indians that I have ever read and it does a fine job of illustrating an important use of cultural evolutionary theory.

The North American Indians, of course, are subjects of an enormous amount of fiction. Unfortunately, however, they are largely a genre, like our romanticized cowboy, rather than a reasonable depiction of the aboriginal reality. There is, to be sure, a fairly large body of specialized anthropological theses and monographs, but these are not literature. Most are academic, pedantic, unreadable. La Farge's *Laughing Boy* is a fine book, but it is also a grand exception.

Man's Rise to Civilization is not a novel like *Laughing Boy*, however, but a scientific work designed to be informative in a very general way. I believe it is scientifically accurate. But it departs strikingly from the standard works, such as Wissler's classic in anthropology, *The American Indian*, by being readable. Peter Farb studied his subject hard for years, but he writes like a breeze, and the reader is thus not conscious of the labor.

Such a wonderfully interesting subject, the American Indians, yet how demeaned by the mediocre literature, both literary and academic. But I am not saying that

Peter Farb's book is merely the best of a poor lot. It is a very good book in an absolute sense.

Equally important is the other virtue of the book, its contribution to the theory and practice of cultural evolutionism. For over half a century American and British academic ethnology has been actively antievolutionary, or at best, passively nonevolutionary. The antievolutionary phase seems over and a few articles and fewer books have recently appeared with proevolutionary arguments. But they are, naturally, mostly general and theoretical arguments with little actual application that demonstrates the intellectual potentiality of the theory.

Evolutionary theory, basically, is about the rise of complexity, whether of the movement from simple to complex biological organisms or simple to complex cultures. The American Indians are highly variable in cultural complexity, ranging from simple hunting–gathering bands of only a few hundred people, through intermediate tribes like the Iroquois, to the affluent chiefdoms of the Northwest Coast, and finally the flamboyant empire of the Aztecs of Mexico. The average White American is not at all conscious of the tremendous cultural differences that are related to these vast differences in size and complexity.

The Indians of both North and South America are one race. Yet no cultural similarity, however general, can be discerned that is ascribable to that fact. On the other hand, literally hundreds of diverse language *families* (not just separate languages) are found among them. But here again there is no important sociocultural characteristic attributable to a language family. Some of the simplest bands, the Shoshone of Nevada, are of the same language family as the imperial Aztec!

Evidently a theory of cultural evolution is a substitute for racist and language-family accounts of the origin of cultural diversity. It holds that the origins of the major divergent forms of culture are functional concomitants of the rise of societal complexity—that is, of the evolutionary process itself. But evolution is not a simple, one-way process. The key to modern evolutionary theory lies in the concept of adaptation: Every society has a culture that adapts, more or less successfully, to an environment. Some of the Indian societies reached a dead end of adaptation, while others continued adapting in ways that made for (or allowed) the rise of greater complexity. This interesting book illustrates clearly the uses of the theory.

Many American readers romantically love the American Indian and will never stop. This is a great book for them (us). But some of us are also, perhaps unexpectedly, intellectuals: interested in science, theory, logic, history, abstractions, data, art and literature, among other things remote from adventurous Indian scouts. Here for once is the romantic subject we love, and the intellectualism we love, served up at the same time by one single author. Peter Farb is plainly one of us.

Elman R. Service, Professor of Anthropology, University of California (Santa Barbara)

Part One

◻

The Evolution of
Culture

I

An Example for
Modern Humans

THE FIRST AMERICANS

"They all go naked as their mothers bore them, and the women also, although I saw only one very young girl," reported Christopher Columbus in his journal for October 12, 1492, after making his landfall in the West Indies. "Some of them paint their faces, some their whole bodies, some only the nose. They do not bear arms or know them, for I showed to them swords and they took them by the blade and cut themselves through ignorance."‡*

Columbus was certain that he had arrived at an island off the mainland of Asia, or even in the fabled Indies themselves. The name he gave these people, Indians, has remained in use to this day. Among themselves, of course, the American Indians had no name to distinguish their people from any other, and they had no knowledge that other varieties of humankind might exist. Usually an Indian group called itself simply "the

---

* I have avoided burdening the text with footnotes, yet I realize that some readers will want to pursue further the subjects discussed. The appearance of the symbol ‡ indicates that a comment, a source, or a further amplification appears in the Notes and Sources section that begins on page 313, arranged by chapter and by page. This section is cross-indexed with the Bibliography that begins on page 331 and lists my principal sources.

people," although sometimes a descriptive adjective was added. Such descriptive names—*Chiluk-ki* (Cherokee), "the cave people," and *Hopitu* (Hopi), "the peaceful people"—were often later adopted by European settlers. Some of the names, though, came from epithets given one Indian group by another. The Sioux Indians' contemptuous description of one of their neighbors as *sha hi'ye na*, "speakers of an unintelligible language," resulted in our calling these people the Cheyenne.

As the Spanish explorers probed the contorted shoreline of the North American continent, and finally penetrated inland, they were bewildered by the great variety in the Indian societies they encountered. Many Indian groups in the West Indies and in the Southeast lived under the rule of powerful chiefs. When Cortés conquered Mexico he came into contact with a glittering culture and elaborate systems of government that much resembled those found in Europe. As Coronado's expedition of 1540–42 pressed northward into the Southwest and the high plains, eventually reaching Kansas, still other kinds of Indian societies were encountered: small bands of impoverished hunters in northern Mexico, Pueblo Indians living as tribes in large compact villages, and seminomadic bison hunters.

The Spaniards observed the diversity of customs, laws, beliefs, tools, and crafts among neighboring Indian groups, as well as the resemblances between widely separated ones; and the Spaniards did not know how to explain what they saw. Some Indian groups erected large monuments, irrigated their fields by an extensive system of canals, lived in permanent villages, and performed elaborate ceremonials; whereas others living nearby wandered about in bands consisting of a few families, collected whatever food was available, whether grasshoppers or lizards, and had no elaborate ceremonials. One group appeared remarkably democratic, whereas another had a rigid system of classes based on wealth. A few groups were leaderless; some paid attention to a headman; other groups appointed temporary leaders; and still others carried a semidivine chief around on a litter. As a succession of Spanish, French, and English explorers traveled the length and breadth of North America, the differences and similarities became even more bewildering. The Iroquois practiced torture; the Choctaw took heads as trophies; the Kwakiutl enslaved captives. The Mandan lived in earthen lodges, the Sioux in bison-skin tipis, the Choctaw in mud-daubed houses. The Sac and the Fox, when first encountered by explorers, lived close to each other in what is now Michigan, and they were very similar in language, customs, traditions, and religion; yet, inexplicably, Whites* clearly found the Sac much easier to deal with.

Most people attributed such diversity among Indian cultures to chance and were willing to leave it at that. They saw merely a continent to be won and inhabitants to be pacified. They had little time to speculate about the exotic Indian customs, or even those customs that so uncannily seemed to mirror European ones. But later it became clear that the multitudes of different Indian groups in North America, the thousands of them, could be fitted into categories that ranged from the simple to the extraordinarily complex, from the condition of "savagery" to that of "civilization." The important thing about all these speculations, though, is that long before Darwin and Wallace brought biological evolution to the attention of the world in 1858, observers of the American Indian had recognized that cultures do evolve.

---

* Great difficulty attends the search for a fitting word to describe the various peoples, mostly from Europe but also from parts of Asia, who came to the New World, made contact with the native inhabitants, and ultimately destroyed the cultures they found. Some writers describe the explorers and settlers as "Europeans," but such a word would include such people as the Swiss, who obviously were not a European colonial power. The use of "Europeans" also ignores the important influence of Asiatic Russians who made early contacts with Eskimo bands and with Indians from Alaska southward to California. Other writers have used the word "white" (spelled with a lower-case *w*), but that is unsatisfactory also. In this book I am not referring to all the members of a particular race; that would be quite unfair to the Caucasoid population of Pakistan, for example, who of course played no part in the conquest of North America. So, with much reluctance (and with an avowal that no racism is intended), I have settled upon "White." I hope the fact that I have spelled it with a capital letter imparts to the reader that I am really not writing about any particular Caucasoid but about an abstraction—a composite of social, political, and economic attitudes held by certain people, whose skin is usually whiter than most of the world's population and who exploited native peoples wherever they were encountered around the globe.

Various attempts were made to plot the Indian's cultural evolution. One well-known sequence was proposed by Lewis Henry Morgan, who saw seven stages through which all cultures must inevitably progress: lower savagery, middle savagery, upper savagery, lower barbarism, middle barbarism, upper barbarism, and finally civilization.‡ Morgan believed that each of these stages was ushered in by some particular new advance; a group went from upper savagery to lower barbarism, for example, when it learned the art of pottery. Karl Marx in 1857 proposed an evolutionary theory that began with Primitive Communism and proceeded through Pagan Society, Ancient Classical Society, Feudalism, and two kinds of Capitalism, up to the ultimate —Communism. Aside from the fact that Primitive Communism probably never existed, these stages were too much shaped by the ethnocentric ideas of European culture.

Another commonly accepted evolutionary sequence was based on the increasing complexity of family life. According to this theory, the family originally centered around the mother, and the father served merely in procreation. But as societies grew in complexity, the father spent more and more time with the family until, as in the European civilizations, the father's name was the one the child inherited. The question of whether a family or a group is oriented toward the male or the female is, however, much more complicated than this theory would suggest. Some of the Great Basin Shoshone, among the most "primitive" peoples in North America, based their descent on the father and not the mother. The Indian peasants of Guatemala are patrilineal—yet the families of mixed-bloods or ladinos, who are also peasants, are most often headed by women. And the whole problem is further complicated by economics. In some modern societies, particularly among the lower classes, the father is unable to contribute much income or prestige to the household. As a result, the major influence in the family is maternal; such a situation exists among the people of East London, England, those of Appalachia, and many Black families inhabiting the ghettos of North America.

An evolutionary sequence that has been popular from time to time shows human groups progressing from hunting to agriculture and finally to civilization. But such a broad sequence is too generalized to provide useful categories, as a comparison of the Northwest Coast Indians with the neighboring Eskimo demonstrates. They live close to each other and the societies of both are based on hunting—but that is about all they have in common. The Northwest Coast Indians were organized as elaborate chiefdoms, the Eskimo into small bands. The two groups differ also in settlement patterns, social organization, religion, crafts, and practically everything else. Lumping two such diverse cultures into the single broad category of Hunters explains nothing.

However inadequate these and other theories‡ have turned out to be, the very fact that they were proposed in such number and variety demonstrates the intense interest of Europeans in the diverse cultures of humankind. Many of the great philosophers of the Enlightenment (Rousseau, Turgot, Condorcet), like the earlier English theorists (Hobbes and Locke, to name only two), were thinking in terms of American Indians as proofs for their theories. It soon became obvious that those cultures could shed much light on the customs and behavior of modern humans.

North America is the place in the world most nearly ideal for observing the evolution of human societies and customs, institutions and beliefs, for these are revealed there with all the clarity of a scientific experiment. The story of the Indians in North America provides modern humans with what can be thought of as a living test tube, in which the major ingredients, the intermediate reactions, and the final results are largely known.

For hundreds of millions of years the North American continent was there, untrodden by humans until the ancestors of the Indians arrived, tens of thousands of years ago. They became the ingredients of this experiment in the evolution of human institutions. They brought with them only a meager cultural baggage when they migrated to North America: a social organization at the level of the small band, crude stone tools, no pottery, no agriculture, no domesticated animals (except possibly the dog). Most of what Indians were to become they would invent for themselves, for once they arrived in North America they were almost entirely isolated from the Old World. They would evolve unhampered their social and political institutions, their religion and laws and arts.

The ways in which these interactions took place are now known; and so are the many stages to which the Indian had evolved by 1492. At that time, the cultures of the American Indians represented all stages of pre-industrial political and social development, from the simplest kind of band up to the complex state. More than five hundred distinct languages were spoken in North America alone, some of them as different from each other as English is from Chinese. Every known category of religious system, including monotheism, could be found somewhere on the continent. More than two thousand kinds of plant food had been put to use, and economies had been developed for harvesting the products of the seas and the lands.

Here, in the Indian societies, was the evidence by which the nature of humans as social beings might be charted—their relations with other humans and with the environment itself, their political and social institutions, their religious systems and legal codes, and their multiplicity of customs. Answers to the problems that have bewildered thinkers since the earliest humans speculated about themselves might be found in North America. And that is exactly what has happened. The evolution of the Indians' culture has shown that human societies around the world are something more than patchworks or haphazard end products of history. The study of the tribal organization of the Iroquois, for example, gives hints about the ancient Hebrews at the period when they, too, were organized as tribes. What is now known about the power of the Aztec state can suggest much about why the Assyrians acted as they did. The varying responses of the North American Indians to the invading Whites shed light on colonialism in Africa and Asia, and its aftermath.

HOW CULTURES CHANGE

A major influence in anthropology in recent decades has been the notion of cultural evolution—as set forth by Elman R. Service, Leslie A. White, and Julian H. Steward—and this book is written from their general point of view. These three scholars, although they differ as to details, believe that cultural evolution is as much a fact as biological evolution has been shown to be. They do not, though, hold with earlier theorists who maintained that all societies necessarily passed through certain stages—from matriarchy to patriarchy, from hunting or pastoralism to agriculture, from savagery to forms of barbarism and then to civilization. Nor do they regard cultural evolution as steady "progress" toward some inevitable goal. Impoverished bands of hunters in Mexico thousands of years ago did not know that their descendants would someday be part of the sophisticated Aztec culture, any more than an apelike primate fifteen million years ago knew that its descendants would someday evolve into humans.

How, then, do cultures evolve? Why have some peoples evolved from small bands to larger tribes, while others have become chiefdoms or states? The answers to questions about different human societies usually cannot be found solely by looking at the environments they inhabit, or by noting great historical events or the arrival on the scene of great leaders. Rather, an analysis must be made of the cultures themselves. Every society is composed of multitudes of cultural elements, from baskets to religious beliefs, including social practices, tools, weapons, preferred foods, attire, and so on. Some cultures, as in Modern America, have millions of such elements, whereas some of the southern California bands probably possessed no more than several thousand elements at the time of their first encounter with Whites.

These cultural elements are in a continual process of interaction; new syntheses and combinations are constantly being produced. But whether or not the new combinations survive in a human group depends on whether or not they work in the existing cultural context. An invention or a new combination can be successful only if all of the elements necessary to produce it are present in the culture. An excellent example of this rule is Leonardo da Vinci's plan for the submarine—which was not built because his culture possessed neither the technology nor the need for it.

The Cheyenne Indians demonstrate the way in which a new combination and a new synthesis may take place in a culture. Just before the arrival of Whites, the Cheyenne had migrated from Minnesota to the plains where they practiced a primitive agriculture. All around them thundered bison, but the Cheyenne lacked the technology to substitute bison-hunting for agriculture as the base of their economy. In the eighteenth century, though, the Cheyenne obtained Spanish horses—together with the techniques of riding them—and the result was a new combination of cultural elements. Once the Cheyenne began to exploit the abundance of the bison, changes swept through their culture. New styles of dress and ornamentation were adopted. Village life was abandoned in favor of wandering in pursuit of the migratory herds. Social stratification based on wealth in horses arose in a society that until then had been largely egalitarian.

These were only a few of the more apparent changes that occurred in the Cheyenne way of life, solely because of a new cultural element, the horse. It might seem to a modern observer that the Cheyenne would have recognized instantly the superiority of the horse for use in killing bison, but that is not necessarily true. The Cheyenne possessed certain cultural features that permitted them to accept the horse and to integrate it into their society. After all, the Paiute of the Great Basin also obtained horses from the Spaniards. But instead of using the horses for hunting, the Paiute ate them.‡

Every culture is similarly made up of shreds and patches from other cultures. Consider that this book is printed by a process invented by a German, on paper invented in China. It uses written symbols that are a Roman–Etruscan variant of a Greek form of the alphabet, in turn obtained from the Phoenicians, who originally got the idea from Egyptian hieroglyphics. Our "American" culture of today is composed almost entirely of such imports and borrowings from every continent. Nevertheless, despite all the borrowing, our culture is distinctly American. The important point is not so much the borrowings as the particular ways the culture has combined the home-grown and the imported into a harmonious whole—and as a result evolved to a new level of complexity.

DIFFERENCES AND SIMILARITIES IN THE CULTURES OF HUMANKIND

Are the apparent differences and similarities in human cultures merely the result of random changes, or does some pattern exist that will explain them? Most social scientists do not believe that cultures are haphazard. But they disagree considerably about the patterns to be detected. According to one commonly argued theory, the basis of culture is biology. Those subscribing to it would trace human culture to the structure of the human brain, the nature of muscular responses, and the workings of the nervous system and glands. But here is a fallacy in logic: A biology that is common to all people cannot account for particular kinds of behavior that occur among some groups of people but not among others. A theory that traces eating habits back to the human digestive system cannot explain why people in one society obtain and prepare food in different ways from those of another, or why some observe food taboos and others do not. People in all societies possess the biological equipment for removing their hats and shoes, but it is having been born within a particular culture that motivates a Jew to keep his hat and his shoes on during worship, a Mohammedan to take his shoes off, and a Christian to keep his shoes on but remove his hat. Sweeping changes took place in most areas of English cultures between 1066 and 1976, yet in that time the English people underwent no appreciable changes as biological organisms. The shared biology of humans everywhere cannot explain culture changes and differences between societies. As a logician might state it: A variable (in this case, culture) cannot be explained in terms of a constant (the human biological makeup).

The psychological interpretation, as popularized by Ruth Benedict in her *Patterns of Culture* (1934),‡ is a variant of the biological one. To Ruth Benedict, the Pueblo Indians of the Southwest were a placid, non-aggressive people, whereas the Indians of the Northwest Coast chiefdoms were warlike. When she wrote her book, she had virtually no field experience in observing American Indian societies and her interpretations were based on observations by others, which she either misinterpreted or romanticized. The psychological description of a culture in terms of its ethos or world view fails to answer really basic questions. How did such a world view originate in the first place? Why did one society embrace a particular world view, whereas a neighboring society did not? No one denies that the human personality is shaped by the culture into which a person is born. But no one has ever demonstrated the reverse —that a culture itself is created by the personality or temperament of the individuals who compose it.

A goodly amount of data has been collected about the Yurok Indians of California; an examination of this data permits us to see whether psychology can offer really basic insights. The Yurok inhabited an earthly paradise with equable and invigorating climate, salmon in the rivers, and acorns in the forests. In fact, the Yurok had so much food available that their population was much more dense than that of most other groups living in primeval California. Yet if the Yurok society had been an individual, it would be labeled "paranoiac." Psychologically-oriented observers have described the people as being pessimistic, hypochondriacal, extremely superstitious, and fearful. Yuroks did not drink water from unknown sources because it might be poisoned; they did not mix deer and whale meat at the same meal; nor did they eat at all while in a boat. After eating deer meat they washed their hands, but they did so in a stream and not in a container of water. The bows they used had to be made from wood cut from a certain side of a particular species of tree. From the moment the Yuroks opened their eyes in the morning, their life was circumscribed by prohibitions and magic of every sort.

And it is precisely at this critical point that the psychologically-oriented anthropologists drop the matter. They have described the way in which a typical Yurok individual behaves. If pressed for an explanation as to why the Yurok behave that way, the psychologist might answer that the Yurok learned such behavior from their parents, who in turn learned it from their parents. Still, the anthropologist has failed to explain what it was that caused the very first Yurok ancestor to become paranoiac.

A much more satisfactory explanation than the psychological is possible. Anyone who closely examines Yurok economy can see that it was organized at the uncomplex level of those groups that forage for wild food—even though an accident of geography had provided them with a superabundance of food and they had developed a technology to exploit it. This interaction of technology and environment had produced an increased population. A large and dense population demands a relatively sophisticated social organization, but the Yuroks had not yet caught up with the increase in their numbers and the resulting necessity for more complex social and political institutions. Because of an insufficient integration between the political and economic levels, Yurok society was exposed to a great many stresses and strains that were manifested through interpersonal fears. The society lacked the built-in checks and balances found in the more successful neighboring chiefdoms of the Northwest Coast. The reach of the Yurok had exceeded their grasp. They were stuck with a complex social structure that they could not manipulate. So the people sought in magic, ritual, and taboos what their institutions were unable to provide.

If the differences and similarities in cultures are not due to human biology or to personality, what then is left? There remains a third characteristic of our species, our sociality—for a human being cannot survive alone and be entirely human. It is through the nature of their social and political institutions that the differences and similarities among cultures are to be accounted for.

HUMANS AS SOCIAL ANIMALS

All people everywhere exist as members of social groups, however small. A group is much more than a random collection of individuals who accidentally happen to share particular customs. The mystifying variety of Indian societies that greeted the explorers of North America can be understood by examining their social structures—that is, the web of relations among people, groups, and institutions. The social structure of a people is the adaptive mechanism whereby its members adjust to the existing ecological conditions. These conditions include not only the physical and biological environment but also the technology available for exploiting that environment, as well as the other human populations with whom they must interact. Social organization is an indicator; it is the common denominator of the group, the integrator. Social organizations are simple or complex, with many gradations in between, in proportion to whether they are composed of few or many elements; as the number of parts increases, more and more social devices for integrating them into a whole are called for.

The members of a society do not make conscious choices in arriving at a particular way of life. Rather, they make unconscious adaptations. Not all societies are presented with the same set of environmental conditions, nor are all societies at the same stage when choices are made. For various reasons, the members of some societies adapt to conditions in a certain way, others in a different way. The people who make up a society almost never quite understand why they opt for certain behaviors; they know only that a particular choice works, even though it may appear bizarre to an outsider.

The adaptation may sometimes appear so irrational as to jeopardize the very society that practices it. An adaptation of the Koryak of Siberia, distantly related to the Eskimo, is likely to strike an outsider as extremely curious. Their religion demands that every year they should destroy all of their dogs, an apparently suicidal step for a people who live by hunting and by herding reindeer. Why, then, does their religion make things even more difficult in an already harsh environment? The truth is that they are not in jeopardy, for they immediately replenish their supply of dogs by purchasing them from nearby groups that impiously breed dogs instead of killing them. The relations between the Koryak and their neighbors now become much clearer. The neighbors are content to breed dogs and to trade them for the Koryak's meat and furs. If the Koryak ever halted their annual dog-kill, the neighbors would have lost their market. They would have to go out and hunt on their own, in that way destroying their peaceful trade relations with the Koryak and substituting one that competes for game.

By examining the ways in which people have organized themselves socially, it is possible to explain why certain elements of culture appear in one kind of society but not in another. It is also possible to categorize societies according to evolutionary stages of increasing complexity. Each stage incorporates some of the traits of a simpler previous stage, to which it adds unique features of its own. An examination of the stages of cultural evolution will explain many of the mystifying aspects of Indian cultures: why Indians living at one stage broke their promises to Whites, and why those living at a different stage did not; why one group of Indians seemed peaceful and another group warlike; why certain groups appeared to waste their resources while others conserved them. Private property, division of labor, the presence or absence of priests, and many other characteristics of societies do not exist at random but only at particular stages.

Several words of caution: The previous paragraph does not state that every people must pass through pre-

cisely the same evolutionary sequence, as was once believed by those who tried to track humankind's tortuous
journey from "savagery" to "civilization." A people
may pass directly from hunting wild game to agriculture
without ever having flocks and herds; this is what happened with all North American Indians except the
Navajo, who stole their sheep from the Spaniards. A
people may even seem to retrogress by giving up agriculture for a return to hunting; many Plains Indian
agriculturists who obtained horses from the Spaniards
and then hunted bison did exactly that. No stage must
necessarily precede or follow any other stage so far as
particular groups of people are concerned. Cultural evolution can indicate major trends, but not necessarily the
inevitable course to be taken by a group, in much the
same way that a life-insurance company's mortality
figures predict life expectancies for categories of people
but not when a particular policyholder will die.

More is known about American Indians than about
any other major indigenous group in the world. They
have been observed, described, catalogued, and cross-
compared. This book will not examine Indians with a
romantic eye, regarding them as nature's noble savages
or as unspoiled children of the land. The romance of
native cultures, to the anthropologist, lies in a different
direction—in what they disclose about the roots of
human behavior. It is now possible to collate the vast
information about Indian societies, to arrange them into
a taxonomic classification that reveals major relationships, differences, and similarities. This taxonomy will
be followed throughout Part One, and will cover Indian
groups at every level of social organization—the family,
the various bands and tribes, the chiefdom, and the state
—in an attempt to understand the intricate web of relationships that makes up the whole fabric of people,
groups, and institutions.‡ Part Two will examine the
origins of the Indian cultures archeologically, beginning
with the peopling of North America, and will also look
briefly at the evolution of Indian physical characteristics and language. In conclusion, Part Three will inves-
tigate what happens to societies undergoing starvation

and disease, economic exploitation, and the pressure of religious conversion—all of which were a part of the White conquest of North America. The answer to why certain societies endured while others became culturally extinct will be found, in many cases, in the varying levels of cultural evolution they had attained.

II
Great Basin Shoshone: Cultural Simplicity

THE "MISSING LINKS"

The "Digger Indians" of the Great Basin, declared the explorer Jedediah Smith in 1827, were "the most miserable objects in creation." Actually, this disdainful name had been given to many different Shoshonean-speaking groups by Whites who saw them, apparently half starved, grubbing for roots. Mark Twain, riding the overland stage west of Great Salt Lake in 1861, reported coming across "the wretchedest type of mankind I have ever seen up to this writing." He went on to describe the Gosiute, one of those groups commonly called Diggers, as people who "produce nothing at all, and have no villages, and no gatherings together into strictly defined tribal communities—a people whose only shelter is a rag cast on a bush to keep off a portion of the snow, and yet who inhabit one of the most rocky, wintry, repulsive wastes that our country or any other can exhibit. The Bushmen and our Goshoots are manifestly descended from the self-same gorilla, or kangaroo, or Norway rat, whichever animal-Adam the Darwinians trace them to."‡

From the moment that the first explorers encountered them, no doubt existed that many of the Shoshonean-speaking Indians, who inhabited one of the driest and

least hospitable areas on the continent, led a miserable existence. The Whites watched with disgust as the Diggers devoured grasshoppers or pried shriveled roots out of the ground with a digging stick. Their clothing was sparse: The men wore breechclouts; the women, a double apron woven from plant fibers. One historian, Hubert Howe Bancroft, even put forward the idea that they hibernated: "Lying in a state of semi-torpor in holes in the ground during the winter, and in spring crawling forth and eating grass on their hands and knees, until able to regain their feet; having no clothes, scarcely any cooked food, in many instances no weapons, with merely a few vague imaginings for religion, living in the utmost squalor and filth, putting no bridle on their passions, there is surely room for no missing link between them and the brutes."‡

To the Whites, here seemed to be people who lived in a state of society no higher than that of the apes. And here, it was thought by some, would be found the earliest customs of humankind to survive into the present. Others thought that the Shoshone might be, if not the missing link, then some sort of transition between the societies of apes and humans. Such a belief is, of course, ridiculous. Neither the Great Basin Shoshone nor any other group of people, no matter how simple the society, has ever revealed itself as one that knows no laws, that consists of unfettered humans free to do what they want when they want. Instead, the Great Basin Shoshone are circumscribed by customs, rules of behavior, and rituals that rival those of the Kremlin or the Court of Versailles. At every moment of life the Shoshone must be careful to observe the complicated folkways of the group, to do reverence to superhuman powers, to remember the courtesies and obligations of kinship, and to avoid particular places. Especially at those critical times of life known as the rites of passage —among them, birth, puberty, and death—an elaborate etiquette regulates their behavior.

The belief that the lowliest human is only a notch above the highest ape and forms a continuum is an old —but erroneous—idea. Darwin was in error when he declared flatly that "there is no fundamental difference between man and the higher mammals in their mental faculties."‡ Some psychologists, sociologists, and anthropologists have continued from time to time to parrot this view. Fundamental differences do obviously exist between humans and apes, both in biology and in behavior. A Digger Indian might have appeared to Mark Twain to be living on a level no better than an ape; but the Digger can classify relatives, distinguishing the different kinds of cousins, and can set up rules about which relatives are appropriate marriage partners and which are not. No nonhuman primate can do that. Economic teamwork is virtually nonexistent among the nonhuman primates, but the Diggers hold formalized rabbit hunts, share food during famines, and observe complicated rules of hospitality and exchange. Prestige among the Diggers is based on who gives away the most

—precisely the reverse of behavior among apes and monkeys. The Digger, unlike the ape, is conversant with spirits and witches, knows holy places and magical procedures. It is not a case of whether the Digger has merely a "better" conception of myth and the supernatural than the apes. It is, rather, a case of either—or. There can be no question of degrees of belief by an ape in the origin myths of its society; either it possesses such beliefs or it does not. Apes and monkeys are, so far as is known, utterly incapable of having any such conceptions. No other living creature can enter the world of human beings and experience what the human experiences, regardless of how simple the society in which that human lives.‡

The social life of a nonhuman primate is governed almost exclusively by its anatomy and physiology, whereas human society is ruled largely by culture. "Culture" is, unfortunately, a word with too many connotations, but it is the best one available for the subjects being discussed in this book. The word can mean good breeding or it can describe a love for the more elevating aspects of human life; it may refer to the tillage of the land, the raising of oysters to produce pearls, the training of the physique, and the propagation of microorganisms. In this book, though, the word is used solely in its anthropological sense. The earliest definition, and still an adequate one, was given (in *Primitive Culture*, 1871) by Edward B. Tylor, the founder of the modern science of anthropology: Culture is "that complex whole which includes knowledge, belief, art, law, morals, custom, and any other capabilities and habits acquired by man as a member of society."

Culture is all the things and ideas ever devised by humans working and living together. It adds up to all the things that go into being human, and without it we would be simply animals. A troop of baboons, for example, has several organizational features in common with a simple human band. But there are essential differences, one of which is that the baboon reacts within the limitations of its biology, whereas humans have learned to transcend their biology to a degree much greater than any other living thing. Baboons do, of course, learn

—as when one animal in a troop long protected in a national park was shot, with the result that the entire troop became wary for many years afterward. But this is a trivial response compared to the cultural reaction of humans. Humans would not only be wary; they would also put up signs, assign round-the-clock shifts of guards, teach their young in school about the danger, and of course convey warnings through the symbols of spoken language. Some scholars in the past have stressed the determinism of culture—that is, asserting that it causes human beings to act the way they do. Debates have raged over whether it is humans who create culture or culture that creates humans. Both points of view are, of course, correct. Culture arrived on the planet with humans and it is thus a human construct. But culture is also creative in the sense that individual humans differ from one another through having been influenced in diverse ways by the varying cultures to which they belong.

The digging stick of the Shoshone, one of the simplest tools used in any human society, provides an example of the relation of culture to humans. Although some apes and monkeys have been observed to use sticks for digging, and chimpanzees use them to "fish" in a termite nest, for a human a digging stick represents something much more complex. To an ape a stick is merely an object, but to a human the stick is an item of culture, denoting ideas as well. It is not just any stick, but a digging stick; it is intended for the special purpose of digging plant roots out of the earth and not for some other use such as dislodging rocks. A Shoshone who wants to pry out a rock uses a stick of a different sort, not a digging stick. Moreover, the digging stick is instantly recognized by all members of the Shoshone band as a digging stick and as belonging to no other category. The stick is also the focal point for traditions and proper usage, and rituals may be connected with its manufacture. To an ape the digging stick is none of these things.

The cultural simplicity of the Diggers (who hereafter will be called the Shoshone; they include Ute, Paiute, Northern Shoshoni, Bannock, and Gosiute bands) can be attributed to two causes, one not very important and the other vital. The unimportant one is that the Shoshone inhabited one of the bleakest places on earth, a stern environment that afforded only limited opportunities. The Great Basin is a land of dry soil, high evaporation, low rainfall. Native plants that can resist drought, such as greasewood and sagebrush, are of little value to humans. Much more important than the environment in explaining the culture of the Shoshone is that they lacked a technology that allowed them to rise above these limitations. The soil and the climate around Salt Lake City today are no different from what they were in primeval times; only the cultures have changed. Yet today Utah is inhabited by many White farmers who produce not only an adequate supply of food for themselves, but even a huge surplus that is exported to other places. The technology of modern Whites has allowed them to nullify the environmental limitations by the use of irrigation, drought-resistant crops, and farm machinery. Modern White culture is based on an economic system that encourages the production of a surplus and that has provided ways to store and distribute that surplus.

How poorly equipped the Shoshone were to cope with this environment can be seen from the paucity of their cultural items, such as tools and social institutions and even religious practices, all of which totaled perhaps three thousand. In comparison, the United States armed forces invading North Africa during World War II unloaded five hundred thousand items of *material* culture alone.‡ Armed forces keep inventories and so this figure is probably close to accurate; but no one has made an inventory of the huge number of cultural items available to a wealthy White farmer near Salt Lake City today—to say nothing of the enormous number of such items available to Americans, which surely would run to many millions.

But we should be careful not to misinterpret this as an unflattering comparison between the impoverished Red and the technologically sophisticated White. No claim for the genetic superiority in intelligence of one people over another has ever withstood scientific scrutiny. Even the sudden "flowering of genius" in a culture cannot be explained in genetic terms. That virtually no geniuses are recorded for a thousand years in ancient Athens does not prove that no geniuses were produced. Nor does the astonishing cluster of them (Socrates, Plato, Aristotle, Sophocles, Hippocrates, Pindar, Phidias, and many others) that appeared in Athens during the fifth and fourth centuries B.C. mean, so far as we know, that biological mutations leading to genius suddenly occurred at that time. The production of people of genius probably remained the same; what changed was the culture, which allowed exceptional minds to flourish.

Culture operated no differently in Indian societies. Probably as many potential geniuses per unit of population were born among the Great Basin Shoshone as among the Athenians. Shoshone culture, though, was different from Athenian. It was not receptive to inventions. Shoshone innovators at various times must have invented permanent dwellings. But the Shoshone populace of course rejected living in houses because their local food supply was unreliable, and the family continually had to abandon its shelter and move on to new foraging grounds. The White settlers ought not to have condemned the Shoshone for living in brush shelters. They should instead have applauded the Shoshone for having had the intelligence not to be tempted by anything so ostentatious, yet so useless to their culture, as a house.

Even a very complex culture may reject an invention that does not fit in with its way of life. All the high cultures of Mexico lacked a component of the ancient civilizations in the Near East: wheeled vehicles. Contrary to what most people believe, though, the Indians of Mexico did invent the wheel also. In 1944 archeologists unearthed, near Tampico, wheeled toys (or possibly cult objects) made of pottery. The principle of the wheel had obviously been understood in Mexico just as well as it had in the Near East. Yet the Mexicans constructed no wheeled vehicles. What they made for play or for cult use, they rejected when it came to utility. One reason why Mexican societies rejected the wheel is apparent. They lacked horses, donkeys, oxen, or other Old World domesticated beasts capable of being trained to pull wheeled vehicles. The wheeled toys of Mexico document the principle that what a cultural novelty encounters in the way of existing conditions is what determines whether or not it is adopted, and if so in what form.

THE IRREDUCIBLE MINIMUM
OF HUMAN SOCIETY

Because of the simplicity of their culture and the limitations imposed by the environment, the Great Basin Shoshone over much of their range lived at a density of one person to fifty square miles, and in some places only one to every hundred square miles. No more than a few families could remain together for any length of time; there simply was not enough food to go around. A few families might come together for cooperative hunts or live in small summer settlements, but they soon dispersed to different foraging grounds.

No human organization can be simpler than the nuclear family, which is a stable association consisting of a man, a woman, and their unmarried children. It is as basic as it is possible to get in interpersonal relations; but simple as it is, the family is the foundation upon which larger bands and more complex social organizations have been built. That is because of the several relationships involving the female: A married female has a conjugal relationship with her husband, a biological relationship with her children, and social relationships with the families into which she was born and into which she has married.

No matter how small and seemingly simple a band may be, it is organized and structured; otherwise it would not be a society. Rules of behavior govern social relations in all societies, and all societies define the differences between right and wrong. Although humans may be thought to have existed once in a state of Rousseauian innocence and freedom, from the very beginning human groups have undoubtedly been regulated by codes, rules, customs, and expectations. One distinction, though, should be kept in mind. Much of the enculturation into the society's social life occurs within the family in parent–child, older–younger sibling, and male–female relationships. Such alignments are domestic and govern the allocation of authority *within* the family. In addition, political authority concerns behavior *outside* the family and governs relations among domestic groups. The distinction is a major one in a simple band. A quarrel between two brothers can be settled by their father or by some other member of the domestic group with higher status than the brothers. But a fight between two males from unrelated families presents a serious political problem, which must be mediated by the society as a whole if violence, revenge, and feuding are to be avoided.

An isolated human in a simple society is usually a dead human, and that is why the unmarried or the widowed always attach themselves to one family or another. A Shoshone family was a largely self-sufficient unit that carried out all the economic activities from production to consumption. In its division of labor, women gathered plant food and small animals; men hunted the larger mammals for meat and also for hides and furs. The male head of the Shoshone family personified its political organization and its legal system. Such an egalitarian society might seem ideal to people in modern societies whose lives are confined by numerous restrictions, but actually egalitarian bands pay a penalty. A leader is often needed for cooperative hunting or for settling disputes, yet it is almost impossible for such a person to lead because the ideal personality in such societies is usually one that is modest, self-effacing, and tactful. A further problem is that only temporary authority must be vested in several people—that is, in those having the personal qualities that are needed at the moment. A leader of a cooperative hunt should be strong, resourceful, and wise in the ways of animals; a person directing a ceremony should be well versed in the band's customs and thus most probably aged; the leader of a war party, on the other hand, must possess youthful vigor and courage. Varying needs explain the shifting leadership that Whites found difficult to understand and to deal with.

The family offered almost all that the Shoshone needed, which is not to say that this is what the Shoshone wanted. Their lot would have been much easier had they been able to form larger social units. As a matter of fact, the nuclear family probably never existed outside of theory, for a tendency was constantly at work to unite several families into a more complex level of social integration: a band. That was done by marriage alliances. As families wandered about seeking rabbits or fruit ripe enough to gather, they from time to time came into contact with other families. Most often these families were ones into which their relatives had already married or which were potential providers of spouses for their children.

All of which brings up the thing which European cultures call love. The Shoshone, as well as those peoples around the world who still survive at the least complex levels of social organization, know that romantic love exists. But they also recognize it for what it is —in their case, a form of madness. Explorers' journals are full of accounts of Shoshone men fleeing at the arrival of the Whites, leaving their women to the latter's mercy. Most people in simple societies joke about the carryings-on of youngsters enmeshed in romantic love; they regard the participants with tolerance and patience, for they know that the illness will soon go away. They treat a youth suffering from romantic love with all the tolerance we devote to a retarded person in our society. To them, only someone mentally backward would base an institution so important to survival as marriage on romantic love.

To a Great Basin Shoshone, marriage is nothing to write sonnets about; it is a life-and-death business. It offers benefits that include division of labor, sharing of food, protection and education for the children, security in old age, succor in sickness. It includes almost everything important in life, but it does not necessarily include romance. And the interesting thing is that most of the world—except European-derived cultures which are definitely in the minority—regards it in exactly the same way. North Americans in industrial society do not base their survival on the partnership of the family when it comes to supplying material needs. A solitary male in that society now survives very well without marriage, whereas in a simpler one he would be unable to live. He dines out or buys prepared frozen dinners; a service company comes in weekly to clean his apartment; when ill he can be cared for in a hospital. Once upon a time, a man had to enter into marriage to receive these and other benefits. Now he can save himself the bother and preserve his energies for romantic love. He does, however, give up the economic benefits of marriage—roughly $8,000 to $15,000 a year that a single man must pay specialists for services he would otherwise receive free from his wife.

MARRYING-OUT

Relatives are important in a simple society such as that of the Shoshone. It is pleasant to see them a few times a year, to sit around the campfire with them and swap stories; they also can be counted upon to avenge wrongs and to share food in times of shortage. The importance of relatives also helps us to understand the reason for universal prohibitions against marrying close relatives (that is, incest and inbreeding).

Inbreeding is banned in almost every known human society, no matter how simple or how complex (the major exceptions being incestuous marriages among some royal families in ancient Hawaii, Peru, and Egypt). Most people confidently explain this prohibition by stating that all humans possess an instinctive aversion to incest. This is, of course, an inadequate explanation—for despite a supposed instinctual aversion, which is reinforced by the prohibitions of law and custom, cases of incest have been reported among many peoples, including "advanced" as well as "primitive" ones. Incestuous sexual relations apparently occur with some frequency in the United States. A psychologist a decade ago estimated that one case of incest may occur for every one thousand people in the United States; and this figure may be somewhat low.‡

Another explanation that is sometimes offered—that the incest taboo eliminates the deleterious effects of inbreeding—is not satisfactory either. For one thing, inbreeding is not always biologically deleterious. For another, it is not logical to suppose that nonliterate peoples, some of whom do not completely understand the physiology of reproduction, would have put incest taboos into operation because they understood the modern genetic principles governing the inheritance of recessive defects. Nor can this argument explain why in one society incest consists of marriage between particular kinds of cousins, whereas in another society marriage is explicitly urged between those same kinds of cousins but forbidden between other kinds. Some incest taboos even apply to individuals who are not biologically related—such as a male's marriage to a stepsister or to an aunt by marriage. A survey was once made of 167 Indian groups living between Vancouver, British Columbia, and Mexico, and eastward as far as Colorado and New Mexico. About seventy-five percent of the groups frowned sternly upon marriage with a stepdaughter; only five percent of them regarded it as proper.‡ Yet marriage between a man and his stepdaughter is not a case of too close a biological relationship; no relationship in blood exists at all.

The reason that psychological and genetic explanations explain nothing is that the problem is not psychological or genetic; it is cultural. (Of course, that is not to say that a cultural prohibition cannot be built upon the biological, behavioral, and demographic characteristics of our species.) The confusion about the incest taboo originated in the nineteenth century when social scientists treated it as a universal prohibition in all societies. They also saw great social value in it because it enforced exogamy—that is, marriage outside of one's social group. Edward B. Tylor in 1888 emphasized this concern with exogamy:

Among tribes of low culture there is but one means known of keeping up permanent alliance, and that means is intermarriage. Exogamy, enabling a growing tribe to keep itself compact by constant unions between its spreading clans, enables it to overmatch any number of small intermarrying groups, isolated and helpless. *Again and again in the world's history, savage tribes must have had plainly before their minds the simple practical alternative between marrying-out and being killed-out.* [Italics supplied.]‡

Tylor and many other anthropologists, though, failed to make a distinction between exogamy and incest. Exogamy refers solely to marriage, whereas the incest taboo may sometimes concern marriage but is primarily the prohibition of sexual intercourse between certain close relatives. The two things are obviously not always the same. Incest prohibition is not universal; father–daughter and sibling incest occur in a number of species of monkeys and apes and, as many a social worker can affirm, in humans as well. What is universal is exogamy, which would explain why many societies prohibit marriage, but not always sexual relations, between people who belong to the same family but are not genetically related (such as in-laws, stepsons and stepdaughters, stepparents, and aunts or uncles by marriage).

Tylor made it clear that marrying a close relative represents a threat to the band because it precludes alliances gained through marrying-out. The smaller the group, the more of a threat it is. If a man marries his own sister, he gives up all possibility of obtaining allies in the form of brothers-in-law. But if he marries some other man's sister and yet another man marries his sister, he has then gained two brothers-in-law to hunt with or avenge his death in a quarrel. An incestuous marriage establishes no new bonds between unrelated groups; it is an absurd denial of the right to increase the number of people whom one can trust.

Marriages in simple societies are thus usually alliances between families rather than romantic arrangements between individuals. Marriage as a political system of alliances sheds light on two customs that are widespread around the world, particularly at the band and the tribal levels of social organization. They are the levirate and the sororate. Levirate (derived from the Latin *levir*, which means "husband's brother") is the rule that obliges a man to marry his brother's widow. The sororate (from the Latin *soror*, "sister") is similarly the practice that obliges a woman to marry her deceased sister's husband. Both customs clearly show marriage to be an alliance, because by the operation of such rules many marriages outlast the original partners to it. The levirate was one of the laws of the ancient Hebrews, particularly before they achieved a complex social organization under King David. Witness the law set forth in Deuteronomy (25:5): "If brethren dwell together, and one of them die, and have no child, the wife of the dead shall not marry without unto a stranger: her husband's brother shall go in unto her, and take her to him to wife, and perform the duty of an husband's brother unto her."

Among the Shoshone, marriage alliances were undoubtedly a great source of comfort and assurance. Shoshone marriages on the whole were enduring, and the alliances between families were maintained during the very long periods in which the families never saw each other. Each family spent approximately ninety percent of its time isolated from other families as it wandered about in quest of food. Yet, when families did meet, marriage alliances served to make interfamily relations less haphazard, for kin cooperated with kin wherever possible.

THE MOST LEISURED PEOPLE

Much has been written about the precariousness of the Shoshone's food supply. Indeed, the occurrence of both their plant and animal food was unpredictable from season to season and from year to year because of variations in rainfall. A particular area might be wet one year —allowing plants to grow, which in turn nourished game animals—but be dry and sparse for several years thereafter. Almost no localities provided a dependable food supply, and so the Shoshone families spent a good deal of time moving from place to place. Each family knew thoroughly its terrain and the exact weeks when the various foods could be expected to become available. The Shoshone had a remarkable amount of knowledge about plants and animals. They harvested about one hundred species of plants; they knew when rabbits would be most plentiful, when pronghorn antelopes would be in the vicinity, when grasshoppers would be abundant.

Most people assume that the members of the Shoshone band worked ceaselessly in an unremitting search for sustenance. Such a dramatic picture might appear confirmed by an erroneous theory many of us recall from our schooldays: A high culture emerges only when the people have the leisure to build pyramids or to create art. The fact is that complex civilization is hectic, and that such hunters and collectors of wild food as the Shoshone are among the most leisured people on earth.

The Shoshone had nothing but time on their hands. Their leisure is explained not by laziness but by an absence of technology for storing and preserving large amounts of food. They might cache some seeds or nuts for the winter, or dry some strips of meat in the sun, but a bonanza in pronghorns did them little good because they did not possess the technology for storage against a future time of need. Whenever the Shoshone caught a fish they had to consume it immediately before it spoiled, because they had never learned to dry and smoke it. They had no way to cope with a surplus. At certain times of the year the Shoshone were surrounded by an abundance of game animals, but they derived little benefit from that abundance. The Shoshone would cease hunting until they consumed what they had already killed. The inability to cope with a surplus is true of most hunting societies, with the major exceptions of the Eskimo, who inhabit a natural deepfreeze, and the Northwest Coast Indians, who achieved a complex system of storage and redistribution of the surplus.

Even when their food supply was nearly exhausted, the Shoshone still did not work very hard. Since they consumed a wide variety of foods, they had the choice of going after whatever was most readily available at the time. If fish were migrating upstream, the Shoshone merely went out and harvested that resource. If not, then they probably knew some place where seeds were ripening. They might have to travel many miles for the seeds, but the undertaking was not haphazard; they knew exactly what was available and in which direction it would be found. Notwithstanding the theories traditionally taught in high-school social studies, the truth is: The more simple the society, the more leisured its way of life.

Also helping the Shoshone to lead a leisured life was their "caloric balance." A Shoshone, like most other humans, needs about 2,000 calories a day to carry on physiological functions. Such a daily intake of calories from food is balanced by the expenditure of calories necessary to produce not only the food but also the culture. Among some Shoshone, nearly two calories of food might be produced for each one expended on hunting and gathering, which would leave somewhat less than a calorie free for all other aspects of culture. But as cultures become more elaborate, the ratio of calories produced to the energy expended must rise very much more. The modern Mayan farmer must feed his family and also set aside seed for the next crop and for feeding his farm animals; he needs a further surplus of calories to give him energy to make tools, to build storage bins and a house, to chase off predatory birds and mammals, and to transport the crop to market. A study of Mayan farmers has indicated that they produce an average of thirty-three calories for each one expended. (An Iowa corn farmer produces about 6,000 calories for each calorie of human energy expended—but the corn farmer is of course using also the mechanical energy in tractors and harvesters, the fossil energy in oil and gas, and the chemical energy in pesticides.)

Humans obviously need surplus production not for physiological reasons, but for cultural ones. The Shoshone were not saddled with an elaborate culture that they had to support with a high caloric output. They did not have to spend calories on building houses and storage bins, caring for farm animals, or supporting the work of artisans and full-time priests who did not produce food. When a Shoshone wanted to eat, fingers did as well as silverware and dinner plates that would have required calories to manufacture. The Shoshone was able to replace the caloric expenditure by working only a few hours a day, and also by keeping the cultural demand for calories low.

COOPERATION

The tendency was always present among the Shoshone for several families to unite and to form a more complex kind of social organization, a band. An important unifier was the cooperation necessary for hunting rabbits or pronghorn antelope. Four elements were essential before a cooperative hunt could be organized: an abundance of game, several families (preferably related), nets, and a leader. If just one of the elements was lacking, then the hunt could not be held. But when all elements were present, the cooperative hunt yielded more game than the same individuals could kill acting separately. In a typical rabbit hunt, several nets, each about the same height as a tennis net but hundreds of feet long, were placed end to end to form a huge semicircle. Then the women and children frightened the rabbits into the enclosure, where the animals were clubbed or became entangled. The most experienced hunter, to whom Whites gave the name "rabbit boss," was in charge of all aspects of the hunt. He selected the locality, decided where the nets should be positioned, and divided the game (giving the net owners a somewhat larger share than the rest).

Although several families cooperated closely during the hunt, there were good reasons why such cooperation established merely temporary bonds. Neither the time nor the place for the next cooperative hunt could be foretold; it could be held only when the game was abundant enough to make the hunt worth the effort, and when families, nets, and a rabbit boss all came together at the same place and time. No one could anticipate which families would happen to be near one another when all essentials for a hunt were present. Since families wandered about a great deal, rarely did even two families hunt together for several years in succession. Nor did the several families, the rabbit boss, and the owners of nets all arrange to be at the same place the following year—for no one could guarantee that game would be available then.

In some areas of the Great Basin a more reliable

food supply permitted several Shoshone families to remain together and to cooperate. In these areas, both the larger population and the need to maintain peaceful relations with non-Shoshone neighbors created a role for leadership. The first White explorers to arrive in such parts of Nevada were delighted to find leaders with whom they could make treaties. The Whites, however, understood nothing about the band level of social organization, and so they mistakenly attributed to this leadership more power than it actually possessed. The leader of a Shoshone band possessed nothing like the political power of a chief. Agreements one Shoshone leader made with Whites in good faith were not kept by other Shoshone, because in band society no mechanism existed to enforce the leader's agreements.

Before the coming of the Whites, the Shoshone, who had appeared so pitiful and lacking the blessings of civilization, had nevertheless achieved one of the noblest aspirations of civilization. They did not engage in warfare. The explanation lies not in some superior Shoshone ethic or in their being Noble Red Men, but in more practical causes. The Shoshone did not wage war because it served no purpose. They had no desire to gain military honors, for these were meaningless in their kind of society. They had no territories to defend, for a territory is valuable only at those times when it is producing food, and those were precisely the times when the Shoshone cooperated rather than made war. Even if they had wanted to steal from richer neighboring Indians, they lacked both the weapons and a political system sufficiently complex to be organized for sustained, concerted action. Whenever other Indians invaded their lands and attacked them, the Shoshone did not fight back but simply ran away and hid.

When that new element of culture introduced by Whites, the horse, spread northward from New Mexico into Shoshone lands, it was greeted in various ways, depending upon the degree of cultural complexity of the different Shoshonean groups. The horse made evident the subtle cultural differences between the slightly wealthier Shoshone groups and their poorer relatives.

The Shoshone living at the lowest subsistence level in the arid portions of the Great Basin found no value at all in horses. In fact, horses consumed the very plants upon which these people fed.

Farther north there was more grass, and there were also bison herds. There, too, Shoshone families had already developed more permanent ways of cooperating than the occasional rabbit drives. The coming of the horse was the catalyst that enabled families to unite into predatory bands of mounted horsemen. When the Ute, for example, obtained some horses, they almost immediately began to raid neighboring Indians, later attacking Mormons and other White settlers in their lands. The mounted Ute even made it a practice each spring to raid their Shoshone relatives in Nevada, who were weak after a winter of hunger; the Ute then fattened them for sale as slaves to the Spaniards in Santa Fe.

The Bannock and the Northern Shoshoni bands, who obtained their horses by theft and by trade early in the eighteenth century, went even further in changing their culture from primeval Shoshone ways: They practiced the same sort of bison hunting from horses as the Plains Indians did, and they increasingly hunted the eastern side of the Rocky Mountains—so efficiently that by about 1840 they had already exterminated the bison in the Great Basin. Although some of the mounted Shoshone bands took on the trappings of the Plains tribes with whom they were in contact, that was all show. The mounted Shoshone adopted only the material cultures of the Plains Indians, such as horses, feather bonnets, and hide tipis. They failed to adopt what was really important for survival: a more complex social organization. The mounted Shoshone, despite their sudden acquisition of wealth, were still organized basically at the family level. Their leaders had almost no authority, and they could not coordinate attacks or defense.

ADJUSTING TO A WHITE WORLD

For more than ten thousand years the Shoshone and their ancestors had scratched out a precarious living in ways that had changed very little. Then for perhaps fifty years some of them became the temporary lords of an immense region between the Rocky Mountains and the Sierra–Cascade ranges. By 1870, though, their burst of splendor had been extinguished. They had been defeated by other Indians and finally by the United States Army. Their lands were quickly filling up with White settlers, who built ranches at oases in the desert and let livestock graze on the Shoshone's food plants. Miners threw up boomtowns in the midst of Shoshone foraging grounds. In 1872 Major John Wesley Powell, explorer of Grand Canyon and founder of the Bureau of American Ethnology, described the effect of the White settlement on the Shoshone: "Their hunting grounds have been spoiled, their favorite valleys are occupied by white men, and they are compelled to scatter in small bands to obtain subsistence . . . They are in an exceedingly demoralized state; they prowl about the mining camps, begging anad pilfering, the women prostituting themselves to the lust of the lower class of men."‡

Shameful as the conditions of the Shoshone were—and to a great extent still are—these people were spared the complete disruption experienced by some other Indian groups that possessed more elaborate social organizations. The Shoshone had little to lose. No complex fabric of culture, meticulously woven strand by strand only to be ripped apart suddenly by the invasion of whites, united them. When White families settled on the lands that had once been theirs, the Shoshone went on as they had before, except that they attached themselves to White families instead of to Indian ones. When they were forced to move about to find work, they did not suffer the extreme anguish many other Indian groups did under similar conditions; the Shoshone had never been tied to any particular localities in the past. There was little for the Whites to disrupt—few bonds of community and no complex political organization. The Shoshone continued to maintain themselves as they always had, on the family level. All their family customs —kinship relations, child-rearing, belief in magic, and even games—continued as before. Their leaders easily switched over to a role not much different from organizing a cooperative rabbit drive: They negotiated for several cooperating families in dealing with Whites. For all these reasons the Shoshone managed to survive the wars, epidemics, famine, and humiliation that destroyed numerous other Indian societies.

III

Eskimo:
Environment and Adaptation

THE FAR-FLUNG PEOPLE

The Eskimo were the first inhabitants of the New World to be seen by Europeans, for the Norse encountered them at least as early as 1005, probably on the southeast coast of Labrador. The Norse saw three kayaks on shore, with three men under each, and wantonly killed all but one. This was the first recorded contact of Europeans with native Americans. Surprisingly, the numerous Norse sagas made little mention of the Eskimo at first. But soon they were being described with the exaggeration and lack of understanding that later came to typify the European's view of the natives of the New World. The anonymous author of the thirteenth-century *Historia Norvegiae* wrote: "Hunters have found some very little people, whom they call Skraelings, and who, when they are wounded with weapons while still alive, die without loss of blood, but whose blood, when they are dead, will not cease to flow."‡ (*Skraeling* or *Skrelling* was a Norse term of contempt, equivalent to our "barbarian" or "weakling.") Nor does much reliable information exist about the numbers of the Eskimo. The population probably never was very high, perhaps 100,000 at its maximum. But soon after contact with Whites their numbers plummeted because of epidemics of measles, smallpox, and other European diseases that they had not previously encountered and therefore had no immunity to. The Eskimo population is believed to have risen again in this century to roughly 45,000 people, who live from extreme northeastern Siberia across Alaska and Canada to Greenland.‡

The Eskimo circle nearly half the globe along the Arctic coast, thus inhabiting a broader stretch of land than any other preindustrial people on earth. This is a considerably smaller area than they inhabited in primeval times, for in the seventeenth century the Eskimo were reported as far south as the Gulf of St. Lawrence, and archeological evidence indicates that they once occupied a large part of eastern Siberia (about fifteen hundred or so Eskimo still live in the Soviet Union). No other people has ever shown an equal uniformity in physical type, language, and culture over such a wide area. No matter where they live, most Eskimo are readily identifiable by their stocky build, long heads and short faces, and the narrow slanting eyelids with the Mongoloid fold. Their dialects, with the exception of a few in Siberia and in Alaska, are mutually intelligible; a new song or joke introduced into Alaska makes its way from one-scattered camp to another and may turn up in Greenland a year or so later. They refer to themselves as *inuit*, which is simply the plural of *inuk*, "human," in that way emphasizing their own identity in contrast to the Indians around them, who differ in physical type, language, and culture. The Whites' name, Eskimo, was coined in 1611 by a Jesuit who heard neighboring Indians call them *eskimantsik*, which means "eaters of raw meat."

A common thread that runs through all Eskimo cultures is adaptation to the stern Arctic environment. The latitudes in which the Eskimo live are marked by enormous differences between summer and winter. During the winter the sun does not shine for weeks; during the summer it never sets. Summer is the only time in which mean daily temperatures rise above freezing; but it is also the season of biting flies and of melted water lying over the tundra without draining away, forming an impenetrable morass. Tree growth is nearly impossible

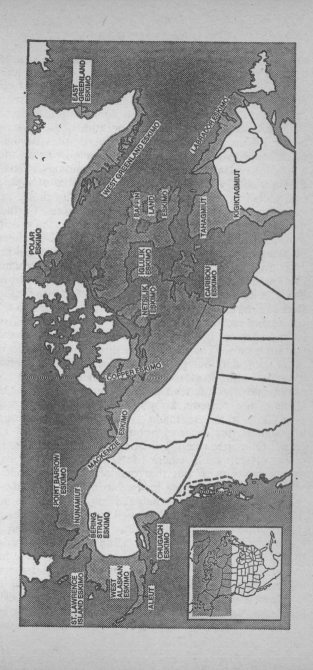

under such conditions, and in only a few places occupied by the Eskimo do even low tangles of willow and alder grow. For their supply of wood, the Eskimo must rely on the drift brought into the Arctic Ocean by rivers that drain the interiors of North America and Asia.

Despite these unpromising conditions, the material culture of the Eskimo shows a very complex development, more than that of any other people living on such a simple level as the family. Their technology is adaptive in that they manufacture a large number of specialized tools from a small number of locally available raw materials: ice, animal skins, bone, and stone. Furthermore, these tools are ingeniously adapted to the specific environmental conditions they face. Everyone has heard of at least a number of their adaptations. Some Eskimo erect an igloo, or snow house, the best possible structure that can be built with the materials available; it is strong, easily constructed, and durable. They often use the dog sled and the kayak, and they tailor their clothes so that the seams are waterproof. Slit goggles are made from ivory to protect against the blinding sun as it is reflected from the snow. They have even devised a beater to remove snow and thus prevent fur clothing from deteriorating in the humid atmosphere of the igloo.

Anyone who has seen the tools and weapons of the Eskimo in a museum knows how carefully, and often beautifully, they are made. That fact has interesting implications for theories about the beginnings of art. In the far north, where humans must face the constant threat of starvation, where life is reduced to the bare essentials—it turns out that one of these essentials is art. Art seems to belong in the basic pattern of life of the Eskimo, and of the neighboring Athapaskan and Algonkian Indian bands as well. Samuel Hearne, an eighteenth-century Hudson's Bay Company trader, in midwinter on the desolate Canadian tundra came upon the tracks of a snowshoe with a strange shape. He followed the trail to a little hut; inside he found a lone woman who explained she had been kidnapped by another band but had escaped seven months previously. Since that time she had lived alone, supporting herself by snaring what small game she could. "It is scarcely possible to conceive," observed Hearne, "that a person in her forlorn situation could be so composed as to contrive or execute anything not absolutely essential to her existence. Nevertheless, all her clothing, besides being calculated for real service, showed great taste, and no little variety of ornament. The materials, though rude, were very curiously wrought, and so judiciously placed as to make the whole of her garb have a very pleasing, though rather romantic appearance."‡

An inventory of Eskimo technology and inventiveness could be extended for pages and even chapters. We can measure, describe, photograph, and make a diagram of a kayak, and we can put it on display in a museum. But no matter how perfect this kayak specimen is, it still has not captured the reality of kayak-ness. A kayak is not an end in itself; rather, it was manufactured to achieve an end. The physical presence of the kayak in a museum cannot be regarded as a substitute for the idea of kayak-ness, for no one can ever transport certain aspects of a kayak to a museum. These aspects, no less a part of it than the wooden frames and skin cover, include who owns it, who is allowed to ride in it, taboos concerning it, rituals connected with its launching and its use, and so on. Only when these and many other things are known can anyone understand what the kayak truly means to an Eskimo. And the same principle applies to all other aspects of Eskimo material culture as well.

The Eskimo used to be put forward as evidence of a people molded by their physical environment. Although now rejected as fallacious by almost all anthropologists, this outmoded theory of "environmental determinism" nevertheless has subtly entered our way of thinking. Some educated people still maintain that Massachusetts has produced more scholars than Alabama because New Englanders have long winters for snowbound study, whereas the South is too hot for study anyway. Massachusetts has indeed produced many more scholars than Alabama, but not because of the climate or any other aspect of the physical environment. Other factors—such as the superior educational system in Massachusetts, the earlier founding of its schools, and the intellectual receptivity of its settlers—are much more important than the long winters. And if any connection did indeed exist between long winters and scholarship, then the Eskimo surely ought to have produced even more scholars than the people of Massachusetts.

Of course the natural surroundings do influence the broad outlines of a culture: An Eskimo inhabitant of the Arctic ice could no more become an agriculturist than the Pueblo Indians of the southwestern desert could ever base their economy on harpooning walruses. The environment does not determine the character of human culture; it merely sets the outer limits. The advance and the retreat of the ice sheet in North America did not determine that the ancestors of the Indians had to act in any particular way; it merely provided them with a particular set of choices from which they selected, unconsciously of course, the ones that worked best. The limits and opportunities of the physical environment are felt in varying ways by different peoples, depending upon the level of their culture. Drought represented a disaster to a Great Basin Shoshone band. But inhabiting an equally arid environment in Mexico were the Mixtec, a culturally advanced people who had largely liberated themselves from their environment by the construction of irrigation works. To the Mixtec, drought was no more than a hardship from which they soon recovered.

The Arctic demonstrates with almost textbook clarity the fallacy of environmental determinism—for if humans have been able to make different kinds of adjustments there, then it is clear that environment influences cultures only in the most general way. The Eskimo of the North American Arctic have exploited their environment with great ingenuity in producing the igloo, kayak, sled, harpoon, and snow goggles. In the Siberian Arctic, the environment is exactly the same and the land is inhabited by close relatives of the Eskimo known as the Chukchi—yet the Chukchi have evolved quite a different kind of culture. The Chukchi do not make snowhouses; instead, their dwellings are built by attaching skins to wooden frameworks, even though wood is as scarce in the land of the Chukchi as it is in the land of the Eskimo. Nor are the Chukchi very proficient hunters, unlike the Eskimo. Before the coming of Whites, the Eskimo hunted caribou (reindeer), whereas the Chukchi herded them. The fact that the Chukchi have survived shows that they adapted to the Arctic environment just as successfully as the Eskimo—but they did so in a different way. Clearly, other factors besides the environment must have influenced the different kinds of cultures the Eskimo and the Chukchi developed.

SOCIALITY AND SURVIVAL

Interest in the environment of the Eskimo and the drama of their response to it has blinded us to other important things the Eskimo can reveal about humankind. The material technology of the Eskimo, sophisticated as it is within narrow limits, may obscure the reality of the Eskimo's life and what it can show about the simpler stages of society. Less dramatic, and ultimately more important, are the Eskimo's social adaptations, their customs and laws and religion. For example, the Netsilik Eskimos northwest of Hudson Bay follow a regular annual migration circuit during which they hunt certain kinds of animals in certain ways and with different combinations of hunters. In winter, the Netsilik must rely almost exclusively on the seals, which keep open a large number of holes in the ice whereby they obtain oxygen. It is thus advantageous for a large number of hunters to cooperate, one at each of the breathing holes with harpoon in hand. Winter then becomes the time when several large families come together and form a temporary community. It is also the time of much ceremonial activity. In the summer, on the other hand, the Netsilik break up into small groups that move inland, fishing and occasionally hunting caribou with the bow and arrow. Constantly changing opportunities and pressures have favored those Netsilik who are most flexible in their social organization, fissioning and fusing again as conditions demand. Even so, some Netsilik are not always successful at the hunt—in which case they share whatever food is available.‡

The precarious existence of the Eskimo has placed certain demands upon them. The primary one is that of having to find a way to survive in small and isolated groups and at the same time lead a nomadic life. Because the Eskimo subsist upon migratory animals rather than upon stationary plants, every morsel that they eat must be sought out, often over great distances. (Some Eskimo have been able to dispense with plant food because they eat at least half of their meat raw, and that half includes the fat and the internal organs of the animal. With such a diet, they obtain from the meat every vitamin and mineral, as well as all the protein, necessary for adequate nutrition.) The Eskimo have improved upon the lot of most hunters by devising sleds to carry possessions, but even so, the amount that they can transport is small. Because of the extremely low population density, contacts between families are rare. The local group that comes together during the winter is usually composed of fewer than a dozen families, perhaps related, although actual kinship is not emphasized.

The only leadership in these groups of families is that of a headman (whose title in the Eskimo language means "he who knows best"). He obtains his position solely by achievement; he does not campaign for it, nor can he pass on the office to his sons or other relatives. In a republic of equals, he is only slightly more equal than others. The family group usually does not have definite marriage or residence rules. Among some Eskimo groups, the older sons might live with the father and the younger sons might live with their wives' families. Religious ceremonies are rarely concerned with the group as a whole, but rather with the rites of passage of the individual and the immediate family: birth, puberty, and death.

Yet certain things do tend to unite families. Among the Copper Eskimo of Canada, for example, all the inhabitants of a settlement are connected by blood or by marriage. Each owes special duties to the others: to care for them in sickness, to feed the aged and the infirm, to protect widows and orphans. In this way, a group of separate families takes on a corporate unity. It eventually is referred to by the same name, which is usually the suffix *miut* added to the word for a prominent topographical feature in the region it inhabits. *Kogluktokmiut*, therefore, is the name of the group that frequents the Kogluktok, or Coppermine, River. Physical propinquity, a similarity in habits and dialect, and intermarriage have given them a sense of closeness that sets them off from neighboring Eskimo groups—but that nevertheless has failed to unite them into a tightly knit band.

SPOUSE-LENDING AND OTHER EXCHANGES

Marriage is at the center of Eskimo life, even though some explorers have maintained that the Eskimo, because of spouse exchange and other sexual irregularities, do not much revere the institution. But the Eskimo are enthusiastically in favor of marriage. A man marries just as soon as he can hunt with sufficient skill to feed a wife, and girls often marry before they reach puberty. A man is destitute without a wife. He has no one to make his clothes or to cook for him. A woman without a husband must live like a beggar, since she has no one to hunt game for her. Marriage is an economic necessity, and that is one reason why no elaborate courtship displays or marriage celebrations take place. A man and a woman arrange to live together with less pomp than modern Americans display when they contract with a carpenter.

The thing that most bewilders a prudish White about the Eskimo's connubial eccentricities—wife-lending, spouse-swapping, polyandry, and polygyny—is the good nature with which the arrangements are made. Occasionally an Eskimo man will beat his wife for being unfaithful—not because she had sexual intercourse with someone else, but because she took it upon herself to grant rights that are the husband's privilege to bestow.

The next week he himself may lend her to the same man. Spouse-exchange exists to some extent in all Eskimo groups that have been studied; the explanation is that such an exchange is one of the best ways to formalize an economic partnership or a social alliance. With so few opportunities available to create bonds between families, the Eskimo must use ingenuity, and one of the best methods is exchanging sexual rights.

So wife-lending and spouse-exchange should be looked upon not as examples of sexual license, but as social mechanisms that serve to unify small groups. Further, wife-lending is a wise investment for the future, because the lender knows that eventually he will be a borrower. Perhaps he has to go on a long journey, and his wife cannot accompany him because she is sick or in late pregnancy; so then he borrows his friend's wife. He is not necessarily a lecher who wants a woman, but a man who needs essential services. While he is out hunting, his friend's wife makes the shelter habitable, lays out dry stockings for him, makes fresh water from melted ice—and is ready to prepare the game he brings back. Similarly, polyandry and polygyny are essential, for a lone Eskimo cannot survive. He or she must become attached to some family, even though another spouse is already present.

Wife-exchange usually is an essential ritual in the formation of a trading partnership between hunters. Trade takes place over long distances among Eskimo groups living in various ecological zones and with varying ways of life. Voluntary associations are thus established between unrelated individuals for the purpose of trading and also of exchanging services. Although such partnerships are not hereditary, a strong tendency seems to have existed for the children of trading partners to create their own partnerships, thereby perpetuating them from generation to generation. When two men agree to become partners, they have symbolically extended the bonds of kinship to each other. They become in effect related by marriage when they then exchange wives for a few days or a week, but sometimes longer than that—and occasionally the couples set up a joint household.

An anthropologist who studied one Eskimo group estimated that a fifth of the couples had entered into such exchange agreements. In northern Alaska in particular, wives were exchanged as a sort of attestation to the formation of a partnership. The wives rarely objected since, among other reasons, each stood to profit herself from her husband's new economic bond. The partnership arrangement also extended to the children. A child called his father's partner by a special name, which freely translated means "the man who has had intercourse with my mother." The child also used a special name—*qatangun*—for his father's partner's sons, who might be his half brothers. He knew that if he was ever in trouble he could call on his *qatangun* for help and his request would be honored.

Alliances are important among the Eskimo because of the minimal social organization that exists beyond the family. This is the major way that they can maintain bonds across social boundaries so as to bring disparate segments of the group into relation with one another. The catalog of alliances is truly impressive; it includes, to mention only some, betrothal, adoption, spouse-exchange, trading partnerships, godparenthood, meat-sharing, ritual feasts, and wrestling partnerships. Betrothal is a basis for alliance particularly among the Greenland and Canadian Eskimo. Two families become united when their children are betrothed, at birth or at a very young age. Betrothal often does not lead to marriage when the children reach maturity, since at that time they are free to choose marriage partners for themselves. Meanwhile, though, an alliance has been forged between the parents which will have endured for many years, for as long as both partners consider it valuable. If the alliance proves of little value to one set of parents, they can withdraw from the arrangement and instead pledge their child to a family that might offer more benefits. Betrothal would seem to be an ideal social mechanism for the Eskimo, but it had one major limitation. Betrothal can bind no more than two families together because a child can be betrothed to only one person at a time.

Exchange is a necessity of Eskimo life that applies to other things besides wives. The explorers of North America made much of what seemed to them an inordinate preoccupation by the Eskimo and the Indian with gift-giving. Over and over the explorers related their disillusionment when the Eskimo or Indian failed to have the "courtesy" to thank them for gifts. And the explorers invariably expressed amazement that their unacknowledged gifts were later remembered and reciprocated in full. The explorers regarded gift-giving as merely a quaint Eskimo custom and did not recognize it as an aspect of exchange. The explorers emerged with false conclusions about these gifts because they did not spend enough time with the Eskimo or Indian group to witness the entire transaction. What they observed was not gift-giving at all but the first step in what should more properly be called "balanced reciprocity." This is a mode of exchange in which both giver and recipient leave unstated what is expected in return or even when the return should be made—but both the expectation of repayment and the obligation to repay are real. One individual cannot long continue to be a freeloader and accept food or objects without reciprocating with things of approximately equal value. In other words, balanced reciprocity is as much a social compact as it is an economic exchange. It is particularly important in hunting–gathering societies, where no individual could possibly accumulate a surplus, live independently of other members of the band, or become so successful in the quest for food as never to need meat from someone else's kill. So step two, which the explorers rarely saw, was the eventual repayment, sometimes years afterward, with a "gift" of approximately equal value.

Further modifying what looks like gift-giving among the Eskimo is that the "gift" usually goes to a relative or a partner. An exchange among those in some sort of formal relationship is not regarded as a gift, and that is why the receiver does not offer thanks. An Eskimo praises a hunter for the way he hurled the harpoon but not for having shared the meat from the seal the harpoon killed. Sharing is a kinsman's or a friend's obligation, and it is not in the category of a gift. The Arctic explorer Peter Freuchen once made the mistake of thanking an Eskimo hunter, with whom he had been living, for some meat. Freuchen's bad manners were promptly corrected: "You must not thank for your meat; it is your right to get parts. In this country, nobody wishes to be dependent upon others . . . With gifts you make slaves just as with whips you make dogs!"‡

An important basis for exchange is that the Eskimo alternate between feast and famine. One Eskimo hunter may be successful, killing seal after seal, while another hunter is having a long streak of bad luck. People who have been molded by a capitalistic culture know what they might well do if they were the fortunate hunters and others were in need: They would jack up prices. Such a thing could never happen in Eskimo society— not because an Eskimo is innately nobler than you or I, but because the Eskimo know that despite plenty today, quite probably they will be in want tomorrow. They know also that the best place to store a surplus is in someone else's stomach, because sooner or later the sharing will be reciprocated. Pure selfishness has given the Eskimo a reputation for generosity and earned them the good opinion of missionaries and of all others who hunger and thirst after proof of the innate goodness of human beings.

The absence among the Eskimo—and among other peoples at the band level as well—of our conventional concepts of property has been the source of some theories to the effect that communism is a basic condition of humankind. But do the facts really warrant such a conclusion? The Eskimo have the kinds of property known as communal and personal, but they lack private property. The natural resources on which the band depends—the rivers filled with fish, the tundra where the caribou feed, the sea in which seals live—are communal and are open to use by all members of the band. Personal property consists of things made by individuals: weapons, tools, ornaments, fetishes, and so on. These items are not really private property, because they belong not to the individual but to that individual's role in Eskimo society. The Eskimo would consider it preposterous for a woman, who has a specific role, to own a harpoon, even had she been foolish enough to devote her energies to making one. Nor is the concept of personal ownership very far-reaching. It is unthinkable that one Eskimo should possess two harpoons while a less fortunate kinsman lacks even one.

Since no private property exists among the Eskimo, it might appear that they are communistic. But to believe so would be to miss an important point about band society. Communism, as the word is understood in modern society, refers to ownership by *all* the citizens of the means of production and an absence of exploitive relations. In modern communism, the "all" refers to the entire population, related or not. But who are the "all" in Eskimo society? Almost everyone in the group is related by blood or by marriage or allied as a trading partner. The Eskimo band is really one big family that includes also close friends (in the same way that American children might call a friend of their parents "aunt," even though she is not a relative). Even in the capitalistic United States, most families practice this same sort of "communism" within the family. They are generous to children, indulgent with nephews and nieces, hospitable to cousins. So before we hasten to praise the generosity found in the band, let us remember that we act some of the time—in our relations with kin and close friends—the way these people act all of the time.‡

FEUDS AND DUELS

The Eskimo male from time to time engages in conflicts, often violent ones—the cause of which, surprisingly enough in his sexually permissive society, is usually adultery. It is not considered adultery when a husband lends his wife to a friend. Nor is it considered adultery when a husband and wife join other couples in the game known as "putting out the lamp"—during which period of darkness they pick at random a partner of the opposite sex. Adultery occurs only when a woman has sexual intercourse without the express approval and prior knowledge of her husband. Since such approval can usually be had for the asking, adultery has a significance other than sexual gratification. It is one man's unspoken challenge to another. And the offended husband must respond to the challenge, if he is not to live out the rest of his years in shame.

Homicide is almost always the outcome of such a challenge to status. When the Arctic explorer Knud Rasmussen visited a community of fifteen Eskimo families in the early 1920's, he found that every one of the adult males had committed homicide at least once, and in every case the apparent motive had been a quarrel about a woman.‡ It would, however, be a mistake to think that the Eskimo are more preoccupied with usurpation of sexual rights than other people are. The Eskimo's problem lies in their society, which has formulated no clear-cut laws governing marriage and divorce. Marriage is simply living together; divorce is simply creasing to live together any longer. In arrangements as informal as these, no way exists to determine when someone is trespassing on another's rights. Since in Eskimo society things are always being borrowed, no definition has been made of where borrowing a wife leaves off and appropriating her begins. When a wife is borrowed, she does not leave the premises with a return date as if she were a library book. Judgment and good taste—and perhaps an undercurrent of hostility toward the husband on the part of the borrower—determine how soon she will be returned.

The murder, either of the interloper or of the injured husband, must be revenged by the kinsmen of the murdered man, and this in turn may bring further retaliation. No chivalry or bravery is involved in blood revenge. In all Eskimo communities, except those of western Greenland, it is carried out by stealth. Since a murderer is required to care for the widow and the children of his victim, blood revenge sometimes produces an absurd situation. A murderer rears as his own stepson the son of his victim—and when this boy grows to manhood he may be the very one to exact delayed blood vengeance upon his foster father.

Several mechanisms serve as checks on the proliferation of killings and revenge. The Eskimo realize that feuds are potentially dangerous to their existence, and families are quick to punish wrongdoers within their own ranks. Every attempt is made to prevent a quarrel from leading to murder. As soon as a quarrel becomes public knowledge, other people in the group seek out a kinsman common to both parties to adjudicate. A man who has committed several murders becomes an object of concern to the entire community. An executioner is appointed, who obtains in advance the approval of the family of the inveterate murderer. No revenge can be taken on the executioner, for he is acting in the name of all the people.

Short of actual murder, outlets for hostility as a means of ending quarrels include buffeting, butting, wrestling, and song duels. In buffeting, the opponents face each other and by turns give forceful blows until one is felled. In butting, the opponents strike at each other with their foreheads, and the one who is felled is derided by the onlookers. Wrestling, though it might seem safe enough, occasionally has a deadly outcome and is one of the subtler ways of carrying out blood revenge. Such contests are announced in advance, and they take place before the whole group, which regards them as festive occasions. Regardless of which party to the dispute may have justice on his side, the winner is the one who displays the greatest strength.

In Alaska and in Greenland all disputes except those involving murder are settled by a song duel. In these areas an Eskimo male is often as much acclaimed for his ability to win such contests as for his prowess in hunting. The disputants in a song duel sing lampoons, insults, and obscenities to each other and, of course, to a delighted audience. The verses are earthy and rudely outspoken; since they are intended to humiliate, no physical deformity, personal embarrassment, or family shame is immune. As verse after verse is sung, with the opponents taking turns, the audience begins to choose sides; it applauds one singer a bit longer and laughs a bit louder at his lampoons. Finally, he is the only one to get applause, thereby becoming the winner of a bloodless contest. The loser suffers the disapproval of the community, a thing very difficult to bear in so small a group. How important prestige can be to an Eskimo is emphasized by the following anecdote. Among the Chugach Eskimo, a thief once entered a house in which an old woman was eating. She began to sing:

> *Old Turd, Old Turd.*
> *He makes me ashamed.*
> *He was looking at me when I was eating.*

This song may not appear particularly clever, but it was enough to make the thief leave the house without taking anything. Soon the children in the band were singing the song whenever they saw him. The result was that he was cured of stealing.‡

THE BIRTH OF THE GODS

People reared in the context of European culture will also find the religious beliefs of the Eskimo quite different from those they are used to. The Eskimo faith is among the simplest known, and it incorporates the two common denominators of all religions: belief in spirits and in magic. The Eskimo are completely without most of the beliefs or practices found in complex societies, such as revelation, a redeemer, a priesthood, orthodox rituals, and articles of faith.

The debate as to where "magic" ends and "religion" begins is an old one, and it appeared to have been settled some decades ago when scholars concluded that no discernible boundary was to be found. As a result, the two were often lumped together in the adjective "magico-religious," a compromise word that originated in much the same way as the word "socio-cultural." Nevertheless, at least one distinction between magic and religion must be made. The practitioners of magic believe that they can directly affect other humans and nature, either for good or for ill, by performing certain acts. Magic is therefore instrumental—and some of its instruments are witchcraft, sorcery, oracles, divination, and cures of various kinds. Although many "religious" people do use religion for instrumental ends, the primary emphasis in religion is on social and cosmological relationships.

Eskimo magic differs from Christianity, Judaism, Mohammedanism, and Buddhism in that it is not concerned with regulating behavior in the society as a whole or with propagating a code either of conduct or of belief. It is concerned not with the totality of the invisible world, but simply with the individual's relation to the food supply and to the physical environment. Eskimo magic operates through an elaborate system of taboos, hundreds of them, that constrain every action. A wise Iglulik Eskimo once said to Knud Rasmussen: "What do we believe? We don't believe; we only fear." Eskimos as well as other peoples in band societies inhabit a world of anxiety, frustration, inadequacy, and vulnerability in which the spirits control everything that cannot be explained rationally. Modern Americans do not suffer the same kind of anxiety, since they have exerted technological control over many of the things that make the Eskimo fearful. In place of science, the Eskimo have only magic to bridge the gap between what they understand and what is unknown. Without magic, their life would be one long panic.

To violate a taboo is a sin, and the most notable thing about the Eskimo attitude toward sin is that it lacks our holier-than-thou connotations. The group does not revel in an upsurge of indignation; there is no righteous lecture, no public stoning of the miscreant. Instead, the community unites in compassion and tolerance around the sinners. They are encouraged to purge themselves, and they do so by hiring a part-time religious practitioner known as a shaman who draws forth from each sinner's mouth the exact details of the taboo violation. The villagers sit in the background, chanting cries of forgiveness for the pitiful sinner.

For the Eskimo, illness in the soul of the wrongdoer usually is the result of sin—but they also believe that illness may result from witchcraft by another shaman. Witchcraft is not the malevolence of one who goes out to murder, but rather is evil worked in the privacy of one's own shelter. Social scientists used to think that witchcraft was correlated with the food supply: the more precarious a group's subsistence, the more prevalent the fear of sorcery. But this is not true. Compared with the Eskimo, the Navajo of Arizona and New Mexico are surrounded by abundance, yet they are even more haunted by witchcraft. When an Eskimo male falls sick and attributes his sickness to witchcraft by a hostile shaman, he assumes that he must have done something to the shaman that cannot be settled publicly through a song duel or even by murder. In such a case, the afflicted person must fight poison with poison, so he hires a friendly shaman to locate the secret attacker and nullify the witchcraft.

Now we come to grips with a basic characteristic of witchcraft: It is aggression for which a society has not provided other channels. In fact, an examination of witchcraft in simple societies around the world shows that it appears when people attempt to handle their vital problems in the absence of formal social controls. The surprising thing about witchcraft in Eskimo society is not that it exists, but that it is not much more prevalent. Its relative infrequency is due to the various social constraints mentioned earlier: public ridicule, prestige, the use of kinsmen in settling quarrels, and a public executioner. Although these are not the same social controls as the laws, courts, and police familiar to us, they serve somewhat the same function.

THE SHAMAN, DEALER IN THE SUPERNATURAL

The word "shaman" comes from the Tungus language of Siberia, but the shaman is important among all the Eskimo bands and among many American Indians. This is particularly true in western North America, where shamans were often called "medicine men" by Whites. Wherever shamans exist, they move with ease in the supernatural realm. They are in the business of going to the invisible world and contending with the spirits on their own ground. An Eskimo believes that spirits must be coerced, and a widespread Eskimo myth tells how the sea spirit Sedna had to be harpooned to force her to release sea mammals for the hunt.

A vast difference exists between a shaman and a priest. A priest is a legally constituted specialist; he is a member of a group set apart from the rest of the social organization. An Eskimo shaman, on the other hand, dresses no differently from anyone else; he (Eskimo shamans are almost always males, although occasionally a woman past menopause may become a shaman) lives like the rest of the community. He hunts, or he joins a whaling crew; he may be married and have children. He has no special privileges or insignia except often a tambourine (a skin drum open on one side), a head-dress, and a special belt. He can be recognized, though, by certain signs. Search out the least skilled hunter in the group, one who is also physically or emotionally handicapped and who makes nervous movements with his hands or feet. You have probably located your man. The Eskimo are smart enough to recognize that the shaman is different from everybody else, and to put this fact to work in their society. Some Eskimo maintain that they can identify a future shaman, even while he is still a child. He will be meditative and introverted; he may have fits or fainting spells; he is disturbed by dreams and suffers from hallucinations and hysteria. The sha-man might in our society be diagnosed as neurotic, a borderline schizoid—which is perfectly all right with the Eskimo, since they believe that the shaman needs extraordinary abilities in his traffic with the supernatural. The shaman comes to the fore because Eskimo culture encourages his hallucinations, provides such situations as the curing ceremonies in which he can flourish, and even pays him for his psychological condition.

Some anthropologists have stated that the shaman fills an important function by draining off the potential "Arctic hysteria" of the group. But what he does is not so simple as that, and the shaman may actually represent an element of hostility in Eskimo culture. The person who becomes a shaman is almost always more misanthropic, more covertly aggressive, and less physically skilled than the ordinary man. Whatever the shaman himself envies—the successful hunter, the virile man with many women, the owner of a boat—are also what the rest of the group envies. Unlike the ordinary Eskimo, the shaman can do something about his malevolence: He can call down sickness upon the envied one. A skilled hunter may suddenly no longer be able to kill game—and he attributes his misfortune not to chance but to the hostility of some shaman or other. He employs his local shaman to perform a ceremony that removes the evil influence. The hunter emerges from the experience a humbler man; he is careful in the future not to boast of his skill, and also to leave game for others and to share more generously. The shaman and the rest of the Eskimo group have had the satisfaction of seeing the mighty brought low.

In any discussion of shamans, the question naturally arises: Are these people frauds? Shamans use many tricks to heighten the effect of their performances: ventriloquism, hypnosis, legerdemain, and general stage magic. Houdini-like escapes are a specialty. A shaman often impresses his audience by vomiting blood; he does this by having previously swallowed a small bladder filled with animal blood, then breaking it with his stomach muscles at the appropriate moment. Although the shaman is perfectly aware that he is at times merely performing tricks, he nevertheless is firmly convinced of his power to deal with spirits. When he falls into a trance, it is a real trance; when he has a fit, it is a real fit. He regards his ultimate purpose as an honest one, and if he can intensify the supernatural experience by slightly hoodwinking his audience, then he goes ahead and hoodwinks them. So convinced of their own efficacy are the shamans that, like psychiatrists, when they are sick in spirit they call in a fellow practitioner to administer treatment.

The life of the Eskimo is hedged in by numerous taboos that would seem to handicap them in their struggle to survive. One taboo, for instance, prohibits any work during a time of mourning; so if someone dies during the long winter of privation, hunger is inevitably the result. A taboo prohibits the use of whaling tools for more than one season, despite the scarcity of raw materials. Such prohibitions would seem to run counter to the best interest of the Eskimo. Is there some hidden value in these apparently irrational taboos, or has the Eskimo managed to survive despite them?

No doubt many of the religious observances work to the Eskimo's detriment. Yet these observances are continued because they afford certain social benefits that cannot be achieved by other methods, although the Eskimo themselves undoubtedly have no conscious understanding of these benefits. The taboos are almost always concerned with rather trivial matters, and at the same time are all very demanding, just as the hazing of freshmen at some college campuses demands that freshmen pay scrupulous attention to minor observances. Both taboos and hazing have the same result: They promote cooperation because all members of the group are made to suffer together. In the simple society of the Eskimo, the sharing of fears and the scrupulous attention to details of conduct create a social bond. Compliance with folkways, no matter how seemingly foolish or trivial, has provided the Eskimo with a better unifying social mechanism than they probably could have devised consciously.‡

Today the life of the Eskimo has changed, for the technology brought by the Whites has meant a new relationship to the environment and to other bands. In place of harpoons, kayaks, and sleds, the Eskimo now use repeating rifles, motorboats, and snowmobiles. Commercial fishing has encouraged small groups to merge into large villages; the Eskimo import canned and preserved foods from the temperate and tropic zones; they have switched to a cash-and-credit economy and often earn morney by working at a fish-canning factory or by turning out soapstone carvings for tourists. Yet, despite the apparent alterations in culture, the first of the native Americans to encounter the Whites have managed to preserve much of their primeval heritage.

IV
The Sub-Arctic:
Living with Expediency

COMPOSITE AND PATRILOCAL BANDS

South of the tundra domain of the Eskimo, from New-foundland westward nearly to Bering Strait, lies a thick green carpet of Sub-Arctic coniferous forest. Game animals of every sort abound here: deer, elk, moose, bears, and a variety of fur-bearing mammals. Herds of barren-ground caribou live in the tundra, and their woodland relatives are, or at least used to be, plentiful in the ever-green forests. Fish swim through the cold glacial lakes and the fast streams. Late each spring the sky fills with birds. Almost everywhere this forest grows are Indians who belong to two large language families, the Algon-kian and the Athapaskan. Those living to the south and east of Hudson Bay speak Algonkian and include such bands as the Montagnais and Naskapi of Labrador, the Micmac of New Brunswick, the Penobscot of Maine, and the Chippewa or Ojibwa of Ontario. The Indians to the west of these speak Athapaskan and include the Chipewyan, Kaska, Slave, and Beaver. Despite the difference between the two language families, the Indian cultures over this immense area have many things in common. In primeval times both Algonkians and Atha-paskans hunted a variety of mammals, fishes, and birds, but with the coming of the French and British they very soon switched to trapping. Their environment is no less rigorous than that of the Eskimo, and their technology is certainly as sophisticated. They build conical skin tents (wigwams) rather than igloos; they use toboggans instead of dog sleds; their feet are shod with moccasins rather than sealskin boots; they use the birchbark canoe instead of the kayak. In addition, they have invented a variety of ingenious deadfalls and snares, calling devices to attract game, nets and weirs for catching fish under varying conditions, and numerous tools that demand exacting workmanship.

Only a meager amount of information about the cultures of the Northern Algonkians and Northern Athapaskans in primeval times exists, for their ways of life were altered very rapidly and very early by the pervasive influence of fur traders. The Whites also brought with them diseases, the severity of whose ravages is difficult to imagine today. Lacking any immunity to smallpox, almost the entire Indian population of Canada suffered very greatly from a series of epidemics. A Hudson's Bay Company explorer reported that one epidemic alone, occurring about 1780, wiped out nine-tenths of the Chipewyan Indians. In addition to disease, population disruptions resulted from warfare among Indian groups, from starvation, and from migration to other areas.

It is, therefore, very difficult to generalize about the band organization of the Sub-Arctic Indians. At various times, these northern peoples traced descent through the male, the female, or through both male and female; the wife might go to live with the husband's family (patrilocal), or the husband with the wife's family (matrilocal), or the newly married couple might take up a new place of residence (neolocal). At times the Sub-Arctic Indians seem to have had a strong social organization based on clans and totemic animals; at other times they have had little organization beyond the family and a leader to represent them at the trading posts. When they first came in contact with Whites, they hunted such big game as caribou and moose; later they concentrated on such small game as hares. Depending

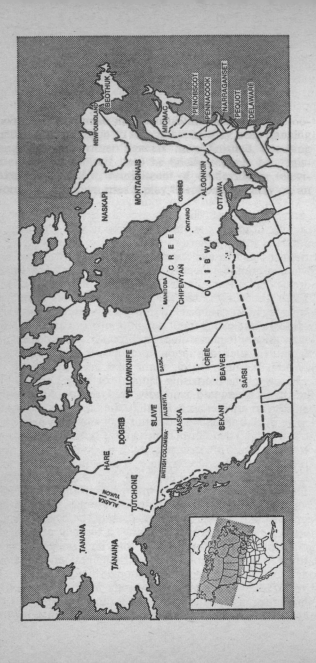

upon the kind of hunting and the season of the year, they lived either as huge bands, numbering more than a thousand people, or as isolated families that hunted and trapped in restricted territories.

The Northern Ojibwa furnish an example of the difficulty involved in reconstructing the primeval life of the Sub-Arctic Indians, owing to the early and persistent influence of European fur traders. The Northern Ojibwa nowadays consist of approximately 25,000 Indians in northern Ontario and eastern Manitoba. But when the Ojibwa were first visited by French traders and missionaries more than 350 years ago, no such group as "Northern Ojibwa" existed. Instead, about twenty groups lived much farther to the southeast, around the northern shores of Lake Superior and Lake Huron, and each group numbered between one hundred and three hundred people. But almost immediately after the first contact with Whites, important changes took place. During the 1620's, enormous groups of Indians—not only Ojibwa but members of neighboring bands as well —began to congregate around Sault Ste. Marie to carry on trade. Further disruption took place just before 1800, both because the big game had been killed off and because of the increasing demand for furs. The size of the bands decreased markedly, and the population dispersed over a wider area. By 1820 the trade in beaver had declined drastically and reports of starvation became common. The Ojibwa bands adapted by more and more splitting into small family units.

To conserve the beaver, White traders soon encouraged the practice of trapping only a portion of the territory each year, a practice which led to the formation of family hunting territories. This change, in turn, influenced many aspects of Ojibwa life. The functions of the clan that had centered around a totemic animal soon atrophied. Hunting groups that had once been identified with one another as patrilineages, and had also shared their food and trade goods, found that they had to break up to survive. The newly married couple who might formerly have gone to live with the husband's family no longer could do so because of the splintering of family groups. And once a subsistence based on hare and fish rather than on moose and caribou became established, the social organization was further fractured —for the reason that small game can support large numbers of people only if these people are evenly dispersed in small family units.‡

In short, before discussing the band organization of a group such as the Northern Ojibwa, one must be clear about the exact historical period in question. The very earliest accounts of the Sub-Arctic bands reveal that armed conflicts between unrelated bands were a major consideration, accounting for their strict rules of residence, their concern with marriage alliances, and the forging of bonds among adult males for defense as well as for hunting—all of which would indicate that they were organized as patrilocal bands. Additional indications that the Northern Algonkians were originally patrilocal come from a linguistic reconstruction of the languages spoken before the arrival of Whites. The kinship terms used were those of a society organized into patrilocal bands.‡ Finally, anthropological knowledge about similar bands, elsewhere in North America and around the world, would seem to support the view that these were originally patrilocal.

Modern American culture has no strict rules about residence after marriage and does not prescribe whether a couple live with the husband's family, the wife's family, a grandparent, or in a house of their own. But to people who are organized along the lines of a patrilocal band, such rules are important. The male is valuable to his family because of his ability to hunt and to trap. If the male hunter went to live with his wife's family after marriage, he would then not be cooperating in the hunt with other males he has known all his life. He is likely to be much more successful by continuing to live with his father and cooperating with males he can count on.

To us, people in simple societies often seem unduly concerned with kinship. Their concern, though, is real. If a strange male wanders into the lands of another band, he cannot be accepted until he traces some sort of family relationship to someone in the band. It will then be known just where he fits into the society and what is the proper way to behave toward him. Otherwise, he would represent a danger that must be driven off or killed outright. Edward B. Tylor long ago pointed out that the English words *kinship* and *kindness* have the same root, "whose common derivation expresses in the happiest way one of the main principles of social life."‡ A similar derivation is found in certain other languages also. In some languages spoken in East Africa, the same word can mean "kinship" or "peace." In Polynesia, "to be relatives" is conveyed by the same word as "to live in peace." For a band to survive, a relationship based on kindness and peace must exist among its members. If it does not exist as a result of blood relationship or if the precise relationship is not known, then the fiction of such a tie must be created to reinforce the solidarity of the band. So the patrilocal band retains its unity by accenting such things as mythology and totems in place of any actual determination of kinship.

Within a mere few decades after the arrival of the Whites, though, the band organization had been ripped apart almost everywhere in the Sub-Arctic. The Northern Algonkians and Northern Athapaskans became wards—or more accurately, debt–peons—of the fur-trading companies. Ever since then, the "peace of the marketplace" has replaced the patrilocal bands which had been in conflict with one another. Those Indians who had survived the warfare, famine, disease, and migrations ended their former hostilities. Their remnants merged into a "composite band," a confederation of families based on expediency, in which rules of marriage, kinship, and residence have become blurred. The composite band is more complex than the social organization of the Eskimo and the Shoshone, but less so than the patrilocal bands that existed in the Sub-Arctic before the Whites arrived. The important thing about the composite band is that it is an aggregate of families, sometimes numbering a few hundred people, which is based on cooperation rather than on actual kinship. Any man and woman can marry so long as they are not closely related. No rules are observed as to whether after marriage they should live with the husband's family or the wife's family—or with neither.

Considerable confusion has existed among White observers about leadership in the composite bands. They have been variously described as leaderless or as having leaders with great power—a power they almost certainly did not have. One reason for this confusion is that although leadership positions did exist, the power inhering in them differed from group to group and from one historic period to another. Among such groups as the Dogrib and Chipewyan, who engaged in communal hunting on a large scale, leadership positions were more important than among such other bands as the Slave, for whom hunting was more an individual matter. Also, as the size of the bands declined and they dispersed into family units, a new need arose for someone to represent the families at the trading posts. Thus the "captain" came into being, a person so named by the Whites. They imagined him to have greater powers than he really did, and they gave him a special "captain's coat," a keg of rum, medals, and other trinkets symbolic of status they had largely invented.

Among the Sub-Arctic bands—and among many other egalitarian groups as well—a person who assumes leadership in response to a specific situation is not so much an executive as an adviser. For example, Father LeJeune wrote of the Canadian Cree in 1634: "All the authority of their chief is in his tongue's end; for he is powerful insofar as he is eloquent and will not be obeyed unless he pleased the Savages." And of the Montagnais–Naskapi of Labrador, Father LeJeune pointed out that the individual Indian will not "endure in the least those who seem desirous of assuming superiority over others."‡ The leader totally lacked the political or legal mechanisms whereby, in a more complex tribal society, he might have enforced his wishes. A war leader is reported on occasion to have killed someone who disobeyed his orders, but that was an individual action and not one taken as a policy of the band.

CAPITALISM: INNATE OR ACQUIRED?

The composite band usually controls in common the principal resources in its hunting territory: the herds of caribou, the fishes, the birds, even the maple trees, which are tapped for sugar. Alongside communal ownership, though, small-time capitalism exists in the form of family ownership of territories for trapping fur-bearing mammals—particularly beaver, but also marten, otter, and lynx. The territories are fairly rigid, and their boundaries are known to all the inhabitants of the area. No longer ago than early in this century, it was still possible to map the hunting territories of twenty-two families of the Penobscot Indians of Maine, even though their lands had been taken over by Whites centuries earlier. Such ownership among bands of simple hunters might appear to demonstrate that capitalism may, despite the absence of private ownership in the Shoshone and the Eskimo, after all be a basic "urge" of humankind. But is it really so?

Those who seek in these Indians the prototype of some inborn tendency toward a form of capitalism will be disappointed. In the first place, strong doubts exist whether hunting territories such as have been described were established before the arrival of Whites. The Northern Algonkians were among the first Indians on the continent to be exposed to White influence, beginning long before the formation of the Hudson's Bay Company in 1670. French companies had been founded during the sixteenth century, and as early as about 1550 French ships were sent to Canada for the sole purpose of trading with the Indians. Indian bands near Quebec and Tadoussac were already acting as middlemen in the trade with isolated bands farther to the north and west.

Even at this early date, the scramble of the French for furs had given the Indians a brief course in capitalism. Champlain in 1611 wrote that the Indians were becoming canny, for they "wanted to wait until several ships had arrived in order to get our wares more cheaply. Thus those people are mistaken who think that by coming first they can do better business; for these

Indians are now too sharp."‡ In 1632 Father LeJeune observed: "Now that they trade with the French for capes, blankets, cloths, and skirts, there are many who use them."‡ The displacement of native crafts by European kettles, axes, knives, and iron arrowheads was just about completed by 1670. Reports exist that by then more than one thousand Indians at a time were gathering to trade their pelts, striving to strike the best bargain between the competing French and British traders. Trade had become so much a way of life that the Indians were already largely dependent upon supplies obtained from the posts. So it is clear that the native economic system was early disrupted by Whites who introduced many notions of European capitalism.

Thus the Indian's attention switched from the ancient concern with the products of the land to the land itself. Before the arrival of Whites, a typical Algonkian band hunted cooperatively and shared its game. Because the outcome of the hunt was uncertain, a custom grew up whereby several families looked out for one another; such an arrangement represented a simple form of insurance, guaranteeing a supply of food when hunting was poor. But a shift in economic patterns took place when the Algonkians started to produce for trade rather than for use. The most important economic ties were no longer within the band; they now extended outside the band to include the White trader. Rather than being in a cooperative relationship with the rest of the band, the band members were now in a competitive one. Neighboring families no longer were insurance against hardship; instead, they became hindrances to the limitless acquisition of furs.

In times of shortage, an Indian could always obtain a loan from the trading post. To repay such loans, and also to obtain the alluring merchandise on display, he had only to increase his take of furs. If the Northern Athapaskan and Northern Algonkian Indians husbanded the land and its wildlife in primeval times, that was only because they had neither the technology to kill very many animals nor the market for so many furs. But once White traders entered the picture, supplying the

Indians with efficient guns and offering an apparently limitless market for furs beyond the seas, the Indians went on an orgy of destruction. As far back as the early seventeenth century, Father LeJeune complained of the wholesale slaughter: "When the savages find a lodge of [beavers], they kill all, great and small, male and female. There is danger that they will finally exterminate the species in this region, as has happened among the Hurons."‡

Given the circumstances of white commerce, it was almost inevitable that territories should come into existence. Because the Europeans placed a premium upon furs, the Sub-Arctic bands settled down to trap beaver and other sedentary mammals instead of traveling great distances after game that moved about from place to place. And once they laid their traplines, they as a matter of course established their own settlements near them. These practices do not constitute a territory as we would envison it. The traplines do not indicate an encircling boundary; rather, they follow a network of trails, lakes, and streams that are used by the same families year after year. Ownership is not permanent, but instead is based on uninterrupted use. A trapline that is not used by a family for a few years in a row can be taken over by anyone who wants it. But so long as the family maintains it, the concept of ownership as we understand it holds sway; the owner has exclusive use, can restrict trespass, and is entitled to dispose of the land.

Anthropologists have long been in dispute over whether the hunting territory existed before the coming of Whites. Most think it did not. For one thing, individual territories among such groups as the Montagnais are most firmly established in those areas where the fur trade has been carried on the most intensively; the importance of the territory decreases markedly farther away where the Montagnais hunt migratory caribou and other large mammals. For another, the resources available in a small territory simply were not varied enough to support even a small band. Fish might be present in one territory, small game in another, and large game in yet another. One anthropologist who has studied the

Northern Algonkians concluded that any band "that was forced to remain on a particular 'hunting territory'-sized tract would probably starve to death, at one time or another, within a generation."‡ Further complicating survival on a small territory was the way the critical resources—moose, caribou, snowshoe hare, fish, and waterfowl—fluctuate in abundance greatly from year to year. But it was eventually possible for families to survive on territories once the needed resources could be obtained at trading posts.

Considering their lack of experience with a capitalistic market and individual ownership of land, these Indians adapted rather well to the changed conditions. Their societies did not become either so thoroughly capitalistic or so competitive as anthropologists once supposed. Every family had the right to trap on land of its own, and if that land proved insufficient it was possible to obtain an increase. Requests for such adjustment were almost invariably honest and justified, for an Indian family obtained no advantage by claiming more territory than it could trap. No institution existed for the buying and selling of real estate, so the Indians lacked an incentive to enlarge holdings or to aggrandize at the expenses of a neighbor.

What is truly impressive about their adaptation to capitalism and land ownership is how well these Indians maintained the band's traditional cooperation. Trespass was now defined as the entrance of one hunter upon the territory of another—but only with intent to obtain furs *to sell*. An Indian might kill a beaver on someone else's land if he was hungry, but after consuming the meat he had to give the fur to the owner of the territory. It was usually not considered trespass if he entered another family's territory to fish, to collect berries, or to strip bark from trees for a canoe. The products of the land were still owned communally. Trespass applied only to those items—the fur of beaver and other mammals—that were desired by the White trader. So it appears that the hunting territory is in some ways less significant than was once thought, and in others more so. The territory is not proof that some urge to ownership is innate in humans even at the simple level of the band. Rather, it demonstrates the way in which a social organization bound together with rather loose strands, and thus resilient, can meet a new challenge and adjust to it.‡

THE SOCIAL FUNCTION OF ANXIETY

The question arises as to why these Indians so respect the others' territories, why they engage in such courtesies toward each other—whereas we would be likely to capitalize on the lack of such social controls as ministers, police, courts, and jails. But although the Northern Athapaskans and Northern Algonkians have no such religious or civil institutions, something else serves to govern their personal conduct—anxiety. Their concern about performing a multitude of little observances would appear exaggerated to us. "Fearful of their environment and numerous demons which they believed inhabited it," writes one social scientist, "they were mutually suspicious of each other, warlike, and aggressive."‡ Several attempts have been made to explain the causes of this anxiety. One cause is probably the kinlike relationship by which the northern bands are involved with totemic animals which they are nevertheless forced to kill for food and furs. Another is what the Athapaskans and Algonkians envision as their role in a harmonious universe—a role that involves an equal measure of being controlled and of attempting to exert control. Such perfect balance, in a rigorous environment that no person could hope to master even partially, is an obvious impossibility. Whatever its source may be, studies both of personality types and of folklore and myths among the Sub-Arctic bands reveal an extraordinary degree of anxiety.

The social functions of anxiety have been studied among the Salteaux branch of the Ojibwa, who live east of Lake Winnipeg in Manitoba. Among the Salteaux, the major sanction for regulating conduct is fear of disease. A headache or a raspy throat may cause mild anxiety; any greater distress brings with it trauma that is out of all proportion to the possible danger of the illness. Every disease is the penalty for what the Salteaux call "bad conduct." The deeds that can cause illness are many, and they include failure to share with others, insults, insufficient attention to the dead, cruelty to other humans or to animals, incest, sexual perversions, and homicide. Bad conduct, it is thought, does not usually cause illness right away. The transgression may lie around quietly for years, ready at any time to unleash its aftermath; people may commit deeds in their youth that decades later will produce illness in their children. Whatever the cause, the ailing person can never be certain how serious the sickness will become. It may be only a passing indisposition, but on the other hand the sick one may feel that life is in jeopardy and suffer an attack of anxiety: a feeling of helplessness that cannot be alleviated until the precise cause of the illness has been discovered.

The illness can be combated in only one way—by confession. But the Salteaux have a different idea of confession from what most people brought up in White societies are used to. We assume that any confession made to a priest, psychoanalyst, friend, or lawyer is a private matter and will be held in strictest confidence. But among the Salteaux—as among the Southern Baptists and Fundamentalist Protestant sects in North America—the whole point of confession is that it must be public; the transgressor must suffer all the shame of self-exposure. By confessing guilt, by telling the members of the band exactly what wrong was committed, the sinner deters others from making the same mistake in the future. Thus the sinner reinforces the society's value system. Details of the confession quickly spread; the young hear it discussed endlessly, and in that way they learn the kind of conduct that is expected of them.

TOTEM AND TABOO

The single most consistent feature of the religious beliefs common among Northern Athapaskans has to do with the relation that exists between humans and the animals on which they depend for food, furs, and hides.

Any distinction between humans and animals—particularly any notion that one is in some way superior to the other—is blurred as a consequence of their belief that humans may be reincarnated in animal form. The Tanana Indians, for example, believe that an animal which a hunter fails to kill must be such a reincarnated human. The spirits of animals therefore have to be placated if humans are to continue to exploit the natural environment. Each family has a particular animal as its emblem, and personal names are often derived from these animals. Descent is claimed either directly from the animal or from legendary ancestors associated with it. The very word "totem" is derived from the Algonkian language of the Ojibwa; their expression *ototeman* means, roughly, "He is my relative."

A branch of the Penobscot living near the Maine coast demonstrates the complexity of the belief in totemism. Groups of families claim association with certain aquatic creatures that fit into two categories: salt-water totems (Whale, Sculpin, Crab, Sturgeon, Perch, and Lobster) and fresh-water ones (Frog and Eel). All the Penobscot, regardless of their own totem, explain their association with the particular animals by the same origin myth: A giant frog swallowed the world's water, causing a universal drought, but a mythical hero slew it and in that way released the water. Some of the people were so thirsty that they rushed into the water, where they were transformed into various aquatic animals. Relatives who escaped the transformation then assumed the names of these animals and became the founders of the various Penobscot families. As time passed, the descendants of these founders gradually assumed some of the traits and peculiarities of their totems. Those, for example, whose totem was the Sculpin—a spiny and ugly fish of the New England coast—were generally regarded as unattractive, even though an objective observer might consider some of them to be quite comely. Each group of Penobscot believes that the particular animal whose name it bears is especially abundant in its territory. The totemic animal may be eaten, although certain rituals often have to be performed. Permission first has to be asked of the animal to kill it, and apologies later are made to it. Many Penobscot Indians also believe that each totemic animal offers itself more willingly to hunters and fishermen of the group bearing its name.‡

Before ridiculing these beliefs, people brought up in White cultures should first consider whether equivalent ones do not occur in their own society. That, as a matter of fact, they do, was demonstrated by a study during World War I concerning the development of totemism in the 42nd Division of the United States Army. The soldiers in this division came from so many states that the regimental stripes were in every color of the rainbow. The notion of a rainbow took hold, so that by the time the 42nd arrived in France, soldiers belonging to it, when asked what their unit was, promptly replied, "I'm a Rainbow." Before long, many of the men in the Rainbow Division became convinced that the appearance of a rainbow in the sky was a good omen for them. Soon most were stating with conviction that a rainbow appeared every time their unit went into action—even at times when the facts of meteorology made it impossible for a rainbow to form. The unit soon took to painting its vehicles with a rainbow emblem and to wearing a rainbow patch on the shoulder. Any use of the rainbow emblem by outsiders was resented—and punished—by those entitled to wear it.‡

Probably no anthropological subject has had so many pages of learned discussion expended upon it as has totemism, which appears in many different cultures around the world. Psychologists, sociologists, anthropologists, and folklorists, among others, have all had a crack at explaining it. Not only is there no agreement, but many theorists wish the troublesome aspects of the subject would simply go away. Freud's well-known study, *Totem and Taboo* (1918), demonstrates the lengths to which a theorist will go to find an explanation. Freud stated that each male child strongly wishes to have sexual intercourse with his mother and so wills the death of the father, his rival. In the Primal Horde,

according to Freud, murder of the father by his jealous
sons actually took place. Ever since, though, such murder has been vicarious, the ritual slaughter of an animal
having been substituted for the original act of patricide.
In that way, reconciliation with the father is achieved
by way of a substitute, the totemic animal. Examination
of cultures around the world has failed to substantiate
Freud's theory, either as a whole or in part. Anthropologists today regard it as totally discredited—which
may be the one thing about totemism they are able to
agree upon.‡

One common denominator of totemism is that it deals
with dualities or opposites that share at least one characteristic, thus allowing a comparison to be made. The
dual totems may be as closely related as two species of
the same kind of animal, or they may be two birds that
are known to be rivals, such as the eagle and the crow.
The crow usually attempts to get its food by subterfuge
or theft from the eagle, which nevertheless is much
stronger. The crow and the eagle are both birds, but the
habits of one will never become the habits of the other.
All the totems of the Penobscot belonged to a single set
of aquatic animals, within which the salt-water and
fresh-water species were opposites. Those Ojibwa Indians of Parry Island who took birds as their totems
divided them into the opposite categories of aerial birds
(such as the Eagle) and aquatic birds (such as the
Loon); those who selected mammals for their totems
divided these into the categories of terrestrial (Moose,
Wolf) and aquatic (Beaver, Otter).

Anthropologists misunderstood totemism for so long
because they thought "primitive" people were concerned
only with filling their stomachs. But as Claude Lévi–
Strauss put it, ". . . natural species are chosen not because they are 'good to eat' but because they are 'good
to think.' "‡ People who have totems are not thinking
about the single totemic animal so much as about the
duality. An isolated totem is meaningless; it becomes
important only when it can be related to one or more
other totems that are generally similar but particularly

different. So when Indians talk about two species of totemic animals, they are not stressing the animality— rather, the duality.

An important reason for accenting such a duality is social, not psychological: Totems serve to define important marriage relationships. In most bands and tribes, genealogical sequences are usually remembered for only two or three generations. Some method must therefore be found for a man and a woman to determine that they are not related and are thus suitable marriage partners. They cannot rely on memory alone, for disease, famine, and old age cause too many deaths among the elders who might have been able to recall who one's ancestors were. But they can rely on their allegiance to totems. If both a man and a woman belong to the Eagle totem, then they are considered related (even though in actual fact they may not be) and they cannot marry. But if one is an Eagle and the other a Loon, then the duality of the totems guarantees that they are unrelated—and so they are permitted to marry.

When the duality of totems is recognized as a way to define descent, it becomes clear that what in Modern American society are sometimes regarded as totems are not really that at all. Some authors have assigned totemic status to the names of sports teams (Bears, Bruins, Tigers, Lions, and so on); to the Democratic party's donkey and the Republicans' elephant; and to such social and fraternal organizations as the Elks and Lions. These symbols are not totems because they do not indicate common descent or who may marry whom. They are, though, similar to totems in that the names serve to set one group apart from another and may become a symbolic focus of allegiance.

The societies of the Shoshone, the Eskimo, the Northern Algonkians, and the Northern Athapaskans—uncomplex as they seem to be—nevertheless possess many characteristics that give them unity, that raise them above the organizational level of the family. Also constantly at work is a tendency toward stability and permanence, a tendency for cooperating families to formalize their relations. The band organization possesses a potential to grow and to become more complex —to become a tribe, the subject of the next section.

V

Zuñi:
Unity Through Religion

THE PUEBLO INDIANS

The Pueblo Indians include the Hopi and Zuñi tribes in northeastern Arizona–western New Mexico and the eastern Pueblo (such as those of Taos, San Ildefonso, and Isleta) near the upper Rio Grande River in central New Mexico. Only about thirty pueblos (Spanish for "villages") still survive out of seventy or so that were inhabited at the time Don Francisco Vásquez de Coronado made contact with them in 1540, during his search for the mythical Seven Cities of Cíbola. The ancestors of the Pueblo Indians once occupied an extensive territory in Utah, Colorado, Arizona, and New Mexico; the Spaniards, however, cannot be blamed entirely for their decline. A drastic shrinkage in territory and a great reduction in the number of villages had already taken place before the Spaniards arrived. A prolonged drought in the thirteenth century accounted for the abandonment of numerous villages; others were evacuated or destroyed because of inter-Pueblo warfare and possibly also because of depredations by Ute, Apache, and Navajo groups.‡

Although the number of villages today is less than in Coronado's time, few other North American Indians have survived with so much of their culture intact. Despite pressures by the Spaniards and later by Mexicans and Americans, the Pueblo have clung tenaciously to their traditions. Important aspects of their life continue with remarkably little alteration. Their clans still function; their social structure is generally unaltered. Although the world around them has changed markedly in the last four centuries, they have largely remained insulated against many changes and have striven to maintain their culture. Some of their dances are open to White spectators, but most of the ceremonials are not; even the "open" ones convey much esoteric lore about which the White onlookers are ignorant. Pueblo Indians who happen not to be members of the participating clans are likewise often excluded from such events. Most of the villages have kivas, secret ceremonial chambers that are usually built partially underground, although the six at Zuñi are above ground.

All of the Pueblo Indians are organized as tribes, which at first thought might seem very much like bands. Like the band, a tribe is based largely on the family; it is egalitarian; no full-time specialists such as soldiers, artisans, priests, or political officeholders are maintained. Differences, though, do exist. The most apparent of these is that a tribe is much larger than a band. It has merged the local, exogamous lineage into a more complex social and political entity made up of several lineages. Not only is the tribe composed of a greater number of groups than a band; in addition, specialized functions are carried out by different groups.

The tribe is an inherently fragile structure. Without any strong political organization or permanent authority that might give stability, it is regulated by a variety of social institutions—among them clans, secret clubs, and specialized societies. The tribal "chief" belongs to no political hierarchy or dominant group; he is merely a sort of consultant, an adviser who may or may not be listened to. In the absence of political authority in the tribe, the lineages take unto themselves the right of self-protection. As in the band, disputes tend to be perpetuated as feuds, with each act of revenge generating a reprisal.

Anthropologists have not had opportunities to witness the growth of a band into a tribe, but the transition can be imagined. First, there would have been a band, with its low population density and its scattered lineages. As agriculture developed, or as the environment was exploited more efficiently in some other way, one result would be a denser population—either more people would come to occupy the same amount of land, or the same number of people would need less of it. In either event, new lineages would be established and their search for food would bring them into the immediate vicinity of other lineages, once again increasing the

density of the population. At first a continued respect for kinship relations would be sufficient to unite several lineages into a tribe; but as the population grew larger, the memory of exact kinship relations would fade. Nevertheless, the fiction of kinship would have to be maintained in order to guarantee solidarity; in what are called lineal tribes, this is largely the function of clans. Besides stressing the common ancestry of the group, clans are also ceremonial societies, landholding corporations, recruiters for war—but above all, they police their own members and maintain good relations with other clans in the tribe. Among the better known lineal tribes are the Zuñi and the Hopi, the Navajo, the Iroquois, and the Huron.

THE CLAN

Not far from the Arizona–New Mexico border, nearly 5,500 Zuñi live in their brown, sunbaked pueblo of adobe and stone, which the chronicler of the Coronado expedition described as "a little crowded village, looking as if it had been crumpled together." The people of Zuñi are organized into thirteen clans, each one named for a different totemic animal or plant; no taboo exists against eating the totem, nor are any special observances concerning it usually required. Marriage between members of the same clan is prohibited. Both the marriage prohibition and the absence of restrictions against eating the totem apparently reinforce the hypothesis discussed earlier: that totemism really is concerned with group solidarity and the identification of approved marriage partners rather than with the food supply. The members of a clan cooperate in the harvest and help one another in building houses; each clan possesses its own sacred fetish, which is kept in one of the clan households.

The clan was foreshadowed in the band when hunting groups cooperated and held joint ceremonies. In the patrilocal band, such cooperating groups were by-products of residence with the husband's father and brothers. Clan membership, though, is based not on one's place of residence but on who one's parents are. Rather than accenting the territoriality of groups, the clan is pan-tribal; it cuts across boundaries and emphasizes common ancestry, mainly through special insignia and ceremonies, the use of the same name, and a shared mythology and clan history. The very fact that two Zuñi belong to the same clan is sufficient to establish their kinship, even though the actual blood ties are not known and, in fact, might be nonexistent. A blood relative in the clan, such as a first cousin, is not considered to be closer than someone who is not a blood relative but with whom the fiction of kinship is maintained. The situation is not much different from a college fraternity where one's blood cousin would be no closer a "fraternity brother" than any other member.

Clans emphasize the alliance of various families, and in that way they reinforce the solidarity of the lineal tribe. They possess an assortment of secret paraphernalia—costumes, fetishes, and sacred altars. They usually also display esoteric insignia in face decoration, in clothing designs, and even in symbolic patterns painted on houses. Each clan carries on its own rituals, and great secrecy is maintained. Punishment for disclosure to an outsider is severe; it may be flogging or even death. The influence of the clan reaches into other areas as well: It controls agricultural fields, maintains burying grounds, and preserves peace among its members. A clan may specialize in a particular duty for the entire tribe, or it may be responsible for performing a ceremony. Various clans hold the rights to particular offices and rituals. For example, the Priest of the North is always a member of the Dogwood clan and the Priest of the South a member of the Badger clan; the leader of the Kachinas comes from the Deer clan. Each clan is therefore essential to the welfare of the whole tribe, and all clans are bound together by their dependence upon one another.‡

THE WOMAN'S ROLE

The Zuñi kinship system is matrilineal and matrilocal. The husband goes to live with his wife's family, who may add an extra room for the daughter's new family. The constant addition of rooms is one of the reasons for the jumbled look of a Zuñi village. The household is really an extended family, sometimes numbering twenty-five people, that includes the grandmother with her husband, her unmarried daughters, her married daughters with their husbands and children, and her unmarried brothers and sons. The women own the house, and all the men except the unmarried brothers and unmarried sons are outsiders. The fields also belong to the matrilineal clans, with the women holding the rights to what the land produces. The men labor in the gardens, but whatever they harvest goes into the common storage bins maintained by the women of the household.

Marriage at Zuñi is best described as "brittle monogamy." A wife can divorce her husband simply by placing his possessions outside the door. No property claims must be resolved since she and her lineage own almost everything; her sons, her unmarried or divorced brothers, and her sisters' husbands can easily enough provide the necessary manual labor until she remarries. Similarly, the divorced man can always expect a welcome if he returns to his mother's and his sisters' household; they are happy to receive the windfall of his labor. The husband feels that his real home is in the household of his mother and his sisters. He interests himself deeply in their affairs; he is concerned with bringing up his nephews and nieces; and he returns to their household on ceremonial occasions.

Matrilineal descent and matrilocal residence present a problem that did not exist in the patrilocal band: the change in the husband's role as an authority figure in the family. He has married into his wife's family and household but remains a member of the lineage into which he was born; he is the one who is the stranger.

In Zuñi and in many other matrilineal societies, the wife's brother (her closest male relative who is a member of her lineage) assumes from the biological father the role of authority over the children. Certain readjustments in family relations result: The biological father is much less likely to be domineering and authoritative, as he is in a patrilineal tribe; his wife's family is always prompt to remind him that he is, in both the literal and the metaphorical sense, "out of line." He is in competition with his wife's brother for the affection of his own children, particularly his sons. As a result, he is apt to be mild in the treatment of his sons and lavish in giving them presents.

Although many tribes trace descent through the male and have rules providing for residence with the father's family, many other tribes have become matrilineal in the way the Zuñi, Hopi, and Iroquois have. Among bands of hunters, an important reason for residence with the father was that brothers could cooperate in hunting a territory they had known all their lives. An emphasis on cooperation among women also seems to explain why some tribes have become matrilineal. Most of the matrilineal tribes known about have one thing in common: They practice gardening based on natural rainfall rather than on the building of irrigation works, which would have required male cooperation to build and to maintain. As the primary food producers, women tend the gardens, collaborate in processing the food, share storage places, and sometimes even cook together. Males continue, of course, to cooperate in hunting, fighting, and ceremonial activities. But since the space utilized by a horticultural tribe is much less than that by a hunting band, males continue to be near one another anyway, whether or not the residence pattern is patrilocal.

Whether a society will be matrilocal or patrilocal often depends on the relative importance of either warfare or subsistence. The Mundurucú Indians of the Amazon jungles of Brazil provide documentation for the way in which a horticultural tribe may change from a patrilocal to a matrilocal one in only two generations as the relative importance of these two factors changes. Before Whites became a major influence in their jungle domain, the Mundurucú women collaborated in growing manioc and in processing flour from these plants—an activity that was overshadowed, however, by the unremitting warfare between the Mundurucú and their neighbors. Male cooperation in warfare served to emphasize the patrilocal marriage rules instead of the matrilocal ones that might have been expected in the presence of a subsistence based on gardening. Then the Whites who settled the area became a profitable market for the sale of manioc flour produced by the Mundurucú women; at the same time, the Whites prohibited warfare between tribes. Within a period of about fifty years, female participation in Mundurucú society became paramount, and the tribe switched from patrilineal to matrilineal rules.‡

ZUÑI RELIGION

The Pueblo Indians spend about half their waking hours in religious activities, and practically everything they do is restricted by their religious strictures. Each village is governed by a council made up of the leaders of the various religious societies. The priestly foundation of Pueblo society was recognized by the chronicler of the Coronado expedition: "They do not have chiefs . . . but are ruled by a council of the oldest men. They have priests, who preach to them, whom they call 'elder brothers.' They tell them how they are to live, and I believe that they give certain commandments for them to keep, for there is no drunkenness among them, nor sodomy, nor sacrifices, neither do they eat human flesh nor steal, but they are usually at work." Hardly a week goes by in which some ceremonial event is not enacted to bring rain, to keep the crops growing, to bring blessings to the village and health to the individual.

The Zuñi have been characterized by Ruth L. Bunzel, an anthropologist who several decades ago made an extensive study of their ceremonialism, as "one of the most thoroughly religious peoples of the world."‡ Zuñi is an almost complete theocracy. Control is vested in a council composed of three members from the principal priesthood, plus the heads of three other priesthoods. The priests also have the power to appoint the officers of the secular government, for the priests are concerned primarily with matters of ritual and leave the day-to-day affairs of the village to the tribal council. This secular arm is concerned with settling disputes within the village, with nonreligious crimes and their punishment, and with the conduct of external relations, which nowadays means dealing with the various bureaus of the federal and state governments.

The Zuñi religion extends its influences in a variety of ways into the clan as well as into the household and the government of the village. Each of six specialized religious cults—the Sun, the Uwanami ("rain-makers"), Kachinas (also spelled Katcinas), the Priests of the Kachinas, the War Gods, and the Beast Gods—possesses its own priesthood, its own fetishes, and its own kiva. Each devotes itself to particular rituals in its own cycle of ceremonies, and each is dedicated to the worship of a particular set of supernatural beings. Outsiders are not likely to realize how very complex the ceremonials of these cults are. Every color and every piece of material in the dance costume, every step and every gesture—all are replete with significance. Each of the six kiva groups dances at least three times during the year, and the preparations may take several weeks or even several months. Membership in a kiva is not hereditary; rather, a youth is sponsored by a ceremonial "father" whose kiva he joins. This further weakens the bonds linking the boy to his biological father. The boy is emotionally and socially attached first to his mother's lineage, then to his uncles on his mother's side, next to his ceremonial sponsor into a kiva, and only last to his biological father.

The cult at Zuñi that Whites are most likely to have heard about is the one devoted to the kachinas, the nearly two hundred happy spirits who live beneath the surface of the waters. The Zuñi believe that the kachinas visit the village each year—at which time they are impersonated by Zuñi men wearing costumes and large masks. The masks are treated with great reverence, for it is believed that a dancer who dons one becomes temporarily transformed into the kachina itself. The owner prizes his mask above all else. The kachina dolls often purchased by White tourists along roadsides in the Southwest have no spiritual significance, contrary to the usual belief. They are pedagogical devices to educate the young in the identification of the numerous kinds of kachinas. Nothing sacred or divine is attached to them —though the proprietor of the roadside curio shop may make such a claim. What are sacred are the masks used in the dances, and that is why a Zuñi will almost never sell one, no matter how much money is offered.

The solidarity of Zuñi culture, so obvious even to the casual observer, is due to the interlocking relationships of clans and religious societies. People are born into a household, a lineage, and a clan, and they can choose to belong to various social and religious groups as well. Many loyalties serve to integrate the entire village by linking people in all directions: Someone might belong to household A, kinship B, clan C, society D, kiva E, priesthood F, and so on. Nearly every Zuñi in a village is linked in some sort of formalized relationship with fellow citizens.

At the level of the band, the shaman performs for the individual alone. But at the level of the lineal tribe, religion is an activity for the entire group. Individuals are no longer lonely souls in quest of the spirits; they become part of a social group that has specific methods for dealing with the supernatural. That does not mean that all the showmanship has gone out of religion. The Zuñi cult of the Beast Gods, for example, is made up of twelve medicine societies, and each society has developed its own secret tricks of swallowing sticks or walking over hot coals. But in the tribe such prestidigitation is controlled by society and not by religious entrepreneurs. Nor do the Zuñi humble themselves before the supernatural. They dicker with it. The Zuñi priest tells the supernatural agencies exactly how he has fulfilled his part of the bargain by the performance of the ceremonials. Now, he says, it is up to the spirits to deliver. The Zuñi often conceive of the spirits as being human and therefore susceptible to emotional appeals. So the Zuñi not only bargain; they also flatter and appeal to the pity of the spirits.

Something else also appears in religion at the level of the lineal tribe. In the band, various classes of spirits control particular places and people, perhaps a spirit of the house or of the fishing boat. But a new concept emerges in the lineal tribe—that of superior gods who control more than only a certain house or a hunting territory. Each reigns over a specific activity and, by extension, therefore protects all people who engage in that activity. Each superior god is important, although no single one is all-powerful. The superior gods of the Zuñi in this way resemble the gods of the ancient Greeks and Romans: Mercury or Hermes, winged messenger; Poseidon or Neptune, ruler of the sea; Mars or Ares, god of battle. Nor are they much different in function from the patron saints of the Roman Catholic Church. Among the Zuñi, the water serpent Kolowisi is the guardian of springs wherever they may exist; Chakwena Woman aids in rabbit hunts; each of the medicine societies possesses its own Beast God, which assists it in the practice of its specialty, whether it be curing colds or removing bullets.

The superior gods of Zuñi are not as clearly delineated as are the superior gods in the more complex societies of the chiefdom and the state. At Zuñi, all men work in the fields and hunt, and little occupational specialization is apparent. The superior gods of the fields and the hunt are therefore not very sharply delineated from one another. But in the more complex societies of the chiefdom and the state, occupations become increasingly more specialized. Some men hunt only particular kinds of game, others only farm, and still others may devote themselves entirely to producing works of art. In the chiefdom and the state, human society with its various specializations provides a model for the superior gods, who are endowed with distinct personalities and very specific areas of responsibility.

A man in the Eskimo or Shoshone band is considered poor if he lacks kin whose aid he can count on. In Zuñi, the poor man is the one who does not take part in the religious rituals or who does not own ceremonial property. Wealth among the Zuñi is equated with ceremonial activities: Only the wealthy man has the time and the resources to participate to the fullest in religious ceremonies. Masks are always kept in certain wealthy households. Particular families also vie to entertain those Zuñi who are masked as kachinas, both during the ceremonies and for several days afterward when the dancers go into retreat. Wealth once again becomes a factor, for not every family can afford the large expenditure necessary for food or for preparing rooms to house the dancers.

Zuñi ceremonial observances, for all their strangeness to a modern American, really do not differ very much from the annual round of religious–secular holidays in the United States: Veterans Day, Memorial Day, Thanksgiving, and Christmas. All are legal holidays, and all have their holy and their secular aspects; all are celebrated both in places of worship and in the social and economic sphere. For example, on Memorial Day an American family may go to church in the morning to commemorate the dead, and in the afternoon to a holiday doubleheader at the baseball park to cheer on the living. On this day, Americans, no matter where they live or how rich or poor they may be, express stereotyped sentiments and platitudes. The common heritage of all Americans is emphasized, even though it is largely a myth—for the ancestors of many people alive in the United States today immigrated to the United States after the first Memorial Day was observed, following the Civil War. Many American towns nevertheless, as they go through the roster of war dead, will try hard to find among the names a Jones, an O'Connell, a Goldberg, a Russo, a Royinski.

THE "PEACEFUL" PUEBLO?

A myth has grown up about the Pueblo Indians in general and the Zuñi in particular, largely as a result of the popularity of the book *Patterns of Culture* (1934) by Ruth Benedict. According to her, Zuñi represented the ideal human society, one of "Apollonian" noncompetitiveness. Everyone was devoted to religion; sobriety and inoffensiveness were highly valued; life was orderly, pleasant, unemotional. If a man regularly won races, he was supposed to withdraw in the future so as not to spoil the contest for others. Everyone was seemingly well adjusted, with no more attention paid to sex than it deserved. Children grew up as unfettered spirits without the strictures of discipline.

Benedict's view of Zuñi is totally misleading; in fact, she never did sufficient field work there to justify her conclusions. Most anthropologists who have studied the Zuñi closely have come away with a far different picture. One found the Zuñi (and the nearby Hopi as well) to be anxiety-ridden, suspicious, hostile, fearful, and ambitious.‡ Florence Hawley Ellis has effectively demolished Benedict's view of the "peaceful" Pueblo: "Pueblo people are endlessly bickering, with covert expressions of hostility against anyone who does not quite fit into the Pueblo pattern, who has more or different possessions. Like any other human beings, these people are subject to jealousies, angers, and the desire for retaliation."‡

The Pueblo Indians may appear peaceful on the surface, but their history belies that appearance. Every village had—and most still have—a war priest, with rank equal to the leading civil priest, and a warrior society, which served as a military force outside the village and which still serves as a police force within it. Each village was always mobilized. No recruitment or special preparations had to be made for war; the war priest and the warrior society stood ready to meet violence at any time. Other anthropologists have shown Benedict's assertion that drunkenness is "repulsive" to the Zuñi to be erroneous. The most common crimes at Zuñi are drunkenness and reckless driving.

The Chinese scholar Li An-che, in reporting on his three months at Zuñi, raised the obvious point that we should not rely too much on appearances. In reply to Benedict's assertion that the Zuñi eschew ambition and are afraid of becoming leaders lest they be accused of sorcery, he wrote:

The problem is not the contrast between leadership and its denial, but the valuation of the ways and means of achieving it. In any face-to-face community, it is safe to assume that no individual with common sense will try to make himself ridiculous by seeking what is obviously beyond his reach, and that even the most eager and legitimate aspirants to high position will make the ordinary official declination of an offer. Modern societies have asylums to take care of the insane, but a primitive community would have to charge the mentally dangerous with sorcery in order to follow the policy of "safety first" for the communal welfare.‡

Further, Li found in the very presence of so many secular and religious functionaries at Zuñi clear evidence that ambition is not lacking. Li also concluded that Benedict had been much deceived about the subject of sex; promiscuity seemed to have won out over fidelity. Young men, wearing large hats to mask their identity, would slink past a fence or dart around a house to arrange their meetings. After a hasty supper, they kept the assignations they had arranged during the day. Li did not consider an exaggeration what one youth told him—that he could have intercourse with any woman at Zuñi whose husband happened to be away or who was not married.

Finally, Li did not find Zuñi child-rearing so worthy of emulation as Benedict did. She praised the permissiveness of Zuñi parents and maintained that as a result Zuñi children were rarely disobedient. Once again she was misled. Responsibility for the discipline of Zuñi children falls heavily on no one in particular, since in a matrilineal society the authority of the biological father has been weakened. The end result, though, is the opposite of permissiveness: Instead of being subjected to the authority of one biological father, the Zuñi child is disciplined by everyone in the household, which may amount to some twenty-five people. And almost all adults in the village, even those not associated through a kinship or a ceremonial relationship to a particular child, will take pains to correct any slight misbehavior they happen to note. The child who gets out of line is immediately hushed by a disapproving glance from some adult. At Zuñi the preferred method of chastisement, which the people consider more effective than physical punishment, is ultimately much more cruel to the child: It consists of constant ridicule and belittling.

RITES OF REBELLION

Even though Benedict drew the wrong conclusions, some of her observations about Zuñi are true. Its society is rigidly structured, and its members behave without display of emotion. But do people actually survive, day after day, with no escape from the psychological strictures imposed by their society? Or are there hidden mechanisms that allow repressed aggressions to be worked off?

Assuredly there are at Zuñi. Before the enforced peacefulness brought by Whites, the Pueblo Indians had

enthusiastic war cults that channeled aggression into
socially acceptable behavior. Before the coming of the
Spaniards, and even for some time thereafter, considerable internecine warfare took place between various
Pueblo tribes, a common excuse being a suspicion of
witchcraft. The warrior society, which nowadays functions solely as a police force, in pre-White times must
have allowed a tremendous amount of internal aggression to escape. To become a member of the Bow
Priests, for example, a warrior had to bring back an
enemy's scalp. The war ceremonies in recent times have
of necessity become more symbolic than real. In place
of the scalp of a fresh victim, the ceremonies make do
with an old one from those still kept in the Zuñi kivas.
The scalp is kicked into the village by four aunts of the
"warrior" while the onlookers whoop it up and shoot off
guns. If a mere symbolic dramatization produces such a
frenzy today, we may imagine what the commotion
must have been when a warrior returned with the actual
scalp of a Navajo or a Ute. Witnesses report that, in
those days, dances around a scalp pole erected in the
plaza continued for twelve nights.

Rebellion against expected behavior also shows up
in certain rites that mock the gods, ridicule the ceremonials, revile the conventions, and merge obscenity
with religion. During such rites, the hostility that the
members of Zuñi society keep repressed during most of
the year comes to the surface in a socially approved
fashion. The prime agents of these rites are members
of the Priests of the Kachinas cult, who are known as
Koyemshi or Mudheads. They are sacred clowns, gro-
tesque in appearance, wearing mud-daubed masks in
which the nose and eyes appear as bulging knobs; the
mouth is a gaping hole, and the entire face is disfigured
with large warts.

The Mudheads are said to have been born of an incestuous union and therefore to be excused from
conventional behavior; hence the obscenities and the
mockery of things ordinarily held in reverence. They
cavort around the serious dancers, giving vent to what-

ever their unconscious feelings may dictate concerning the ceremony or the audience. Their antics are funny in the same way a circus clown is funny and partly for the same reason, both being excused from conventional behavior. A Mudhead may satirize the dancers by a too-meticulous attention to ceremony; he may keep dancing long after the other dancers have finished, focusing attention on himself until he finally realizes his "mistake." In one skit, reminiscent of vaudeville or television, a Zuñi clown uses a play telephone to carry on an imaginary conversation with the gods.

Some observers have suggested that these routines originated only in recent decades, perhaps inspired by movies or by television—but one account of clowning at Zuñi in 1881 shows that they are not new.‡ According to this account, twelve Zuñi males dressed themselves in odd bits of clothing to caricature a Mexican priest, an American soldier, an old woman, and several other identifiable types. The principal performance of the evening was a devastating parody of Roman Catholic ritual. The dancers rolled on the ground, and with extravagant beating of the breast mocked a Catholic service. One bawled out the paternoster; another took the role of a lecherous padre; a third mimicked old people reciting the rosary. The dancers then started to eat such things as corn husks and filthy rags. One called out, in the same way that a diner might summon a waiter in a restaurant, for a portion of dog excrement. In place of sacramental wine, several of the dancers took long swallows of human urine, smacked their lips, and pronounced it tasty. The account reports that the audience of men, women, and children responded with uncontrolled merriment.

What do these rites of rebellion indicate? Are they as infantile as they seem, or is some more complex social mechanism at work? Obviously, they release the audience emotionally by permitting it to tread forbidden ground, without the usual consequences. Comic relief, though, is probably not the only explanation for these rites. Far from being entirely negative, they give positive support to the Zuñi social order. At one level, the effect of the burlesque is negative because it undermines convention; but at the same time, through contrast and the very outrageousness of the buffoonery, it reinforces what everyone in the audience has known all along—the social behavior that is proper.‡

VI
Iroquois:
A Woodland Democracy

"THE GREEKS OF AMERICA"

At the time the Whites arrived, the most powerful Indians in northeastern North America were those centered in New York State—various groups who spoke dialects of the Iroquoian language. Some scholars used to believe that they were invaders of the area, recently arrived from the south. But though they are indeed related linguistically to the Cherokee of North Carolina and Tennessee, their culture is now known to be indigenous and to have emerged from that of the lower Great Lakes several centuries before the arrival of Whites. They had trained systematically to equip themselves for warfare in the woodlands; they grew in population, in prosperity, and in the complexity of their culture. After the Whites arrived, they responded to the fur trade by expanding in all directions so as to control the rich beaver territories. Some American romantics have called the Iroquois "The Greeks of America"—but it would probably be more accurate to regard them as our native Prussian Junkers.

To the European explorers, the culture of the Iroquois tribes obviously differed considerably from that of the neighboring Algonkian bands. The Iroquois village was constructed on flat land alongside a stream or a lake, and was protected by a palisade of logs. The village became a permanent fixture of the landscape; around it the forest was cleared to make space for gardens. Inside the palisade were large rectangular longhouses made of elm bark on a wood frame, each containing many compartments that were occupied by several related families.

The sedentary, agricultural Iroquois were much admired by the Jesuits of New France, particularly as contrasted with the nomadic Algonkian bands. The Jesuits described in laudatory terms the villages, which sometimes numbered several hundred people; the extensive fields of maize and other vegetables; and the dignified governmental councils. Underscoring the differences between the Iroquois and the Algonkians, one of the Jesuits wrote: "The Iroquois and Hurons [also an Iroquoian-speaking people] are more inclined to practice virtue than the other nations; they are the only savages capable of refined feelings; all others are to be set down as cowardly, ungrateful, and voluptuous."‡

Despite such virtues, the Iroquois were noted for the havoc they spread among Indians as far south as Virginia and Tennessee and westward to Michigan. The fiercest of the Iroquois were the Mohawk (the name means "cannibals"), who lived just west of the Hudson River in New York State. To the west of them were the extraordinary fierce Oneida, and then came the Onondaga, a relatively peaceful tribe; farther west were the Cayuga, a small group. The most westerly Iroquois, and the most numerous, were the Seneca, who harassed the Indians living along the Ohio River and its tributaries. These five tribes formed the *Hodenosaunee* or League of the Five Nations (becoming the Six Nations when the remnants of the Tuscarora were admitted in 1722). During the period of English colonial rule, several other groups, such as the Delaware, were brought under the protection of the Iroquois. The League eventually might have extended its control from the western Great Lakes to the Atlantic Ocean—had it not been checked by the White colonists.

THE DEMOCRACY OF THE LEAGUE

The story of the League's origin has been pieced together from numerous sources, a good many no doubt fictional. It seems that around 1570 a saintly prophet named Dekanawidah, born of a virgin mother, put an end to warfare among the five tribes and established the "Great Peace." Dekanawidah was supposedly inspired by a dream in which he saw a huge evergreen tree reaching up through the sky to the land of the Master of Life. This was the tree of the sisterhood (not brotherhood, for the Iroquois were a matrilineal society), and its supporting roots were the five Iroquois tribes. What Dekanawidah envisioned was brought into being by Hiawatha, his spokesman, who was said to have paddled his white canoe from tribe to tribe, eloquently urging peace among them, and eventually to have brought about the formation of the League. The noted poem by Longfellow has caused much confusion about the historical Hiawatha. Longfellow used as his source a number of legends from Ojibwa bands; casting about for a main character to tie together these legends, he chose the name of Hiawatha, the hero of a group of tribes not at all like the Ojibwa bands.

An impetus for Iroquois confederation more likely than any vision of a prophetic Dekanawidah may be traced to the first probings by French ships into the Gulf of St. Lawrence, early in the sixteenth century. The Iroquois could hardly have been unaware of the Whites just beyond their borders. Cartier, for example, is known to have sailed up the St. Lawrence River, and he had probably reached the vicinity of Montreal about thirty-five years before the League was formed. Again and again, all over North America, Indians challenged by White invasion either ran away (as did the Great Basin Shoshone) or settled their petty differences and confederated (as did the Pueblo Indians when they rebelled against the Spaniards in 1680). The very practical question of how the Iroquois were to defend themselves against the alien Whites may have given religious sanction by the visions of Dekanawidah.

The League favorably impressed the White settlers, and some historians believe it to have been one of the models on which the Constitution of the new United States of America was based. In organization the League did somewhat resemble the union of the original thirteen colonies, but in other ways it was closer to the United Nations. The League had a constitution, which was orally transmitted, but it could not levy taxes, and it lacked a police force to carry out its decisions. The hereditary leaders, the Council of Sachems, were concerned solely with external matters, such as war and peace and the making of treaties. The Council could not interfere in the affairs of the individual tribes—a situation that is analogous to the small influence the federal government originally had over the internal affairs of the thirteen states. Each tribe had its own sachems, but they also were limited in their powers; they dealt with the tribe's relations with other tribes and not with clan matters.

The tribes were not equally represented in the Council of Sachems, but the inequities were more apparent than real. The Iroquois had worked out their primitive democracy in a way unfamiliar to Modern Americans. Of the fifty hereditary sachems, the Onondaga had fourteen; the Cayuga, ten; the Mohawk and Oneida, nine each; and the Seneca, even though they were the most numerous, only eight. Before any vote was taken, the sachems of each tribe met in private so that the tribe could speak with one voice—just as, in a presidential election in the United States, each state casts its entire electoral vote for one candidate. The major difference between the Iroquois system and our own was that decisions reached by the Council of Sachems had to be unanimous. If four of the tribes were in favor of a motion, but with the fifth against it, they would simply argue until the fifth gave in—or until the single recalcitrant tribe won over the other four. So the inequality in representation between the Seneca, with only eight sachems, and the Onondaga, with fourteen, was ultimately meaningless.

The Iroquois system was not, though, as democratic

as it appeared to the early settlers. The approximately
fifty sachem titles were rigidly controlled. Only males
belonging to certain matrilineages within each tribe
could hold the title of sachem. When a sachem died, his
successor could be selected only from the matriliny
holding that title, and the females were the ones who
did the choosing. The headwoman of the lineage assembled all the women of her clan and discussed with
them her choice for a successor sachem. The women's
control over the sachem did not end with his selection.
If he failed to perform his duties as they liked, the headwoman gave him three stern warnings, after which he
was removed and his badge of office was given to a new
candidate. So even though the women did not themselves rule, they had the sole power to appoint and to
remove from office.

All of which only emphasizes the control exerted by
women among the Iroquois. Property and goods were
inherited entirely through the female line. The women
owned the longhouse, the garden plots (even though
they were cleared by the men), and the tools used to
cultivate the land. Peace and order in the longhouse
were maintained by the women. Husbands came and
went, either through losses in warfare or through the
simple process of divorce, and the children of these
unions belonged to the mother's lineage. In the political
sphere, women not only appointed the sachems and
named their successors when they died; women might
even act as regent for a sachem too young to rule. In
warfare, they had the power of life or death over
prisoners. They also helped to select the religious practitioners known as "keepers of the faith," and half of
these had to be females.

For all these reasons the Iroquois are usually regarded as having come as close to matriarchy as any
society in the world. In actuality, though, females cannot be said to have ruled, since they did not directly
serve in the positions of leadership in the supreme council. Furthermore, males were clearly dominant in the
society, as Lewis Henry Morgan pointed out: "The
[Iroquois] Indian regarded women as the inferior, the
dependent, and the servant of man, and from nurtur-

ance and habit, she actually considered herself to be so." Numerous anthropologists nevertheless agree with a recent conclusion that Iroquois females "enjoyed unusual authority in their society, perhaps more than women have ever enjoyed anywhere at any time."‡

How can this unusual power be accounted for? One explanation that seems to fit the known facts is based upon the almost total control of subsistence by the Iroquois women. They were sedentary horticulturists while the males were nomadic—nearly always away making war, hunting, trapping, or trading. So, by default, the males had allowed the females to become economically self-sufficient. Iroquois women not only totally controlled the lands they cultivated, the implements they used, and the seed supply. They also maintained the right to distribute all food, even that obtained by males through hunting. The females could thus prevent the formation of a war party, if they disagreed with the action, by withholding supplies of dried corn needed for the expedition. In other words, the unusually high status of females is not explainable as some historical curiosity but rather as the direct result of controlling the economic foundations of the tribe.

GREAT LEADERS AND GREAT EVENTS

This would seem a good place for a pause to speculate about what might have happened to the Iroquois League had Hiawatha not been born. Would the League itself ever have been established—and if it had, would the events that followed have been any different? The question really being asked is: Do great leaders and great events determine the major course a culture will take?

People who believe that the answer to this question is in the affirmative usually point to sudden spurts in the history of cultures. The culture of Classic Greece lasted for about 1,250 years, but most of its achievements were concentrated in the 150 years around the fourth century B.C. and primarily in the small area occupied by Athens. During this brief time Greek democracy developed, the population increased, military ventures were almost always successful, the arts and sciences flourished. Similarly, much of the grandeur of Rome was compressed into a few decades under the reigns of Julius and Augustus Caesar. Similar bursts of cultural energy took place under the Chou and Han dynasties of China, during the Age of Pyramids and the Middle Kingdom in Egypt, during the Renaissance in Italy, and in the England of Elizabeth I.

Most of us were taught in school to explain such climaxes in culture by the birth of great leaders or by great historic events. If the logic of such an explanation is carried to its conclusion, then Shakespeare must have been inspired to write his plays by the reign of Elizabeth I and the defeat of the Spanish Armada; and Rome's burst of creativity in architecture, roadbuilding, sculpture, and literature occurred because the Gauls were conquered and because Augustus succeeded Julius Caesar. Such explanations are demonstrably nonsense. A close look at the chronology of events in Elizabethan England and Augustan Rome reveals that the creative burst had already begun before the onset of the great events or the arrival of the great personages.

We are in the habit of thinking in terms of great leaders largely because the leaders themselves want it that way. The pharaohs ordered that a record of their accomplishments be carved on stone; medieval nobles subsidized troubadours to sing their praises; today's world leaders have large staffs of public-relations consultants. No culture can be explained in terms of one or more leaders, whether the leader be Pericles, Augustus, Joan of Arc, Elizabeth I, Franklin Roosevelt, or Hiawatha. The great leader is not the culture's prime mover but rather its manifestation. If James Watt had spent his time in Glasgow writing poetry instead of tinkering, someone else would no doubt have perfected the steam engine—because the culture of the time was ripe for such a discovery and because the intellectual and technological groundwork for the acceptance of that discovery had already been laid. No great intellectual leap was required for the invention of the steamboat: Steam is a principle known to the ancients, and the use of boats also goes back thousands of years. The combination of

MAN'S
RISE TO
CIVILIZATION

UNEASY ENCOUNTERS

Left: The first attempt by Europeans to portray the inhabitants of the New World is this engraving from Columbus' letters, published in 1493. A small boat from one of Columbus' ships is making a landfall to barter with the natives, who, Columbus wrote, were "as naked as their mothers bore them."

Below: An Indian view of the Spaniards is that of the Pueblo Indians living near the present-day Cochiti Reservation in New Mexico. Their cave painting shows what impressed them about the invading Spaniards. Amid the older and more traditional Pueblo symbols, designs, and kachina masks are Spaniards on horses and a church with a cross.

GREAT BASIN SHOSHONE: CULTURAL SIMPLICITY

Top: Paiute woman, making a basket outside of her brush shelter, was photographed near Grand Canyon during the Colorado River Expedition of Major John Wesley Powell in 1871–75.

Bottom: Wheeled toys from Mexico, a dog and a cayman, demonstrate how a culture may reject an invention. The peoples of Mexico obviously understood the principle of the wheel as well as did the peoples of the Near East. But the Indians constructed no wheeled vehicles because they possessed no domesticated beasts of burden to pull them.

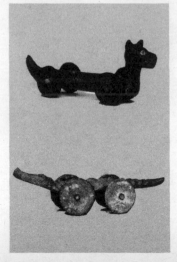

ESKIMO: ENVIRONMENT AND ADAPTATION

Top: This earliest surviving picture of an Eskimo, dated 1577, was probably drawn by John White at Frobisher Bay.

Bottom: Wooden mask of Alaskan Eskimo represents the spirit of cold weather and storms. The Eskimo believe the sad expression is because he must leave the people in the spring. The mask is carved from driftwood, the only source of wood in this timber-poor country, yet it is burned each year after use and a new one carved for the following spring. Because the mask is usually too fragile to be worn, the dancer holds it in front of his face to identify himself to the other participants in the ceremony.

THE SUB-ARCTIC: LIVING WITH EXPEDIENCY

This Ojibwa tomahawk, although carved about 1900
and somewhat more decorated than those made in primeval
times, remains faithful to the traditional form and
shape of the Northern Algonkian war clubs.

ZUNI: UNITY THROUGH RELIGION

Pueblo village of Zuñi, when photographed in 1879,
still looked much as the chronicler of Coronado's expedition
described it—"as if it had been crumpled together."
A Spanish innovation is the beehive oven in the foreground.

Top: Kiva scene in Zia pueblo shows priests
conducting a curing ceremony. This photograph was
taken in 1890, just before the Pueblo Indians began
to enforce strict prohibitions against Whites
inside their ceremonial chambers.

Bottom: Rain dancer at Santa Clara pueblo,
New Mexico, is symbolism in motion, from the evergreen
sprigs on her arms to the intricate designs on her
headdress, from the kinds of feathers that adorn her
to the colors of the material in her skirt.

The myth of the "peaceful" Pueblo Indians is disproved by the figure of the Zuñi war god, which was placed at a shrine following ceremonies for war. The carved stick emerging at a right angle is not a phallus but rather the umbilical cord which in Zuñi mythology represents the center of life.

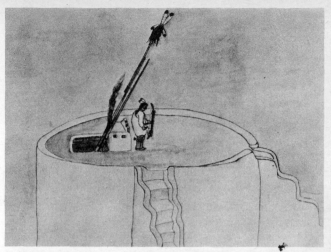

Left: Ceremonial clowns of the Rio Grande pueblos, similar
to the Mudheads of Zuñi, act as intermediaries between
the Indians and the gods. The clowns are also privileged
beings who can express the rebellious thoughts of the people.
This painting was made about 1920 by the well-known
San Ildefonso pueblo artist Tse Ye Mu.

Above: A secret Isleta painting portrays part
of the war ceremony and shows that the Rio Grande
Pueblo were as much inclined to war as the Zuñi.
The painting shows the portion of the ceremony
during which the scalp dancers withdraw into the
kiva, leaving a single member of the war society to
watch over the scalp tied to the kiva ladder.

IROQUOIS:
A WOODLAND DEMOCRACY

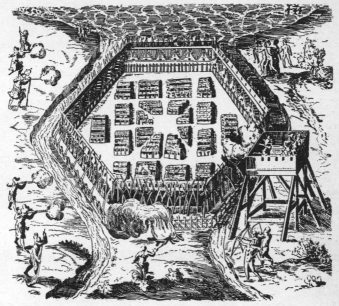

Left: Portrait of a Mohawk "king" was engraved in London
in 1710 when four Iroquois were brought to visit Queen Anne.
His totem, the bear, is in the background.

Above: Champlain's attack on an Onondaga fort in 1615
is depicted in a contemporary French engraving. Note the
elaborate fortifications typical of Iroquois villages: the moats,
a double stockade, and a location near water. The platform
on the right was erected by the French so they could shoot
down on the terrified Iroquois.

Top: The false face
mask of the Iroquois was
first carved into the trunk
of a living tree, then
cut out and painted.

Bottom: The Onondaga
mask depicts one of the
most important Iroquois
supernatural beings,
the Humpbacked One.
The distorted features
portray the pain he
suffered when, according
to Iroquois mythology,
he struck a mountain.
The knobbed chin, though,
has nothing to do with the
accident; it merely
enables the wearer more
easily to hold the mask in
front of his face.

PLAINS: EQUESTRIAN REVOLUTION

The make-believe Indians: Rocky Bear
of the Sioux poses in the full regalia of a typical
Plains Indian of the end of the last century.

Above: The Bison Dance of the Mandan was pictured in all its primeval splendor and fury by the artist Carl Bodmer, who accompanied Prince Maximilian on his expedition to the plains in the early 1830's. The dancers portrayed both the game animals and the hunters, and through ceremonials such as this one they hoped to gain power in the hunt.

Right: Exploits of a Plains warrior were painted on bison skins for all to see—and envy. This Pawnee skin from about 1870 shows in picture writing the principal accomplishments of a leading warrior.

Custer's last stand is seen in this drawing by
an Indian veteran of the battle of Little Bighorn,
in which Custer and about 250 men of the elite
Seventh Cavalry were annihilated in 1876,
and which provoked the final White assault upon

steam with the boat took place at a time when European culture was receptive to new ideas and when its technology was sufficiently advanced for a workable steamboat to be made. If the particular inventors had not performed a cultural synthesis of these two ancient ideas, then others would have done so.

The technological aspects of culture are usually easier to discuss in relation to prime movers because much of technological innovation has a precise date, whereas social and political innovations generally do not. Several hundred instances are known of inventions and scientific discoveries that were made simultaneously by two or more people working independently, each completely ignorant of the other's efforts. Some of them are:

TELESCOPE:	Jansen, Lippershey, and Metius, 1608
OXYGEN:	Priestley and Scheele, 1774
TELEGRAPH:	Morse, Henry, Steinheil, and Wheatstone and Cooke, about 1837
PHOTOGRAPHY:	Daguerre and Talbot, 1839
PLANET NEPTUNE:	Adams and Leverrier, 1845
ANESTHESIA BY ETHER:	Jackson, Liston, Morton, and Robinson, 1846
NATURAL SELECTION:	Darwin and Wallace, 1858
TELEPHONE:	Bell and Gray, 1876
AIRPLANE:	Wright brothers and Dumont, 1903
HUMAN-HEART TRANSPLANTS:	Barnard, Shumway, and Kantrowitz, 1967–68 (within a period of six weeks)
SUPERSONIC AIR TRANSPORT:	Soviet Union, Britain–France, 1975

How can the great-leader theory possibly explain why a discovery like the telescope was made not by one man, but by three—all in the same year, and all working without knowledge of the others' investigations? To reply that it is "coincidence" explains nothing and puts a great strain on the laws of chance. And to say that the invention "was in the air" or "the times were ripe for it" are just other ways of stating that the inventors did not do the inventing, but that the cultures did. Such is in fact the probable explanation. All three inventors of the telescope worked in Holland, no doubt because lens manufacture had progressed furthest there. For the same reason, the compound microscope also was developed in Holland, and the major early discoveries in microscopy were made by two other Dutchmen, van Leeuwenhoek and Swammerdam. Human-heart transplants were the culmination of heart surgery that began before World War II, together with the development of the heart–lung machine and of new artificial pumps that assist failing hearts—and finally the discovery of drugs that can suppress the human body's natural tendency to reject a transplanted foreign organ.‡

The seventeenth-century Iroquois, as described by Jesuit missionaries, practiced a dream psychotherapy that was remarkably similar to Freud's discoveries in Vienna two hundred years later. No evidence has ever come to light that Freud knew of these reports or could have had any inkling of this aspect of Iroquois culture. Differences can, of course, be found between the psychotherapeutic systems of the Iroquois and of Freud, but these are no more marked than the differences between, for example, the Freudian and Jungian schools of psychoanalytic theory. The Iroquois explained their concept of dreams to the Jesuit fathers in terms remarkably similar to the words that Freud used:

In addition to the desires which we generally have that are free, or at least voluntary in us, [and] which arise from a previous knowledge of some goodness that we imagine to exist in the thing desired, [we] believe that our souls have other desires, which are, as it were, inborn and concealed. These . . . come from the depths of the soul, not through any knowledge, but by means of a certain blind transporting of the soul to certain objects.

The Iroquois believed further that a person's natural wish was often fulfilled through dreams, "which are its language"—and they were sufficiently intuitive to realize that a dream might also mask rather than reveal the soul's true wishes.

All of this demonstrates a remarkably sophisticated grasp of what in our very different culture has evolved as modern psychiatry. The Iroquois recognized the existence of an unconscious, the force of unconscious desires, the way in which the conscious mind attempts to repress unpleasant thoughts, the emergence of unpleasant thoughts in dreams, and the mental and physical (psychosomatic) illnesses that may be caused by the frustration of unconscious desires. The Iroquois knew that their dreams did not deal in facts but rather in symbols—which then had to be brought to "certain persons, more enlightened than the common, whose sight penetrates, as it were, into the depths of the soul." And one of the techniques employed by these Iroquois seers to uncover the latent meanings behind a dream was free association, a technique employed by Freud and by psychiatrists today. The Iroquois faith in dreams, by the way, is only somewhat diminished after more than three hundred years. The Iroquois still pay attention to hints given in dreams when they have to choose a curing ceremony, select a friend, or join a particular association; they still bring their more vivid dreams to a seer, usually a woman, for interpretation.‡

The conclusions are inevitable: Had Freud not discovered psychotherapy, then someone else would have. Had Hiawatha not united the five Iroquois tribes, then someone else would have. The culture of the Iroquois tribes was sympathetic to such a possibility; its level of social and political organization at the time made confederation possible; and the arrival of the Whites made it imperative.

WARFARE

Much of the warfare carried on by American Indians stemmed directly from contact with Europeans. Indian groups were early set into conflict with one another because of the loss of their lands, the increasing dependence upon Whites for trade items, and the necessity of sharing traditional hunting areas with alien groups that had been pushed westward by advancing Whites. As early as 1640, Iroquois warfare intensified as a reaction to the presence of Whites. The Iroquois needed pelts to barter for cloth, steel, iron, and other trade goods—and they quickly overtrapped the fur-bearing mammals in their lands. The Iroquois either had to give up obtaining trade goods, or else go beyond their traditional boundaries for furs. They chose the latter course, and they began expanding in all directions to raid other tribes and bands. Eventually they had to fight large-scale battles—as they did against the Huron around the upper Great Lakes—to obtain control of the trade networks that extended from Huronia to the vast regions north and west of the Great Lakes.‡

Iroquois war parties carried bows and arrows, but these were used only for ambushes. The warriors preferred close-in fighting with the club that the Algonkians called a tomahawk; they also carried wooden shields and wore a sort of armor made of sticks laced together with buckskin thongs. The Iroquois way of making war was to sneak up on the enemy like foxes, fight like lions, and disappear into the woods like birds. The object was both to kill and to obtain captives. Many captives, especially the young ones, were adopted into the Iroquois tribes as substitutes for the husbands, brothers, and sons lost in battle. Reserved for most of the others, though, was a torture of exceptional ferocity, which continued for as many days as the victim could be kept alive. He was refreshed with water and even given long periods of rest so that he might regain his strength—and also might feel the pain more exquisitely. Father LeJeune describes one torture he witnessed:

One must be there to see a living picture of Hell. The whole cabin appeared as if on fire; and athwart the flames and dense smoke that issued therefrom, these barbarians, crowding one upon the other, howling at the top of their voices, with firebrands in their hands, their eyes flashing with rage and fury—seemed like so many demons who would give no respite to this poor wretch. They often stopped him at the other end of the cabin, some of them taking his hands and breaking the bones thereof by sheer force; others pierced his ears with sticks which they left in them. One of these butchers having applied a brand to his loins, he was seized with a fainting fit . . . As soon as day began to dawn, they lighted fires outside the village, to display there the excesses of their cruelty, to the sight of the Sun. There they began to burn him more cruelly than ever, leaving no part of his body to which fire was not applied at intervals . . . Therefore, fearing that he would die otherwise than by the knife, one cut off a foot, another a hand, and almost at the same time a third severed the head from the shoulders, throwing it to the crowd, where someone caught it to carry it to the Captain Ondessone, for whom it had been reserved, in order to make a feast therewith.‡

Some psychologists have seen in these tortures an emotional escape valve for a people who spent a good deal of their waking hours obedient to rigorous standards of conduct. Such an explanation of torture, of course, contains a degree of truth, but one other explanation should not be overlooked. A tribe is by its very nature a fragile organization; it lacks institutions that promote unity within the tribe. For a tribe to endure, it must find some way to achieve internal unity—and that way usually is external strife. The tribe exists at all times in a state of mobilization for war against its neighbors. The slightest incident, or often merely a desire to increase prestige, is enough to set off a skirmish, and in such circumstances hatred against external enemies must be unremitting.

The actual fighting, though, was usually in the form of brief skirmishes, because neither a tribe's social organization nor its economy can sustain the kind of warfare that is practiced in more complex societies. No specialized class of soldiers existed to devote itself full time to fighting. Nor could male labor constantly be diverted from the needs of clearing fields and building houses. Extending their borders brought no benefits, for the Iroquois lacked both the political machinery and the manpower to administer occupied territory. The best they could achieve was a succession of clashes by which they obtained captives, furs, and booty. The emphasis was not on building a mighty war machine but on becoming expert in psychological warfare. Rather than face-to-face combat, the Iroquois and their neighbors fought a war of nerves whose strategy included torture, ambush, ruthless massacre, and even the fearsome tactic of howling in the night. The Iroquois did in one way improve on the warfare practiced by most tribes: they adopted some of the conquered peoples to replace their own losses. More than half of some Iroquois tribes—particularly in the seventeenth century when warfare had increased—consisted of adopted Huron and Algonkian Indians who had been trained to equal in ferocity any native-born Iroquois.

THE GREAT SPIRIT AND MONOTHEISM

The Iroquois theogony was probably complex to begin with, and it survives in a form made even more so after being garbled by explorers and by early settlers. Three classes of supernatural phenomena—spirits, the ghosts of the dead, and the gods—seem to have been believed in, along with a Great Spirit and his satanic counterpart. At a man's death, his spirit departed for the afterlife—not for some "happy hunting ground," which was a White conception of the Indian afterworld. (The Iroquois did not believe they ate food after death, and therefore would have had no reason to hunt.) The dead man's ghost maintained an interest in the tribe. Special wintertime feasts were held for the ghosts, who were thought to take part unseen in the dancing and the games; they also accompanied raiding parties, even though they could only watch and not participate.

The Iroquois represent possibly the least complex social organization in North America whose beliefs were monotheistic. Monotheism, contrary to what is generally supposed, goes beyond simply a belief in one god. It posits a supreme being who is responsible for creating clusters of other supernatural and sacred beings, which may be angels, demons, or saints. In Judaism, Christianity, and Mohammedanism alike, Jehovah or God or Allah is regarded not as the only supernatural being, but rather as the first cause and creator of the world.

Modern Christians and Jews usually ignore the references in the Old Testament to immortals created by the supreme being Jehovah. The King James Version often translates the original Biblical languages as "sons of God"—but "divine beings" is more accurate.‡ The Iroquois worshipped their Great Spirit for himself—and also for creating the other gods.

The Iroquois raise an interesting question about the origins of monotheism. Some scholars have supposed that monotheism arises whenever people have experienced the power of human rulers who hold sway over empires or kingdoms. A supreme god would then become a celestial reflection of some supreme ruler on earth. That was probably true in ancient Egypt, where the high god Aton was worshiped during the reign of the powerful Pharaoh Ikhnaton. Christianity increasingly came to reflect the political society of the Roman Empire in which it arose as there developed a hierarchy consisting of God, Jesus, angels, the Pope and priesthood, and the saints. Eventually nine orders of the celestial hierarchy were conceived of, supposedly numbering 266,613,336 angels.‡ The Iroquois, by contrast, not only lacked a single strong ruler but did not even have a powerful government. The Council of Sachems, which limited itself mostly to external questions of war or peace, was unable to control its own young warriors. The case of the Iroquois is in some ways similar to the ancient Israelites in the time of the Judges when a potent Jehovah controlled human affairs, yet the earthly government consisted of a weak council of elders.

The monotheistic societies of the Iroquois and others, past and present and around the world, reveal one common characteristic: A hierarchy of numerous allegiances extends from the individual to the outermost boundaries of the society. Among the Iroquois, the individual is part of a nuclear family, which belongs to a household, which lives with other households in a longhouse, which constitutes part of a clan, which goes to make up a tribe, which in turn is part of the League of the Iroquois. The individual Iroquois is thus enmeshed in a widening system of allegiances; the only way to make sense out of it all is to postulate an orderly environment over which rules prevail even at the ultimate, supernatural boundaries.

FALSE FACES

Despite the complexity of much of Iroquois society, its religious rituals remained shamanistic—with the difference that they were not carried on by a religious freelancer but by an organized shamanistic group. The shaman's songs and dances were restricted to the False Face society, whose members cured with the aid of large wooden masks.‡ These were distorted facial nightmares, consisting of twelve basic types—crooked mouth, straight-lipped, spoon-lipped, hanging mouth, protruding tongue, smiling, whistling, divided red and black, long nose, horned, pig, and blind. There are also some additional local types, such as the diseased face, as well as color variations. A catalog of all combinations probably would number several dozen. The society's members always functioned as a group, and would put on a frightening performance for the sick person. They lurched, humped, crawled, and trotted to the house, grunting and issuing cries from behind their masks. They danced around the sick person, sprinkled ashes, shook large rattles made from the carapaces of turtles, and sang out their incantations.

In 1751 a pioneer American naturalist and friend of the Indian, John Bartram, described what it was like to encounter one of the members of the False Face society:

He had on a clumsy vizard of wood colour'd black, with a nose 4 or 5 inches long, a grinning mouth set awry, furnished with long teeth, round the eyes circles of bright brass, surrounded by a larger circle of white paint, from his forehead hung long tresses of buffaloes hair, and from the catch part of his head ropes made of the plated husks of Indian corn; I cannot recollect the whole of his dress, but that it was equally uncouth: he carried in one hand a long staff, in the other a calabash with small stones in it, for a rattle . . . He would sometimes hold up his head and make a hideous noise like the braying of an ass.‡

Considerable dispute has taken place about the significance of the masks. It has been suggested that they represent merely a form of idolatry. It is true that in addition to the large masks intended to be worn, much smaller "maskettes," often only two or three inches long, were made. These were kept partly as charms, much as some people keep a lucky stone, but primarily as compact substitutes for, and reminders of, the larger masks—similar to the Saint Christopher statuettes some drivers place on automobile dashboards. If the word "idolatry" is pronounced with a condemnatory tone, as it often is by White Christians, then the Iroquois must be defended. The Iroquois worshiped—and many still worship today, despite the inroads of Christianity—supernatural beings and not idols. They regard the masks as portraits through which the supernatural has made itself manifest. The wearer behaves as if he were the supernatural being he impersonates. He obtains the mask by carving in the trunk of a living tree the vision he has of a False Face, and then cutting the mask free. During this ceremony, the spirit reveals itself to the maker, who then finishes carving the features and paints the mask. The Iroquois do not worship the images themselves, only what they signify. "Iconism" is undoubtedly a better term than idolatry.

The faces can also be interpreted in light of the great psychological sophistication of the Iroquois' traditional belief in unconscious fears and desires, such as might be supposed to find an outlet in the rituals of the False Face society. Hidden behind the contorted faces of mythical figures, individuals could thus act out forbidden behaviors—and in the process cure psychosomatic illnesses. The False Face society obviously had found a way to vent emotions that in daily life had to be repressed. Under the cover of the masks, the people could indulge an unconscious longing to be irresponsible, to be weak, or to compete with their creator. One authority on the Iroquois has pointed out:

The culture of dreams may be regarded as a necessary escape valve in Iroquois life. Iroquois men were, in their daily affairs, brave, active, self-reliant, and autonomous;

they cringed to no one and begged for nothing. But no man can balance forever on such a pinnacle of masculinity, where asking and being given are unknown. Iroquois men dreamed; and without shame they received the fruits of their dreams, and their souls were satisfied.‡

Historians can speculate endlessly about the Pax Iroquoian that might have spread over much of the East—and might have given rise to one of the greatest confederacies the world has ever known—had the Whites not arrived. But even if the Whites had never intruded, the Iroquois probably would not have achieved that confederation. The Iroquois were hampered not only by the fragility inherent in any tribal organization, but also by the unresolved friction between the hereditary sachems, who sought peace, and the military opportunism of the young warriors. Rivalry between the British and the French—and later the British and the Americans—for the loyalty of the Iroquois served to accent this basic problem but was not the cause of it. The League, formed in 1570 and not known about by Whites until around 1640, was considered by Lewis Henry Morgan to be on the path to extinction when he wrote in 1851:

Their council-fires . . . have long since been extinguished, their empire has terminated, and the shades of evening are now gathering thickly over the scattered and feeble remnants of this once powerful League . . . The Iroquois will soon be lost as a people, in that night of impenetrable darkness in which so many Indian races have been enshrouded. Already their country has been appropriated, their forests cleared, and their trails obliterated. The residue of this proud and gifted race, who still linger around their native seats, are destined to fade away, until they become eradicated as an Indian stock. We shall ere long look backward to the Iroquois, as a race blotted from existence; but to remember them as a people whose sachems had no cities, whose religion had no temples, and whose government had no record.‡

Morgan was unduly pessimistic. Some 35,000 or so Iroquois still survive, the majority of them living on reservations in New York State, Quebec, and Ontario— actually a larger population than the 15,000 estimated to have been alive during their heyday in the seventeenth century. To the casual glance of nearby Whites, their television antennas, automobiles, and ranch houses seem today to indicate complete assimilation; but in fact during recent decades many of the Iroquois have participated in a cultural rebirth.

VII
Plains: Equestrian Revolution

THE GREAT AMERICAN EPIC

To many people, the typical Indian is the Plains Indian, a painted brave in full regalia, trailing a war bonnet, astride a horse ridden bareback, shown in gorgeous Technicolor as he sweeps down upon a wagon train. In actual fact, the picturesque culture of the Plains Indian was a creation of White pressures and influences, and it did not last very long. The amalgam known as the Plains culture was not fully accomplished until the early 1800's—and like the spring grass of the high plains, it quickly withered.

This culture emerged in the middle of the eighteenth century as its catalytic agent, the horse, spread northward from Spanish settlements in New Mexico. Within only a few generations the horse was to be found throughout the central heartland of the continent, and from every direction Indians spilled onto the plains. They originally spoke many different languages and observed various customs, but they all discovered in the horse a new possibility—that of killing greater numbers of bison than they had ever dreamed of before. They also became rich in material goods far beyond their wildest imaginings, and then like a dream it all faded. By about 1860 the Plains culture was already on the wane, pushed aside by the "manifest destiny" of the

United States as it moved ever westward. The fate of the Plains Indians had been sealed with the arrival of the first miners and the first prairie schooner. The battles of extermination between Plains Indians and United States cavalry were to become America's own great epic —its *Iliad,* its *Aeneid*, its Norse saga—and in the telling this epic proved no more true than any other.

Despite the surrounded forts, the saving of the last bullet for oneself, the occasional acts of heroism, and the frequent acts of bestiality on both sides—despite the stereotype played over and over again in the telling and retelling of this Great American Epic—remarkable little formal combat took place. Deaths and hardship there were in plenty as the Plains Indians met their catastrophic end, but far more deaths were due to starvation, exposure, disease, casual brutality, and alcoholism than to bullets. In all the actual battles between White soldiers and Indian braves, only several thousand deaths on both sides took place on the field of battle. The wars of the plains were very little more than mopping-up operations. In the process millions of bison very nearly vanished without any survivors, and the once-proud Indian horsemen were broken in body and spirit.

The Plains Indian culture in all its glory did not exist when Coronado first explored the region. Lured on by tales of rich lands, where kings were supposed to be lulled to sleep by golden bells, Coronado eventually reached Kansas in 1541. Here the Spaniards saw the beast they had been hearing so much about: the remarkable "cow," actually a bison, as large as a Spanish bull. They also met some impoverished Indians who lived in conical tipis "built like pavilions," according to the chronicler of the expedition. That chronicler was particularly impressed by the way the bison seemed to provide most of the materials needed by the Indians: "With the skins they build their houses; with the skins they clothe and show themselves; from the skins they make ropes and also obtain wool. With the sinews they make threads, with which they sew their clothes and also their tents. From the bones they shape awls. The dung they use for firewood, since there is no other fuel in that land. The bladders they use as jugs and drinking containers."‡

Hunting bison on foot was not productive, and it certainly could not support large numbers of Indians. Such hunting was practiced largely by small nomadic groups who lived off the occasional weakened bison they succeeded in killing, or those they were able to stampede over bluffs. Most of the aboriginal cultures on the plains and prairies were based on the cultivation of maize, beans, and squash. Agriculture had spread westward from the eastern woodlands, and it followed the finger-like oases of fertility along riverbeds throughout the arid Dakotas southward to Texas, and westward virtually to the foothills of the Rockies. Hunting bison, for these people, was only incidental to a primary subsistence based on agriculture. They went on a hunt about once a year to supplement their vegetable diet and to obtain hides, sinew, bone, and other raw materials.

Once the horse arrived on the plains, that way of life changed. The nomadic bison hunters became ascendant over the farmers, who either were driven off their lands or abandoned agriculture to become bison hunters themselves. The Indians had never seen the horse until the Spaniards brought it to the New World; thousands of years previously, during the great glacial melt, it had become extinct in North America. The Indians obtained the first horses after the Spaniards settled New Mexico in 1598. (Contrary to previous belief, the Indians captured no horses from de Soto, Coronado, or other early explorers, for these horses either died or were taken back to Mexico and the West Indies.) The Spaniards prohibited the sale of horses to Indians, but some Indians nevertheless learned Spanish riding techniques and stole the animals. Indians soon taught one another how to train horses and they were so apt that by the mid-1700's mounted Apache and Ute were raiding Spanish settlements to obtain additional horses. The revolt of the Pueblo between 1680 and 1692 threw some of the animals on the Indian markets of North

America. The Spaniards restocked their herds, which proliferated, but they were unable to prevent further stealing of horses. From New Mexico the horses—as well as the knowledge of how to break and train them —spread northward through barter or theft from one Indian group to another. Soon a whole new profession, that of the Indian horse merchant, grew up. In addition, some Spanish horses had gone wild and now roamed the plains in herds. The Spaniards called them *mesteños* (from the word meaning "wild"), and from this the English word "mustang" is derived. Even before the mid-1700's, almost every Plains Indian tribe had obtained horses.

At the same time that the horse was moving northeastward, guns were being traded to the Plains Indians from tribes in the east, who had obtained them from the French and British. As the Whites advanced westward, so did guns and ammunition, traveling from one group to another by barter, theft, or capture as the booty of warfare. The combination of guns and horses brought drastic changes in the balance of power throughout the entire plains region. Some tribes owned horses, others guns; a fortunate few had both. At first, mounted warriors using only bows and arrows were driven off by horseless Indians who already had firearms. The Blackfoot tribe, once it obtained both horses and guns, cut a wide swath of conquest. It raided to the south and west, forcing the Northern Shoshoni (who had horses but no guns) to seek refuge in the Rocky Mountains. Farther to the north, the Blackfoot drove the Kutenai westward over the Canadian Rockies and began their period of dominance on the northern plains.

Once the Indians had discovered the effectiveness of rifles, an armament race began on the plains. Just as with the earlier realization of the value of horses, which drove those without them to obtain them by any means, the balance of power was again upset by the acquisition of rifles. And now there was a continuing need not only for rifles but also for powder and for lead. The Indians were driven to take continually greater risks, making raids to steal horses that could be bartered for guns and ammunition. Over a period of nearly fifty years, the plains were an arena of turmoil where from year to year the status quo was upset as successive groups became supreme in supplies of horses or guns, or in the mustering of powerful allies.

A LIVING EXPERIMENT IN CULTURE CHANGE

Indian groups converging on the plains from every direction had soon adapted themselves to an economy based on the bison. The lands of the agriculturists were usurped, and the plains became a maelstrom of varied and often conflicting cultures. The stolen, bartered, bought, or captured horse was a new cultural element in the heartland of North America, and because of it the way of life there was entirely changed.‡ From Alberta to Texas, the plains were now peopled by groups of great diversity, many of whom had come from far away. There were Athapaskans from the north (Kiowa–Apache), Algonkians (Cree, Cheyenne, Blackfoot) and Siouans (Mandan, Crow, Dakota) from the east, Uto–Aztecans (Comanche, Ute) from the west, Caddoans (Pawnee, Arikara) from the south. The plains became a melting pot for more than thirty different peoples, belonging to at least six language stocks. It also furnished anthropologists with a living laboratory of culture change—that is, the way in which a group alters because of new circumstances, or borrows traits from other cultures and fits them into the configurations of its own.

By about 1800 the gross difference in culture among all these peoples had disappeared; the Sun Dance ceremony, for example, was eventually observed by virtually every tribe.‡ Differences could, of course, be discerned by the trained eyes of anthropologists; yet it is remarkable that one people originally from the eastern forests and another from the Great Basin, two thousand miles to the west, within only a few generations should have become so nearly identical. And not only had this homogeneity been achieved with great speed; it had also occurred voluntarily and in the absence of a common tongue except for the "sign language" that served as a lingua franca among the Plains tribes.

The Plains Cree demonstrate how a people originally distant from the plains in both culture and geography could eventually become so typical of the region. The Cree were first recorded in the *Jesuit Relations* of 1640, and at that time they had no connection at all with the plains. They inhabited the forests between Hudson Bay and Lake Superior, where they were roving hunters and gatherers of wild rice. Their culture was typical of the Northern Algonkian bands, and like them the Cree were soon caught up in fur trade with the Whites. The Whites' insatiable demand for beaver pelts caused the Cree to push westward; and having obtained guns from White traders, they were able to dispossess the previous inhabitants. Some of the Cree had already penetrated to the west of Lake Winnipeg by about the middle of the eighteenth century. Their culture by now had changed considerably. It had become dependent on the White trader for weapons, clothing, and cooking utensils— and sometimes even for food, since the Cree spent their time trapping rather than hunting. Then the Cree living farthest west discovered the resource of the bison. Historical records reveal that they were hunting bison as early as 1772, although they still did not possess horses. Within another generation, though, the Plains Cree had emerged—a typical equestrian tribe, very different in customs and outlook from the Cree who still inhabited the forests, although both groups continued to speak the same language.

In the case of the Cree, as with other Plains tribes, no longer were only stray or weakened bison killed; now entire herds were pursued on swift horses and the choicest animals were selected. And no longer was the whole animal utilized for raw materials, as the chronicler of the Coronado expedition had been so impressed to observe; the Indians could now afford the luxury of waste. They stocked the tipi with supplies for the future: meat sliced into thin strips and dried in the sun (jerkee), and meat that had berries pounded into it and had been covered with a coat of fat to become pemmican. Even though few of the Plains Indians ever saw a White close up until they were overwhelmed, the influence of Whites had become profound as goods and trade articles flowed across the plains by means of barter between one tribe and another. Tipis twenty-five feet in diameter were filled to overflowing with new-found riches. An economic revolution, for which the Indians' tradition had not prepared them, took place. The women no longer toiled in the fields—for gardening was not as profitable as hunting, nor could it be practiced in a nomadic hunting society—and the Indians stopped making pottery once brass kettles could be obtained from Whites. Permanent villages disappeared, and with them went many of the crafts, the traditions, the rules, and the customs.

THE MAKE-BELIEVE INDIANS

The Plains Indians in their heyday were a study in hyperbole, and as make-believe as the set for a western movie. They sprang from greatly differing traditions, from farmers and from hunters and from collectors of wild plants. Each contributed something of its own to the creation almost overnight of a flamboyant culture whose vigor was for a time unequaled. In this world of hyperbole, many traditions that existed in non-Plains Indian societies underwent a wild exaggeration. Other tribes also had men's associations, but few so extravagant in ritual and insignia as the Plains warrior societies now became. Indians elsewhere were caught up in religious emotion, but none had so relentlessly pursued the vision quest. Other Indians tortured captives, but none before had so exquisitely evoked pain in their own bodies.

A kind of social organization, known to anthropologists as the composite tribe, developed on the plains. Wherever the composite tribe is found, it signifies a breakdown in culture and a subsequent readaptation. Sometimes the breakdown will have been due to loss of population through migration or stepped-up warfare; this happened to some of the Pueblo Indians around the Rio Grande River of New Mexico. Sometimes it may follow a disturbance of the resource base as a result of economic exploitation by outsiders; this has been characteristic of many African societies. Occasionally, as happened on the North American plains, the breakdown will be due to the abandonment of old culture traits and the substitution of borrowed new ones. Whatever the specific cause, composite tribes usually appear after an alien culture has intervened.

A distinguishing characteristic of the composite tribe is that the reckoning of descent is vague. It can be through either the father's or the mother's line, or both. Marital residence rules also are unspecific, and the newly married couple lives with whichever relatives expediency may suggest. The composite tribe of the Plains Indians was more nearly a mere collection of bands than were the Zuñi or the Iroquois lineal tribes. During most of the year a number of Plains Indian families lived together as a band. They united with other bands to form a composite tribe at the time of the summer encampment, when tribal ceremonies and communal bison hunts took place. An individual's band membership tended to change, and many Plains Indians belonged to several bands during their lifetimes. One reason for this was the constant feuding, which often became so divisive that the only way to preserve any peace at all was by a fissioning of the band. The Plains Indians might thus appear to have been no more complex in their social organization than the Eskimo and the Great Basin Shoshone bands, but that is not really true. They became functioning tribes during their summer encampments, and they managed to maintain that tribal identity the rest of the year when they broke up into small bands.

The primary way in which tribal identity was achieved was not through kinship or residence groups but through nonkinship sodalities. The word "sodality" is derived from the Latin *sodalitas*, which means "fellowship," and in a modern society it is equivalent to fraternities and sororities, political parties, service clubs like the Rotary or the Lions, and religious organizations. The political significance of sodalities is that they cut across the boundaries of residential groups and in that way interconnect them around a common purpose. In the United States, even a sodality as specialized as the Society for the Preservation of Barbershop Quartet Singing includes members from various residential groups and thus plays some role, however small, in integrating the society. When the Plains tribes united in the summer, they were crosscut by a bewildering variety of sodalities with ceremonial, social, and military functions. There were dance societies and feasting societies, and even societies based on a common supernatural experience. Among the Cheyenne, only the bravest of brave warriors could belong to the elite military society known as the Contraries. Somewhat like the Zuñi Mudheads, they were privileged clowns. They did the opposite of everything: They said "no" when they meant "yes"; went away when called and came near when told to go away; and sat shivering in the hottest weather. Other societies were open to both men and women; such were the tobacco societies of the Crow which centered around the raising of special kinds of tobacco for ceremonial use.

A special development among the Mandan, Hidatsa, Arapaho, and Blackfoot was a hierarchy of warrior societies. The members of these societies were ranked according to age; as an individual grew older, he moved up step by step. In this way a warrior society existed for every male from the youngest to the oldest, with the exception of the effeminate male known as a berdache. Little scorn was attached to his position; rather, he was regarded with pity at not being able to fill a male role. But even the berdache found his place in Plains Indian society. He permanently adopted female clothing and became skilled in such female tasks as beadwork or skin-tanning; he was also eligible to join the women's societies.

The richness and diversity of these sodalities is explained by the lack of lineal residential groups among the Plains tribes. The non-kin sodalities were greatly needed on the plains to fill a social void left by the absence of clans. Had these non-kin sodalities failed to develop, with the rules and regulations that sometimes appear so bizarre to outsiders, the tribes would have been reduced to mere collections of bands. The sodalities brought unity to one of the most diverse collections of people on earth.

COUPS AND SCALPING

The various groups had engaged in warfare even before they obtained horses and guns, but with the emergence of the Plains Indian culture during the nineteenth century, warfare became as ritualized as it was for a medieval knight. Only during the very twilight of the Plains culture did large battles take place that pitted Indian against Indian, or Indian against the United States Army, with each group seeking to exterminate the other. Previous to that, tactics consisted of forays and raids by small war parties; the conflicts were brief and often indecisive.

The Plains Indians fought not to win territory or to enslave other tribes, but for different reasons. One conscious motivation was the capture of horses, which had a high economic value. Another kind of reason, less conscious but equally powerful, was that external strife served to unify the tribe internally. A tribe, especially one as fragile as the composite tribe unified only by non-kin sodalities, badly needed a common enemy as a rationale for its existence. A third motivation was the status that could be acquired through raiding, which was regarded as a game in which one's exploits were graded according to the dangers involved. The exploit itself was known as a *coup*, a word borrowed from French trappers and originally referring to a "blow" struck by a brave against an enemy's body with a special stick that was often striped like a barber pole. Eventually, "counting coups" came to mean an immodest recital by the brave of all his war deeds. These recitals went on endlessly. Each time a man achieved a new honor, he used it as an excuse to recount the old ones. If he lied about his exploits, though, or even shaded the truth a bit, he was immediately challenged by someone who had been along on the same war party.

Each Plains tribe had its own ranking for coups. Among the Blackfoot, stealing an enemy's weapons was looked upon as the highest exploit. Among some other tribes, the bravest deed was to touch an enemy without hurting him. A much less important exploit usually was killing an enemy, but even that deed was ranked according to the way it was done and the weapons that were used. The whole business of counting coups often became extremely involved. Among the Cheyenne, for example, coups on a single enemy could be counted by several warriors, but the coups were ranked in the strict order in which the enemy was touched by the participants; who actually killed or wounded him was immaterial. Like a sort of heraldry, these deeds were recorded in picture writing on tipis and on bison robes. Among many Plains tribes, each coup earned an eagle's feather, and the achieving of many coups accounts for the elaborate headdresses of some war leaders.

Scalps taken from dead or wounded enemies sometimes served as trophies, but they were insignificant as compared with counting coups. Many Plains tribes did not take scalps at all until the period of their swift decline, which began in the middle of the last century. It has been commonly believed that all Indians took scalps, and that scalp-hunting was exclusively a New World custom. Neither notion is true. Herodotus, the ancient Greek historian, mentioned the taking of scalps by the Scythians, for example. In North America scalping probably existed before the arrival of Whites, but only in a few areas, primarily along the Gulf Coast. Some historians still question whether scalp-taking was a widespread aboriginal Indian practice in North America, or rather one learned quite early from White settlers.

Whatever its exact origins, scalp-taking quickly spread over all of North America, except in the Eskimo areas. The spread was due more to the barbarity of Whites than of Reds. Governor Kieft of New Netherland is usually credited with originating the idea of paying a bounty for Indian scalps, since they were more convenient to handle than whole heads and they offered the same proof that an Indian had been killed. By liberal payments for scalps, the Dutch virtually cleared southern New York and New Jersey of Indians before the English supplanted them.‡ By 1703 the colony of Massachusetts was paying the equivalent of about $60 for every Indian scalp. In the mid-eighteenth century, Pennsylvania fixed the bounty for a male Indian scalp at $134; a female's was worth only $50. Some White entrepreneurs simply hatcheted any old Indians who still survived in their towns. The French also used scalp-taking as an instrument of geopolitics. In the competition over the Canadian fur trade, they offered the Micmac Indians a bounty for every scalp they took from the Beothuk of Newfoundland. By 1827 an expedition to Newfoundland failed to find a single survivor of this once numerous and proud people.

Among the Plains tribe, apparently only the Sioux and the Cree placed great value on scalps; both tribes were late migrants to the plains from the East, where they probably learned the practice from Whites. Nor did the Plains tribes torture their captives as frequently as was once believed. The White settler who saved his last bullet for himself to avoid a horrible death usually took a needless precaution. Unlike the Indians of the eastern woodlands, the Plains Indians killed swiftly and cleanly. They looked upon the White custom of hanging, for example, as undignified and barbaric.

CAUSES OF WARFARE

The Great American Epic has traditionally depicted the Plains Indians as the most "warlike" on the continent. Indeed, history does confirm that the heartland of the continent was an arena of continual strife. Yet to say that a Blackfoot, for example, was "warlike" reveals nothing. The entire Blackfoot tribe did not habitually engage in war because certain individual members possessed "warlike" personalities. Individuals go to war for individual reasons: for social prestige, for economic rewards and for booty, because of religious convictions —even to escape from frustrations at home. Entire societies, though, do not go to war for such personal reasons. The fact is that the individual Blackfoot was warlike simply because his whole cultural system obliged him to be that way.

The various theories as to why groups of people go to war fall into four general categories. According to the first of these, it is in the very biological nature of humans to be aggressive. This is supposedly because in the remote past those of our species who were aggressive survived to produce more offspring than those who were not. If warfare did indeed become locked into human behavior in this way, then there is little that can be done—an extraordinarily pessimistic view of the human condition. This is an old theory, and it keeps popping up from time to time in some new guise, recently in that put forward by Konrad Lorenz and by some proponents of sociobiology.‡

Nothing in the human physical makeup suggests that we have evolved as a warlike animal. Humans are, in truth, puny creatures, lacking fangs, claws, thick skin, speed, or other adaptations for combat. And even though a good deal of archeological evidence indicates that humans have always warred at one time or another, no evidence exists that *all* of them always have—a fact which would tend to deny that warfare is part of our biological inheritance. Quite a number of the world's hunting groups and simple food-producers are not known to have carried on warfare or to have engaged in combat beyond occasional feuding. Among these are such diverse groups as the Paiute Indians of the Great Basin, the Arapesh of New Guinea, the Tiwi of Australia, the Lepchas of the Himalayas, and the Pygmies of Zaire. In the specific case of American Indians, they often took up arms against Whites only after being pushed to the extreme of their forbearance. Furthermore, a people cannot be regarded as being biologically programmed to respond aggressively when they react in diverse ways to the same provocation. Even after many Cheyenne who were camped peacefully at Sand Creek, Colorado, had been massacred in 1864 by U. S. cavalry, the survivors did not take up arms—although some other Cheyenne did raid White settlements in retaliation.

The second explanation is that humans are warlike because they are warlike. Such an explanation is an affront to logic, but even so noted an anthropologist as Ralph Linton wrote that the Plains Indians would not have been so interested in war if "they had not been warlike."‡ Similar statements are made in Ruth Benedict's *Patterns of Culture.* Obviously, such logic is akin to explaining obesity in middle-aged males by saying that many middle-aged males are obese.

The third explanation is a psychological one, and it probably boasts the most adherents—which is understandable, for these people can bolster their case by surveys, personality tests, statistical analyses, and other impressive tools of modern scholarship. Even before the widespread use of such tests and surveys, Freud, in an exchange of correspondence with Einstein in 1932 about the causes of war, agreed that "there is an instinct for hatred and destruction . . . which goes halfway to meet the efforts of the warmongers."‡ All of these psychological studies, though, can explain only the motivations behind why individuals slug each other in barroom brawl or fire weapons in combat. Individuals do not go to war; only entire societies do that.

That leaves the fourth explanation, which is simply that the causes for war are to be found within the cultures of the contending groups. This explanation avoids confusing the issue with related problems, such as individual motivations or the kinds of warfare practiced. In the case of the Plains Indians, their composite tribes could not have survived without external enemies, real or imagined, against whom the warrior associations could unite. Moreover, the Plains culture came into being as a reverberation across the continent set up by the arrival of the Whites. That event upset delicate adjustments that the Indians had made to one another over very long periods of time. As just one example, the fur trade disrupted relations between the Ojibwa and surrounding groups; some of the Ojibwa spread westward and displaced certain Siouan tribes, which in turn migrated westward and southward to the plains. There the Sioux displaced the Hidatsa and Mandan, who then

stirred up the Cheyenne and others. The whole situation
was unstable in the extreme—very much as though a
series of billiard balls had been set in motion, with
renewed collisions as one ball caroms off another.

Most important, once all these groups were on the
plains and their cultures had been altered by the acquisition of horses and guns, the make-believe of their existence had to be kept in motion or it would collapse.
Horses had to be stolen so they could be bartered for
more guns to aid in the stealing of more horses. Many
White traders encouraged the strife so as to capitalize
on it by selling guns, ammunition, and liquor. The herds
of bison, once thought to be limitless, dwindled; and
as they did so, an additional cause for strife arose over
hunting territories. In any event, cultural—that is, social, political, economic, and technological—causes can
be found to explain why the Plains Indians were "warlike." They were that way not because of their biology
or their psychology, but because this was what their
new White-induced culture demanded.‡

THE NEW RICH

Among the Mandan, Hidatsa, Arapaho, and Blackfoot,
a member of a war society purchased his way up the
ladder of age-grades until he arrived at the topmost one.
At each step, he found a seller from the next older
brotherhood and then purchased his rights. A buyer was
free to select any seller he wanted, but he usually chose
someone from his father's family. Sometimes, as part
of the payment, the purchaser had to relinquish his wife
to the seller for a time; if the purchaser was unmarried,
he had to borrow a wife from a relative.

Membership in other kinds of societies was also
often purchased, and in fact many things were for sale
among the Plains tribes: sacred objects, religious songs,
and even the description of an especially potent vision.
The right to paint a particular design on one's face during a religious ceremony might cost as much as a horse.
Permission just to look inside another person's sacred
bundle of fetishes and feathers was often worth the

equivalent of a hundred dollars. A prudent Blackfoot was well advised to put his money into a sacred bundle, an investment that paid him continued dividends. The investment was as safe, for a time, as today's government bond is. And it was readily negotiable at a price usually higher than the purchase price, because as the Plains tribes became richer, the price of sacred bundles continued to rise. Further, by permitting a bundle to be used in rituals, the owner received fees that were like dividends.

Almost none of these tribes had ever known such wealth before they obtained horses. The Comanche, for example, were once an impoverished Shoshonean people from the Great Basin. Many of the other tribes only a generation or two earlier had been inefficient hunters; in those days all of a family's possessions could be dragged along by a single dog. But the Plains tribes quickly learned the laws of the marketplace, both from each other and from the White trader. The accumulation of wealth became important, but it was not incorporated into the structure of their societies in any significant way. Perhaps it would have been in time, and the Plains tribes might have served economic theorists as a model of the steps by which societies become capitalistic.

But theorists today can do no more than guess what might have happened to the concept of wealth had the Plains culture endured for another century, or even for a few more generations. Some indication is given by tribes such as the Kiowa, who learned to invest wealth to create more wealth. A Kiowa warrior, who had once been forced by custom to share his wealth, soon learned to hoard it and to keep it in his family through inheritance. Classes based on wealth arose in what had once been an egalitarian society. Members of the wealthiest classes could afford to give their sons certain benefits. They equipped them with the best horses and guns and sent them down the road to military glory at an early age. And when the son of a wealthy Kiowa achieved an exploit, everyone heard about it, for the wealthy controlled the channels of publicity through their ability to give gifts. Such publicity paid further economic benefits: The scion of a wealthy Kiowa, whose exploits were well publicized, could increase his wealth even more because he easily obtained followers for a raiding party.

The new-found wealth that crammed the Plains Indian tipis was valued as a status symbol. It became another way of counting coups, of being one up on a neighbor. And since the primary way to acquire wealth was to steal horses from someone else, wealth became a validation of bravery. The warrior also made certain to remind everyone of his prowess by issuing constant reminders in the form of gifts. Gift-giving emphasized that the giver was brave enough to go out and steal more wealth any time he felt like it.

The sudden wealth achieved by the mass slaughter of bison changed customs in other ways also. It took only a moment for a man on horseback to kill a bison with a bullet, but it still remained a long and arduous task for his wife to dress the hide for sale to the White trader. As a result, a shortage of women developed and a premium was placed on them. Men always needed the hands of extra women to dress the skins, and the parents of a healthy girl could negotiate her marriage from a position of strength. At the same time, polygyny, which probably had existed to a limited extent, became widespread, for a good hunter needed as many wives as he could afford. Instances are known of berdaches being taken on as second wives, not for any sexual variety they might offer but because they performed women's tasks. (A corresponding role was possible for females who found a woman's life dull and uninteresting; they might become "manly-hearted women" and hunt with the men.)

VISION QUESTS

Many North American Indians had great respect for visions, but few immersed themselves so deeply in them as did the Plains tribes. Sometimes a spirit might appear in a vision of its own accord, just to befriend a mortal; usually, though, the Plains Indian had to go in active pursuit of his vision. He did this by isolating himself, fasting and doing without water, and by the practice of self-torture, at the same time imploring the spirits to take pity on his suffering. A youth might gash his arms and legs, and among the Crow it was the custom to cut off a joint from a finger of the left hand. Cheyenne vision-seekers thrust skewers of wood under pinches of skin in the breast; these skewers were attached to ropes, which in turn were tied to a pole. All day the youth leaned his full weight away from the pole, pulling and tugging at his own flesh while he implored the spirits to give him a vision.

A spirit might at last take pity on the pain and delirium of the Plains Indian youth and give him supernatural guidance. A successful vision supported the youth for the rest of his life. He now had a guardian spirit on whom he could always call for help and guidance, although from time to time he had to repeat the self-torture to renew his familiarity with the spirit. During his vision, the youth usually learned what items —such as feathers, a stone pipe, a piece of skin, or maize kernels—he should collect for a sacred medicine bundle, which he would keep in a small pouch. A particularly lucky youth might also receive his own songs, which when sung served as a call for supernatural aid; that they sounded like gibberish to everyone else only reinforced the belief that he had received a unique vision.

The entire Plains culture worked toward producing visions. Every Plains youth grew up believing firmly in the reality of the vision, so no resistance to the idea had to be overcome. The youth worked himself into an intense emotional state by starvation, thirst, self-torture, exposure to the sun, and isolation—all of which are known to produce hallucinations. The shape in which the vision came to him was predetermined by the structure of the myths and visions he had heard about since childhood. And when narrating his vision, he unconsciously reconstructed it and filled in gaps, adapting it to the norms of behavior of his culture—much as we do in reporting an incoherent dream, no matter how sincerely we believe we are not distorting it.

A remarkable thing about the visions is that they were not invariably experienced, despite all of the cultural incentives toward that end. Some youths failed to receive any visions at all, even though they tried repeatedly. (Those who could not obtain a vision on their own could sometimes purchase one, as well as a replica of the successful visionary's medicine bundle.) One explanation for this failure is that visions offered a rationale for the differential distribution of power and prestige in the society, justifying the greater rights and rewards that certain individuals already had. This was so nearly the rule that most individuals had the visions that their status entitled them to have. To become a member of the Buffalo Doctor's society among the Omaha, for example, individuals had to receive a vision of a specified type. Since membership in this society was restricted to those with wealth and prestige, only individuals who had the right to enter could be expected to receive the required vision. Anyone who claimed to have received this vision—yet who lacked the appropriate wealth and family connections—was informed that his vision was not deemed acceptable. An individual who received no appropriate vision might thus interpret the failure as proof that he was going to be poor—a self-fulfilling prophecy. In contrast, the son of a man wealthy in horses would probably attain his vision very easily; in the unlikely event that he did not, he could always purchase one.‡

The visions differed from person to person and from tribe to tribe. Some differences can, of course, be explained by individual personalities. An Indian with an auditory personality might hear loud calls of birds or gibberish songs, whereas one who was visually oriented would be apt to see a horse with strange markings. Individual fears and anxieties must obviously have gone into the vision. Despite the Plains warrior's attitude of fearlessness, a common vision was the sudden transformation of rocks and trees into enemies, against whom the youth was made invulnerable by his guardian spirit. Often the vision involved the visit of some animal. An eagle might fly by, flapping its wings with a sound like the crash of thunder; bison, elk, bears, and hawks also appeared quite often. Among the Pawnee (who, alone of the Plains tribes, had an orderly system of religious beliefs, including the idea of a supreme being), the stars and other heavenly bodies entered quite freely into visions.

The belief in visions existed among most of the Indians of North America, and it seems to have developed in two different directions. Among some Indians, it led directly to shamanism, for shamans were believed to be recipients of particularly intense visions and to have the power of summoning up new visions at will. The other line of development led to visions of more limited power that had to be sought after. A great range of variation occurred in this second category—from the Plains youth, who suffered ordeals, to the Great Basin Shoshone, who passively waited for the spirit to find him.

Before the contrasting attitudes of the Plains tribes and the Great Basin Shoshone can be explained, the vision must first be recognized for what it is: a resort to supernatural aid in a dangerous undertaking, one in which individual skill is not sufficient to guarantee success. The Plains culture provided numerous opportunities for dangerous undertakings, such as riding among a herd of stampeding bison or stealthily entering an enemy camp to steal horses. For the Plains warrior, the rewards of such undertakings were certainly great enough to compensate for the few days of self-torture and fasting required to obtain a guardian spirit. The impoverished environment of the Great Basin Shoshone, however, provided no such rewards. The land yielded a bare minimum, and the rewards went not to the man who showed courage and daring, but to the one who was wise in the ways of rabbits. Any yearning for visions that existed among the Great Basin Shoshone was not for protection in the dangers of the hunt or in warfare, but for curing snake bites or disease.‡

The various responses of people in different cultures toward visions partly explains why some Indians took enthusiastically to the White man's alcohol and others did not. The use of firewater was particularly reckless among the Plains Indians, as well as among the woodland tribes who were related to them. Alcohol was promptly seized upon by the Plains Indians as a shortcut method for producing derangement of the senses and hallucinations. In primeval North America the Plains tribes had made remarkably little use of such hallucinogenic plants as peyote and certain mushrooms. The Plains vision-seekers were not even fortunate enough to have available the jimsonweed, whose original range in the West generally covered only portions of the Southwest and southern California. Nor had the Plains tribes learned that tobacco, which they smoked for a few ritual puffs, when swallowed could produce considerable discomfort and emotional upheaval, as it did for many Central and South American Indians.

Only after about 1850, when the Plains culture was rapidly disintegrating, did the hallucinogenic cactus known as peyote take hold. Peyote is native to northern Mexico, but it spread like a grass fire from tribe to tribe as far north as the Canadian plains; it was most widely and promptly accepted by the Plains tribes. Peyote afforded a way to seek visions; it also provided an escape from the humiliation of the complete defeat by Whites in the latter part of the last century.

THE END OF A CULTURE

As White settlers migrated westward after the Civil War, they sealed the fate of the Plains tribes. Treaty after treaty was broken by Whites as the Indian lands were crisscrossed by Easterners covetous of acreage and precious metals. At first the Whites tried to restrict the Plains Indians to valueless areas, but that policy was soon supplanted by a war of extermination. General William Tecumseh Sherman said in 1867: "The more I see of these Indians, the more convinced I am that they all have to be killed or be maintained as a species of paupers." To help clear the Indians from the Plains, the Whites struck at their food base, the bison. They themselves not only destroyed the animals, but they also induced the Indians to collaborate with them by offering to buy vast quantities of such delicacies as bison tongue.

Tensions between the Whites and the Plains Indians increased during the 1870's. On July 5, 1876, newspapers describing celebrations of the young nation's Centennial reported also the delayed news of a humiliating defeat. The elite Seventh Cavalry, a tough outfit of more than two hundred men, which had been organized specifically for killing Indians—and which were led by Lieutenant Colonel George Custer—had been annihilated on June 25 by a combined force of Sioux and Cheyenne under Sitting Bull and Crazy Horse in the battle of Little Bighorn. But the victory over Custer had been empty, and for the Plains Indians it marked the beginning of the end. From that time on, troops pursued them mercilessly from waterhole to waterhole; their women and children were slaughtered before their eyes, their encampments and their riches burned. The glory and the poetry had gone out of the Plains Indians. Mighty chiefs emerged from hiding as miserable fugitives, hungry and without bullets for their guns. The survivors, like so many cattle, were herded onto reservations, where rough handling, cheap whiskey, starvation, exposure, and disease depleted their numbers still more severely.

The end of the Plains culture can be dated exactly. In 1890 the surviving Plains Indians enthusiastically listened to a native messiah who foretold the return of dead Indians and the magical disappearance of the Whites. Alarmed, the United States government sent out troops—once again, ironically, the Seventh Cavalry, which had been resupplied with men after Custer's defeat—to suppress this Ghost Dance, as it was called.‡ While being placed under arrest, Sitting Bull was killed. And some three hundred Sioux, mostly women and children waiting to surrender at Wounded Knee Creek, in South Dakota, were massacred. The soldiers lost 25 dead and 39 wounded, most of them struck by their own bullets or by shrapnel. Wounded Knee marked the end of any hopes the Plains Indians still cherished. The Ghost Dance had proved as much a piece of make-believe as the rest of their improbable culture.

VIII
Northwest Coast:
Status and Wealth

THE AFFLUENT SOCIETIES OF THE PACIFIC COAST

The Northwest Coast culture refers to numerous Indian groups, speaking a diversity of languages, who inhabit the narrow strip of land between the continent's western-most mountains and the Pacific Ocean. This strip extends from eastern Alaska to northern California, a distance of some fifteen hundred miles. The subsistence pattern of all these Indians was hunting-and-gathering —yet, because of a fortuitous combination of environmental factors, their food supply was of an abundance more like that reaped from intensive agriculture. So rich are the products of the sea and the land along this coast that the Indians "harvested" them much as agricultural Indians living on fertile soils harvested their fields.

Much of the food supply along this coast is—or was, before the building of big dams and the effects of pollution degraded the rivers—in the form of fish, particularly the salmon that swarm up the inlets and rivers on the way to their spawning grounds. They used to be so numerous that at places they nearly filled the rivers from bank to bank, and an early explorer averred that "you could walk across on their backs." Since several different species of fish returned from the ocean to the rivers

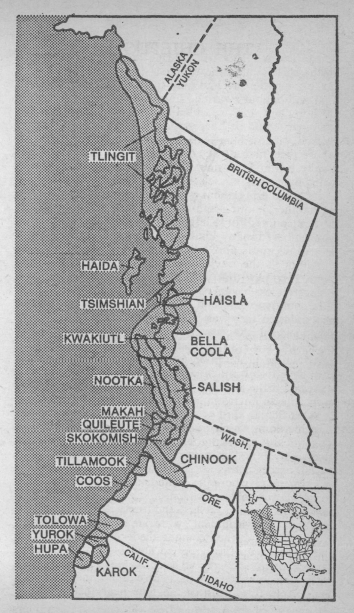

ALASKA
YUKON

BRITISH COLUMBIA

TLINGIT

HAIDA

TSIMSHIAN — HAISLA

KWAKIUTL — BELLA COOLA

NOOTKA — SALISH

MAKAH
QUILEUTE
SKOKOMISH — WASH.

TILLAMOOK — CHINOOK
COOS — ORE.

TOLOWA
YUROK
HUPA — CALIF.
KAROK — IDAHO

at different times, the Indians could often count on from five to seven major runs during the summer and fall. In the spring came the candlefish, so rich in oil that to make a candle one had only to run a wick through it. Cod and halibut swarmed in unbelievable numbers just offshore, and smelt sparkled in the surf. A wealth in sea mammals could be harvested from large canoes: humpbacked whales, hair seals, sea lions, and the sea otters whose pelts first attracted Whites to this coast. In addition to fish and sea mammals, additional food was provided by clams, mussels, abalones, oysters, limpets, and crabs. Gathering them was women's work and, as in most other hunting-and-gathering societies, female efforts accounted for a large part of the diet. The women also gathered many kinds of berries and fruits, as well as various roots and tubers.

Although the environment does not determine the kind of culture that will arise in any particular place, it nevertheless has its own limitations and opportunities. The abundance of food on the Northwest Coast led to a population that was basically sedentary. The incredible yield of the seas and shores, together with the discovery of ways to preserve fish by smoking and drying, resulted in the piling up of vast surpluses, which in turn gave rise to much larger populations than might be expected if the hunting economy were not located in so favorable an environment.

A particular kind of social organization arose here— the chiefdom, which transcends the tribe in two important ways. A chiefdom usually has a denser population than a tribe and is better integrated in its economic, social, and religious life. Chiefdoms arise most often in environments where an abundance of food and materials can be obtained from a variety of sources such as the sea, beaches, rivers, and forests. A band exploits this kind of environment by moving from place to place, fishing the river, then going to the forest to pick berries, later moving up the slopes to hunt big game. A chiefdom, though, can exploit such an environment much more efficiently because the people do not move around. One group lives most of the time near the river, and does the fishing; another lives in the forest, where it specializes in hunting game; a third gathers plant food. Each group channels the food and raw materials to a central authority—the chief—who then redistributes them to all.

Chiefdoms arose in two areas in the New World where such environments exist: the Northwest Coast and the Circum-Caribbean area (southeastern United States, Central America south of Guatemala, the larger islands of the West Indies, and Venezuela). In other parts of the world, chiefdoms were most abundant in the myriad islands of Polynesia, Micronesia, and Melanesia; among the steppe nomads of central Asia (including the Turkic and Mongol hordes of less than a thousand years ago); and in West Africa among the Ashanti, Benin, and Dahomey—before Whites taught them to become slavers.‡

Other places in North America also were blessed with an environment that could have yielded a surplus, yet their hunters and gatherers went on living as bands or tribes and never organized themselves into chiefdoms. These people were unable to store a surplus, and so had no need for a central authority to redistribute goods. The Plains tribes were surrounded by a summer abundance of bison, but the only storage they practiced was to save some of the meat as jerkee or pemmican. For the rest of the year they lived off their meager supplies and hoped to find stray bison. Lack of a technology of food storage can place severe limitations on the complex institutions possible to a society, for it will have no way to sustain its social, economic, and political links during the long periods of scarcity. The Northwest Coast people, on the other hand, were remarkably efficient in developing a technology of food preservation that provided a year-round food supply; and they developed it primarily for fish, a food that otherwise spoils very rapidly. Fish were split open, dried or smoked on racks, pressed together into bales, and then stored in oil. The roe from female salmon was stored in seal bladders, or else it was smoked to produce what White settlers called Siwash cheese.

The chief was basically the group's economist. His responsibility was to lay aside sufficient supplies of food and raw materials and to distribute them as needed. But he was also a figurehead for his people, much as is the monarch of England. For example, the Tsimshian, who lived on the coast opposite the Queen Charlotte Islands in British Columbia, were bound together by loyalty to their chief and by participation in his activities. They took extravagent care of him throughout his life. They built his grandiose house, saw that he performed no manual labor, and financed his elaborate feasts; and when his life was over they buried him with much mourning. If a member of another chiefdom even accidentally caused the slightest inconvenience to their chief, the Tsimshian rose as one to wreak vengeance. Since the reputation of the Tsimshian among their neighbors depended upon the reputation of the chief himself, he could almost always count on support and assistance.

The chief, though, had no formal political power and no way to back up his decisions. His control over his people existed only because of the prestige of his position and the force of his own personality. The weakness inherent in the chiefdom was the chief's lack of legalized authority to carry out his decisions. Those who live in complex modern society think in terms of political authority enforced overtly by the police officer or covertly by agents of the Central Intelligence Agency. Modern Americans assume that political decisions made by their government will be enforced by specialists having legally-sanctioned police powers. The Northwest Coast chief lacked any such powers. He was the central authority, but if his personality lost its charm, then he no longer could function as chief. Thus the Tsimshian chief, for example, always needed to court the favor of the heads of powerful lineages who served as his cabinet and advised in all important affairs. If they did not approve of his plans, they simply withheld their support, and he became politically paralyzed. Sometimes a strong chief successfully overruled opposition; but in most cases the chief realized that his powers were not limitless.‡

RANK AND STATUS

In the evolution of culture, rank appears for the first time at the level of the chiefdom. The band and the tribe are both egalitarian. Once a society starts to keep track of who is who, there is no telling where the bookkeeping will end. In Northwest Coast society it did not end until the lowliest citizen knew his exact hereditary rank, defined by his precise genealogical distance from the chief. A record has survived of one Kwakiutl feast in which each of the 658 guests from thirteen subdivisions of the chiefdom knew whether he was, say, number 437 or number 438.

Most North American Indians do not place great emphasis upon their genealogy. The Iroquois usually remember genealogies going back no more than two or three generations, and the same is true of some Pueblo Indians. The early explorers of North America did not report the same extraordinary recollection of genealogies as had been observed in parts of Africa and in Polynesia (where chiefs are supposed to have been able to reel off genealogies going back fifty generations). This absence of a deep interest in genealogy can be accounted for by the absence of any great amount of inheritable property among the Indians. People who lack domesticated animals, slaves, and rights to grazing lands are not likely to show a great interest in who their relatives were. On the other hand, in societies in which large amounts of property are distributed to kin after the death of the owner, the closeness of kinship may be crucial in determining who inherits what. Genealogy thus becomes important in documenting claims to kinship. In other words, the energy required to retain knowledge of genealogical links is unlikely to be expended except when it serves some purpose considered important in the society. For this reason, genealogy is usually given little attention in societies less complex than the chiefdom. For the people of the Northwest Coast chiefdoms, it was to their benefit as potential inheritors of both property and status to know exactly who their ancestors were.

In most chiefdoms around the world, rank and status have been stratified into classes—chiefs, nobles, and commoners. But the Northwest Coast Indians did not have a true class system. Rather, as we have seen, there was a continuous gradation from the topmost chief downward, a gradation as precise as the marks on a yardstick. The ranking of the aristocracy in feudal Europe was similarly precise, with the major difference that, unlike the Indians of the Northwest Coast, the aristocracy ruled over an ungraded mass of peasants. A specialist on the Northwest Coast cultures has stated: "To insist upon the use of the term 'class system' for Northwest Coast society means that we must say that each individual was in a class by himself."‡ Thus even identical twins were ranked in the order of their birth. Although no distinct class of nobles was set off against a class of commoners, some individuals were generally recognized as "high" and others as "low." In a chiefdom, the members of society are preoccupied with making visible the distinctions in rank and class. On the Northwest Coast, the position of chief was invested with a dignity of its own, and persons of high rank became identifiable by means of sumptuary laws. Such laws govern the dress, ornamentation, and deportment of privileged individuals or classes. The Northwest Coast chief lived in the largest village; his was the most ornate house, and the crests carved on it were the most ostentatious. Only heads of lineages were allowed to wear ornaments made from abalone shell or to have their robes trimmed with sea-otter fur.

Sumptuary laws are to be found in many societies. In the Aztec state, a commoner who dared to build a stone house would probably have been put to death. In Tudor England, only men entitled to be addressed as "Lord" were permitted to wear sable fur. In the seventeenth century, the General Court of the Massachusetts Bay Colony decreed harsh penalties for those who exceeded their rank by wearing lace, gold and silver buttons, silk hoods or scarves, or expensive boots. Sumptuary custom may produce distinction in vocabulary and pronunciation, and may even entail a completely different language; thus, aristocrats in Czarist Russia spoke French, and in imperial China the Mandarins had a language of their own. The rise of a "jet set," which flies to Paris for dinner and the opera and back to New York the next day, is one development in recent years by which wealthy people set themselves apart from the middle classes.

Among the Northwest Coast Indians, the matter of rank was of crucial importance during a potlatch, the extravagant feast at which gifts were made to every guest. Since the gifts had to be distributed in some kind of order to avoid a chaotic scramble, it was logical that the most important guest should receive his gift first, followed by the next highest in rank, and so on down the line. The lavishness of the gifts dwindled accordingly, to a pittance for the lowliest person present. In this way all of the guests became aware of their precise rank among the others; and since everyone at the potlatch also knew, it soon became common knowledge.

The precise rank of each Northwest Coast Indian was acquired mainly through birth and inheritance, and only occasionally through social maneuvering. Opportunities for maneuvering were few, however. Since all parents wanted their children to marry a partner of greater rank, the ambitions nullified each other, and marriages were most often between men and women of nearly equivalent rank. Inheritance was much more important. Just as in Europe, where laws of primogeniture were once common, the Northwest Coast Indians were reluctant to divide up inheritances. So a man usually passed on his estate intact, either (among the matrilineal Tlingit, Haida, or Tsimshian) to his eldest sister's eldest son or (among the Northwest Coast societies that were patrilineal) to his own eldest son.

Rank and status were so important that they applied even to adultery. Among the Tlingit, if an adulterous male held a very high rank, the lower-ranking kin of the offended husband pacified him with gifts, so as to avoid his jeopardizing his entire clan by taking action against an adulterer of high rank. But if the adultery had been between a man of low rank and a married woman of high rank, the high-born woman's clan had to show to the world that it was offended—which it did by killing two of the offending male's clansmen of a rank midway between the ranks of the two adulterers. The adulterous male's clan was then expected to hand over for execution one of its men who was equal in rank to the woman. All through these complicated maneuvers and compensations, the offended husband remained indoors. When the affair had been settled, he grandly emerged and accepted lavish gifts from the adulterer's clan; the words for these gifts translates into English as "they wipe the shame from my face." As for the adulterous male himself, he usually became a debt-slave to his own clan, in partial compensation for the cost of the gifts and the loss of the productive labors of three of their kin who had been executed.‡

SLAVERY

Only one gap existed in the orderly ranking of Northwest Coast society: that between free members of society and "slaves." The latter were usually captives from some other chiefdom, were not related to anyone in the group, and had no rank of their own. Unlike the slaves who figure in the history of European and Arab colonialism, these individuals were not a very productive part of the Northwest Coast economy. They performed only menial tasks such as might otherwise be performed by a free person of very low rank. Most of them did not produce enough even to earn their keep. They were merely tangible evidence of their owners' high rank. The "slave" was more a prestige item than a producer of economic wealth. Nor was the "debt slavery" practiced in some parts of the Northwest Coast, particularly in California and Oregon, actually slavery as it is usually defined. Debts might be incurred in a variety of ways, such as by owing compensation to one's kin for the consequences of adultery or by gambling. A man saved from accidental death also owed a debt to his rescuer, and if he could not pay it, he then became his rescuer's debt–slave until he had worked off the obligation. The rescuer owned only temporary economic services and was not allowed to inflict physical harm on the indebted person. Since no justification therefore exists for calling the Northwest Coast cultures "slave societies," from now on these people will be referred to as "captives."

Some apologists for slavery in the United States used to assert that it is part of human nature to enslave others when the opportunity presents itself; as evidence they have pointed not only to the Northwest Coast Indians, but also to Africans who once put other Africans in chains, and to various peoples in Southeast Asia. But slavery has never been shown to exist as an indigenous institution in any society simpler than the state, other than those societies that learned slave-making from more complex ones. The people in Africa and in Asia who took up the slave trade as partners of the Europeans and the Arabs were responding to the economic incentives of those alien cultures and not to anything inherent in their own.

The lot of the Northwest Coast captive was disagreeable enough. He (or sometimes she) was an object of contempt who lacked any rights. Marriage was allowed only with another captive. The perpetual hope of a captive was to be ransomed by one's kin, who usually attempted to do just that. Once back with his own people, a returned captive might give face-saving feasts, but he never fully recovered his former rank. The stigma was so great that sometimes relatives refused to ransom a captive, simply to avoid the shame of having him back in the village.

Northwest Coast captives could be killed at the whim of their masters. Among the Tlingit, for example, it was the custom to put the body of a captive in the bottom of the main post hole for a new house—not to sanctify or to bless the dwelling, but merely to show that the builder was of such wealth that he could afford to dispose of one of his captives. Also, for the purpose of gaining prestige, the bodies of captives were sometimes offered to a visiting chief as rollers for beaching his canoe. The Northwest Coast Indians apparently did not regard the killing of captives, even those who had

been living in the house for years, as a barbarous act.
The captives seem to have been regarded as dead from
the moment that they allowed themselves to be captured; killing them a few years later merely meant a
delay in executing the sentence. In practice, though,
captives were seldom put to death; they might just as
easily be freed as killed, since in that way also the
owners could show off their prestige.

SPECIALISTS IN RELIGION AND ART

Occupational specialization occurs to a minor degree in
tribes, and very occasionally in bands. At the level of
the chiefdom, though, specialization becomes an inte-
gral part of the economic system and is found at every
step from production through redistribution. The individuals who spend their time carving house posts need
berries to eat, and the individuals who know where to
find berries usually do not know how to carve; and
neither of these will be equipped to hunt seals in the
ocean. The central authority of the chiefdom can arrange to satisfy all their requirements, with the result
that craftworkers, berry pickers, and hunters, among
others, can carry on their own occupations without
interruption.

Specialized work—such as hunting whales or seals,
making canoes, carving totem poles, and netting fish—
tended to be perpetuated in families among the Northwest Coast Indians, with an increase in skill from
generation to generation. Certain families eventually
assumed roles similar to those of the guilds in medieval
Europe. In addition to the manual skills a young man
learned from his father or uncle, something else was
needed—and that was supernatural sanction. He had
first to dream that he could perform the work he was
destined for. Even though he came from a long line of
wood carvers, a vision was necessary as assurance. In
search of such a vision, the Northwest Coast youth
flayed his body with thorns and chilled it by immersion
in lakes. The ease with which visions came to a youth

often depended upon his rank. The son of a man with high rank quickly found the spirit helper who had aided his ancestors to become specialists in a highly valued kind of work. A youth of low rank usually received only inconclusive or uninteresting visions, so he ended up in a less valued occupation, such as the menial one of gathering wood. Apparently the Northwest Coast culture did not encourage dreams of glory in those born at the lower levels of society.

Religion was a specialized occupation also. Superficially the religion of the Northwest Coast Indians may not appear to differ greatly from the shamanistic practices of bands and tribes. But whereas the shaman in a band usually cures or otherwise assists only one person at a time, in a chiefdom he participates in rituals that have a larger societal function. A still more notable difference is that in a chiefdom the role of the shaman comes to resemble that of a priest—in other words, the permanent holder of a specialized religious office. In Eskimo society anyone might become a shaman, but in a Northwest Coast chiefdom, shamans tended to come from certain families that specialized in shamanism. The Northwest Coast shaman thus appears to represent an early stage in the development of the priesthood as an institution.

The achievements of specialization among the Northwest Coast Indians were apparent in their art. That of the Haida, Tlingit, and Tsimshian is especially notable for its size and power. But all Northwest Coast art shares a quality that makes it instantly identifiable to most museum viewers. On totem poles, canoes, wooden boxes, eating utensils, in fact on just about every available object, figures of animals and mythical beings are carved or painted with almost unvarying symmetry and a compulsion, bordering on agoraphobia, to cover every inch of the surface. In the context of a status society, the carving of a house front, for example, is not done to render the house more attractive, but solely to enhance the social and economic position of the owner and to arouse the envy of neighbors.

TOTEM POLES

The best-known and most dramatic manifestation of Northwest Coast art is the totem pole, as Whites mistakenly call it. This huge, upright log, carved with figures of animals plus a few mythological beings, does not serve as a totem but simply as a crest, combining pride in one's ancestry with the ostentation of high rank. To display such a crest was to announce one's status, much as heraldic crests once did among the high-born families of Europe. A person who paid for carving and painting the pole outside his dwelling would order the same combination of figures to be painted or carved elsewhere; on a mortuary pole above the grave of a relative, on household furnishings, on the posts and beams of the house, and on the family's canoes. The totem pole is thus somewhat similar to a southwestern cattleman's brand: an artificial emblem, often incorporating the family initial, together with an arbitrary symbolic element such as a bar or a circle. The Johnson family, having burned a Circle-J brand on its cattle to show ownership, probably will not stop there, but will also carve the same Circle-J over the front gate and the entrance to the corral. The brand may be cast in metal as a door knocker, painted on the mailbox, etched on crystal ash trays, and burned into the leather of boots worn by members of the family.

The reasons given for the production of art in different cultures have been many: religious veneration, magic, esthetic pleasure, and so on. But few other cultures besides the Northwest Coast have had ridicule and boasting as an artistic incentive. A Northwest Coast chief might order a carved and painted record of the way he outwitted another chief; indeed, some poles are hardly more than billboards advertising the humiliation inflicted upon someone else. Several of the carved figures on one pole in the Haida village of Old Kasaan depict Russian priests. The nineteenth-century owner of the pole was extremely proud of having successfully resisted attempts by the priests to convert him. Having defeated them in a contest of wills, just as he might have defeated a neighboring chief in warfare, he felt entitled to record the event on his pole.

Seeing the cracked and weathered poles, either in a museum or still in place in Alaska and British Columbia, one is likely to suppose they are of great antiquity. The truth is that almost all are quite recent—most of them less than a hundred years old, with only some as old as a hundred and fifty years. So a question arises: To what extent are totem poles an indigenous art? The existence of totem poles was not mentioned by Whites until 1791, even though more than a hundred vessels from Europe and the United States had already visited the Northwest Coast to trade over a period beginning twenty years before. Some of these ships had in their crews Filipinos and Hawaiians who conceivably may have passed on the art to the Indians. Indeed, the closest approximation to totem poles elsewhere in the world exists in the islands of the Pacific Ocean. It is also possible that ships from Asia may have reached the Northwest Coast somewhat before Europeans and Russians arrived, and may have had something to do with the development of totem poles.‡ Carving them would have been very difficult without an array of very sharp tools—yet the Northwest Coast Indians lacked iron, except possibly for some that may have reached them from Siberia via the Eskimo, several hundred years before the coming of Whites. Some totem poles might have been carved in primeval times, but the numerous and flamboyant ones we know about were not made until trade with Whites provided large quantities of iron tools.

THE ECONOMICS OF PRESTIGE

In the Northwest Coast culture, social rank went hand in hand with economic wealth. Common to almost the entire Northwest Coast was wealth in the form of dentalia shells. Shells of the same size were strung to a specific length, and the value of a string increased markedly with the size of the shells. Early in the nineteenth century, a string consisting of eleven large shells was worth about $50. A string of the same length containing fifteen smaller shells was worth a mere $2.50. But to equate dentalia shells with money is to misunderstand the Northwest Coast Indians. They did not translate the cost of something into a certain number of shells, as a modern American does with coins or bills, and then decide whether or not it was worth the purchase price. Indians did not need money to purchase the essentials of subsistence; what they did need it for was to purchase social recognition. When one village had to humble another because its chief had been insulted, reparations were often demanded in the form of dentalia. For anyone entitled to a reward, dentalia strings were a greater enhancement of prestige than their equivalent value in a small canoe.

Status was continually having to be reaffirmed through the display of wealth, which often took the form of lavish tipping. A man who wanted to maintain his rank was almost constantly handing out small gifts. On being invited to a feast, he had to tip whoever invited him. Someone who mentioned his name with reverence was immediately rewarded with a gift. If he stumbled at a ceremonial—thereby exposing himself to possible ridicule, with consequent loss of status—he had to restore his dignity by giving presents to the onlookers. For this reason he left his house in the morning draped in several blankets that could be given to people who performed important services for him during the day. He also carried many lesser presents, which he tossed away as casually as a modern American tips a delivery boy.

The really amazing thing about the Northwest Coast economic system was that it worked without laws to enforce it. What kept it going was vanity, prestige, and ridicule. Economic products were assembled in vast surpluses, which flowed to the chief. Such an accumulation was neither tax nor tribute, as it was in the Aztec state. Perhaps the system worked mainly because of the participants' realization that sooner or later they would get back a comparable quantity of goods at a potlatch. (The word originally came from the Nootka *patshatl*, "to give," but the Chinook jargon that was later used by Whites as a trade language altered the word to its familiar spelling.) Potlatches were given as soon as a lineage could amass enough wealth to serve as hosts. But the memorable potlatches were those given by the chiefs; the chiefdom gathered surpluses from the whole population, and then its chief feasted another chief. Everyone understood that in a year or two the guest chief would reciprocate, at which time his surplus goods would be given as presents to the chief who had been his host.

This whole system is bizarrely different from what modern Americans, trained in a market economy, regard as normal. We would be inclined to handle such a series of transactions by trying to get the better of the bargain at each step as goods changed hands. The attitude of the Northwest Coast Indians, though, was just the opposite. Their competitiveness lay in trying to give away more than was received, with the aim of humbling someone else. And what to us is simply an economic transaction, to the Northwest Coast Indians was gift-giving. Their potlatches produced incidental benefits that our system of trade does not. The participants got a lavish feast as a dividend, plus the occasion for good fellowship and for building up peaceful relations with neighbors. By means of the seating arrangement at the feast and the order in which gifts were distributed, the feast also served to validate the rank of each participant.

As soon as plans for a potlatch were announced, vast quantities of fish oil, carvings, blankets, tools, jewelry, and other valued items were assembled; sometimes, for a really memorable potlatch, the preparations could go on for years. Everyone contributed willingly, simply because it was an opportunity once again to validate rank. Anyone who lagged in participation might be dropped down several notches. A potlatch also offered an opportunity to humilate another lineage or another chief by hosting a potlatch grander than had been offered up to them. Over the years, the competition increased, to a point where the catalog of gifts at one Kwakiutl potlatch included eight canoes, six captives, fifty-four elk skins, two thousand silver bracelets, seven thousand brass bracelets, and thirty-three thousand blankets—while the guests consumed the meat of about fifty seals. (My discussion of the potlatch has been in the past tense, for the lavish potlatches belonged to the last century. But it is also true that so deeply embedded was the idea of the potlatch in the Northwest Coast culture that even today the surviving populations of these chiefdoms exchange gifts. Sewing machines, refrigerators, bedspreads, bolts of cloth, and similar goods keep changing hands far in excess of actual use or need.)

INTERPRETATIONS OF THE POTLATCH

Anthropologists have understandably been intrigued by the potlatch and many have attempted to interpret it, with little agreement. At one time the main emphasis was on its destructive and competitive aspects: the burning of property, the killing of captives, the aim of one chief to outdo competing chiefs in generosity. At other times anthropologists have described the potlatch as a ceremony for asserting and validating claims to rights and titles, thus confirming social status while providing a substitute for physical violence. According to a different view, the chief who gave grand potlatches did not become great by giving them, but rather gave them because he was great. In other words, it was not so much his pleasure to do so as his duty.

The potlatch was probably all of these things—and more. A recent comparison of potlatches among the Tlingit and the Kwakiutl indicates that they also served as a sort of "rite of passage" for a society in transition from one critical stage to another. That this might have been their function is suggested by major differences between the two societies in the occasions for the potlatches, the frequency with which they occurred, the guests who were invited, and the nature of the exchanges that took place. The Tlingit and the Kwakiutl likewise differed in their social structure. The Tlingit had rules concerning marriage but none concerning the succession of power; the Kwakiutl had rules of succession but almost none governing group affiliations. In each society, potlatches were given at the critical times for which rules to govern conduct were missing—for the Tlingit, at funerals when the problem of succession arose; for the Kwakiutl, not at funerals but at marriages and other occasions when an individual was initiated into a group. In both instances, the potlatch obviously served to reaffirm the structure of society during a period of change and uncertainty. The guests at the ceremony thus served to validate the shift to a new order of things, whether it was the succession of a new chief or the altered status of an individual. The guests were witnesses to the fact that all was well once again in the society.

Yet another explanation, which perhaps better accounts for the potlatch throughout all the Northwest Coast societies, is the ecological one. The Northwest Coast environment had been described as affording the inhabitants with abundant food from the sea and forests. That was true—for most of the year. But in some years a run of salmon might fail to take place; or, for the groups that depended upon fishing in the open seas, long periods of fog might make fishing impossible. In other words, an environmental limitation was placed on the Indians of the Northwest Coast, the usual abundance notwithstanding, by occasional periods of scarcity, which set the outer limits to the size of the population that could be sustained.

How could this "law of the minimum" be surmounted? One way was to store a surplus, and this the Northwest Coast Indians did. Another way, though, was to assure a surplus in the form of an obligation on the part of other groups, who were spurred on by a value system that encouraged the rivalry for prestige. Suppose that one group whose subsistence was based upon harvesting the sea had a bountiful year. This group might then hold a potlatch to which those living alongside rivers that had not been so productive that year would be invited. The guests would be fed for a time and eventually go home with presents of food. These recipients were undoubtedly shamed—but in a year or two the situation might be reversed. The open-sea hunters might have been landlocked by fog and rough waters, whereas the river people might have reaped a bounty. Now it would be the turn of the river people to hold a potlatch, to lord it over their former benefactors, and also at the same time to repay the debt of food. Furthermore, because of the rivalry connected with the potlatch, all groups were inspired to maintain a high level of productivity so as to counteract the law of the minimum.

This ecological interpretation accounts for most of the known facts about the potlatch, except for the destruction of vast amounts of food and property. Would that not seem to deny the redistributive functions of the potlatch? It must be remembered, though, that the potlatches observed in the nineteenth century were outlandish exaggerations of the indigenous tradition, the result of contacts with Whites. The Whites, in their scramble to obtain sea-otter and fur-seal pelts, pumped vast amounts of fresh wealth into the Northwest Coast societies. The potlatch simply could not handle the sudden flood of mass-produced fabrics, guns, kitchen utensils, metal tools, cheap jewelry, and other products of industrialized Europe and the United States. So one cause for the explosion of the potlatch was a deluge of White wealth.

A second cause is that Northwest Coast populations had plummeted because of disease introduced by the Whites' trading ships and as a result of conflicts brought on by competition for Whites' goods. In one chiefdom, for example, disease and social disruption had caused the population to drop from 23,000 to 2,000 in a mere half century. Fewer Indians were thus available to share the abundance. Furthermore, the numerous deaths left open more noble titles than there were persons of high rank to bear them. The humble man who had previously been among the last to receive his small present at a potlatch might have become in a few years, because of the death of those ahead of him, a contender for the role of heir presumptive to the chief. He would not be the sole contender, however; probably half a dozen other humble men would also have risen for the same reason. A bitter competition then began, in which potlatches of unprecedented lavishness were given, so that one man might claim prestige over others as a contender for a vacant high rank. No longer did the potlatch serve its traditional functions of redistributing wealth, validating rank, and making alliances. The wealth of these new rich seemed limitless, more than they could ever consume at a feast. So they instead destroyed vast amounts of wealth before the horrified eyes of the guests, as well as those of other contenders, to dramatize the extent of their holdings. Fortunes were tossed into potlatch fires; canoes were broken apart; captives were killed. The competing claimants had no alternative but to destroy even more property when they in turn gave potlatches.

Competitive potlatching went completely wild, particularly so among the Kwakiutl, who developed an intricate system of credits to finance the feasts. A typical interest charge for a loan of less than six months would be about twenty percent; for six months to a year, forty percent; for one year, a hundred percent. But if the borrower's credit was poor, the rate might rise to two hundred percent for less than a year. The borrower then promptly loaned out what had been borrowed to someone else, at an even higher rate of interest if possible. Within only a few decades, everyone was in debt to everyone else. In one Kwakiutl village with a population of somewhat more than a hundred people, the actual number of blankets was only about four hundred. Yet the pyramiding of debts, credits, and paper profits had raised the total of indebtedness to the equivalent of seventy-five thousand blankets.

We, trained in a capitalistic society, are horrified to think of the financial panic that would have ensued if just one person called in such loans for repayment. But it never occurred to a Northwest Coast Indian to do that. The point of loans was not to make a profit but rather to validate a higher rank. If a lender called in his loan, it would stop earning prestige and obligations for him. One escape valve, though, prevented the inflated economy from being smothered in imaginary blankets: the destruction of "coppers," which were hammered and decorated sheets of raw metal nearly three feet long. A copper was like a bank note of very high denomination. At first it represented several hundred blankets. But as the demand for the scarce coppers grew, they repeatedly rose in value until each was valued in blankets almost beyond calculation. One Kwakiutl copper, purchased originally for four hundred blankets, rose to a value of twenty-three thousand blankets (worth about $11,500 in the early years of this century). A contender for rank ultimately found himself in such a position that the only way he could humiliate a wealthy rival was to destroy one of the precious coppers. The act was equivalent to wiping out all the debts owed to him. It was an incredible price to pay, but the man who made such a dramatic gesture no doubt rose meteorically in rank.‡

THE RISE AND FALL OF CHIEFDOMS

The chiefdom has the potential for expansion because of its own internal growth, and also because it can absorb additional people through conquest and through the desire of a nearby tribe to become part of the redistribution system. Records exist of bands and tribes that voluntarily joined Northwest Coast chiefdoms, no doubt because they recognized the economic benefits. The chiefdom also benefited, since the new groups usually inhabited a different environment and thus could bring new products into the redistribution system. All the Northwest Coast chiefdoms tended to expand as far as their topographical boundaries—fjords, mountains, dense forests, or the sea itself—would permit.

Anthropologists have disagreed about what part warfare may have played in this expansion. The point was made in previous chapters that bands and tribes do not fight for additional living space or to increase their population, since they lack the complex social organization for integrating conquered peoples into their own societies. Chiefdoms, however, can more easily assimilate conquered peoples and occupy their lands; that is why true warfare appears for the first time at this level of social organization. Northwest Coast warfare was not the skirmish and the ambush of the Iroquois, nor the coups ceremony of the Plains Indians. Rather, Northwest Coast wars were expeditions organized to exterminate or capture enemies and to win their lands and wealth. Records exist of bitter and prolonged wars for the purpose of occupying territory—such as the Tlingit driving Eskimo bands off Kayak Island and the Haida forcing the Tlingit to withdraw from parts of Prince of Wales Island.

Yet, as the chiefdom grows, it contributes to its own decline. It may become so large that it no longer can redistribute goods efficiently. In that event, the citizens whose voluntary compliance is the cornerstone of the economic system may decide to leave it. A man who is number 987 in the ranking system may sooner or later decide to join with number 986 and some other low-ranking individuals to form a chiefdom of their own, in which they will all have higher status. They will be so far removed from the central authority that their departure is scarcely noticed. Nor could the chief force them to remain within the redistribution system, for a chief lacks police power to carry out his wishes.

Expansion and fragmentation were of such common occurrence among the chiefdoms on the Northwest Coast that they are thought to be characteristic of this level of social organization. Some excuse was usually given for the fragmentation: warfare, a revolt by malcontents, or a dispute over succession to the office of chief. Often, though, clear and obvious abuses in the office of the chief were the real cause. The chief, the specialist who directed redistribution, may have given a disproportionate amount of what was produced to his many wives, his rank-conscious kinsmen, his private shamans, and his personal artisans. For whatever cause, sooner or later the chiefdom fragmented into smaller groups, and the whole process of waging wars of territorial expansion would begin all over again. Any new

Northwest Coast chiefdom thus formed would be as unstable as the old. Every chiefdom is fated to collapse eventually, because it lacks one essential: the use of *legal* force, which does not exist below the level of the state.

IX

Natchez: People of the Sun

THE FRENCH ROMANTICS

Of the many glittering chiefdoms in southeastern North America, none outshone those in Georgia, Alabama, Mississippi, and parts of Louisiana and Tennessee that belonged to the Muskogean language family. The Muskogeans include such groups as the Chickasaw, the Choctaw, the Creek, and the Seminole. Of them all, the grandest were the Natchez (a French word of uncertain meaning, pronounced as if written *nachay*). The Natchez occupied at least nine villages, one of which was inhabited by the chief and was therefore known as the Great Village, in the vicinity of the present-day city of Natchez, Mississippi. Their population in primeval times is in dispute, but they are thought to have numbered about 4,000, and perhaps considerably more than that.

Their sedentary village life was based on food production, most notably maize. The names for the thirteen months into which the Natchez divided the year indicate that they relied as well upon a variety of other foods, both wild and cultivated: the months of Deer, Strawberries, Little Corn, Watermelons (which were probably introduced by the Spaniards), Peaches (possibly obtained from English settlements on the Atlantic coast), Mulberries, Great Corn, Turkeys, Bison, Bears, Cold Meal, Chestnuts, and Nuts. The environment and the economy of the Natchez clearly provided one of the essentials for the formation of a chiefdom: a wide diversity of foods that could be directed to a central authority for redistribution.

The Natchez were probably the people about whom de Soto, when he marched through their lands in 1542, reported that they dominated all their neighbors. The Natchez, devout worshipers of the sun, heard de Soto's claim that he was the sun's younger brother, but they were more skeptical than the Indians of Mexico who at first welcomed the Spaniards as gods. The Natchez asked de Soto to prove his claim by evaporating the waters of the Mississippi River. Unable to perform such a feat, de Soto fled down the Mississippi, harassed by fleets of Natchez canoes, and escaped to Mexico. The Natchez do not again appear in the history of colonization until 1682, when La Salle visited one of their villages. From then on, their decline was swift: The French crushed them in a series of wars and sold the survivors into slavery.

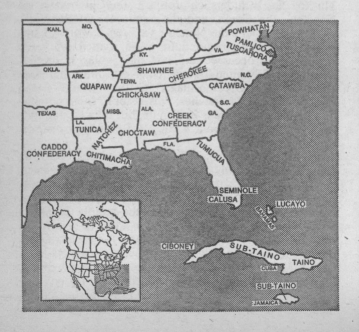

The French were fascinated by the Natchez, perhaps because of all the native cultures they had encountered from Canada to the West Indies, that of the Natchez appeared closest to the standards, the ideals, and even the morality of the Court of Versailles. Poetic metaphor described King Louis XIV as *le Roi Soleil,* "the sun king"; but in their social and political system the Natchez seemed to have brought the metaphor into reality. "The sun is the principal object of veneration to these people," wrote Maturin Le Petit, a Jesuit priest, after a stay with the Natchez in 1699, "and as they cannot conceive of anything which can be above this heavenly body, nothing else appears to them more worthy of their homage. It is for the same reason that the great chief of this nation, who knows nothing on earth more dignified than himself, takes the title of brother of the Sun, and the credulity of the people maintains him in the despotic authority which he claims."‡ Le Petit was particularly impressed by the high temple mounds the Natchez had built so that the chief, who was the earthly sun, could converse with the heavenly sun: "Every morning the great chief honors by his presence the rising of his elder brother, and salutes him with many howlings as soon as he appears above the horizon . . . Afterwards raising his hand above his head and turning from the east to the west, he shows him the direction which he must take in his course."

THE GREAT SUN

In Natchez society the characteristics of the chiefdom were still more highly developed than in that of the Northwest Coast—as highly developed, in fact, as it was possible for a chiefdom to be without becoming organized as a state. The Great Sun and the most important nobles, known simply as Suns, were treated with extreme deference. The people always gave way before them and never turned their backs when withdrawing from these exalted presences. Only wives and a few high officials might enter the Great Sun's cabin. He traveled about on a litter carried at a fast pace by relays of eight men, who passed it from one team to another without breaking step. The French explorer Charlevoix was impressed by the Great Sun's power, noting that he "acknowledges no superior but the Sun, from which he pretends to derive his origin. He exercises an unlimited power over his subjects, can dispose of their goods and lives, and for whatever labors he requires of them they cannot command any recompense."

As the redistributing agent, the Great Sun possessed an authority that would have been envied even by a Northwest Coast chief. He redistributed not only food and raw materials, but also the labor force. Le Petit reported that "the French, who are often in need of hunters or of rowers for their long voyages, never apply to anyone but the great Chief. He furnishes all the men they wish, and receives payment, without giving any part to those unfortunate individuals, who are not permitted even to complain." The admiration by the French for the authority of the Great Sun was no doubt colored somewhat by their own authoritarian political system. Despite appearances, however, the Great Sun was not a complete despot. He could on a whim order the execution of anyone who displeased him, but in matters of general concern to the chiefdom he was very much limited by a council of elders.

When a male heir to the title of Great Sun was born, nobles and commoners alike brought forth their children —and from these the Great Sun's future retainers were chosen. When the Great Sun died, the funeral rites were spectacular. About four days after death his body was borne in pomp toward the temple. His wives, guards, and retainers were expected to die also; and other volunteers vied for the privilege of accompanying the Great Sun into the afterworld. These volunteers swallowed a tobacco concoction that caused them to lose consciousness, after which they were strangled by their relatives. Then the cabin of the Great Sun was burned, and the fires in the village were extinguished. Several months later his bones were exhumed, separated from any flesh that remained, and placed in a basket within the temple; at this second burial a number of temple guardians were also strangled.

The Natchez chiefdom was a theocracy, with both

secular and sacerdotal authority embodied in the Great Sun. His large cabin was built atop a mound; near by stood a similar mound, crowned by the temple dedicated to the sun. Around the two mounds ran, as Le Petit reported it, "a circle of palisades on which are seen exposed the skulls of all the heads which their Warriors had brought back from the battles." Inside the temple were the bones of the Great Sun's ancestors, and there burned the symbol of his authority, the eternal fire. Although only the Great Sun and a few priestly officials appointed by him were permitted to enter the temple, Le Petit had either somehow gained entrance himself or else obtained a good description of its interior, for he reported: "Their Religion in certain points is very similar to that of the ancient Romans. They have a temple filled with Idols, which are different figures of men and of animals, and for which they have the most profound veneration . . . These are figures of men and women made of stone or baked clay, the heads and the tails of extraordinary serpents [probably rattlesnakes], some stuffed owls, some pieces of crystal, and some jaw bones of large fish." He also stated that the Natchez had obtained a glass bottle from the French and that they guarded it inside the temple as a very precious object.

RULER AS SUPREME PRIEST

The cult of the sun represented the official religion of the chiefdom, sanctioned by the chief himself and having a priesthood subject to his official approval. Its theology was quite complex. Central to it was a supreme deity who lived in the sky and was closely associated with the sun (or who may indeed have been identical with it; the early French reports are ambiguous on this point). The Natchez believed that in the distant past the son of this deity had descended to earth and brought to his own chosen people those laws, customs, ceremonies, and arts that gave them power over their neighbors. This deity then retired into a stone that was ever afterward preserved in the principal temple, having left the actual governing of his people to the Great Sun.

One third of the space in the cabin built atop the temple mound was devoted to this stone.

The French priests and explorers reported that every morning and evening the Great Sun came to the temple to worship the idols housed there, and then announced to the people what the idols had foretold. The Great Sun also brought to the temple the first fruits of the harvest, clearly showing that the ideas of redistributor and supreme priest had become entwined. The perpetual fire was maintained in the temple by special guardians, who would be punished by death if they allowed it to go out. This fire could not be profaned for any earthly purposes, even for cooking the Great Sun's meals; it burned solely in honor of the celestial sun. Fire caused by lightning also was regarded as a manifestation of the sun, and a bolt that destroyed a temple was considered a certain sign of divine wrath. In that event, the deity had to be placated, and to do so parents threw their infants into the flames.

The priesthood represented a specialized profession among the Natchez and most other chiefdoms of the Southeast. Priests were in charge of temples and ossuaries, and training them to carry out the complicated rites and ceremonies required many years. The priesthood naturally opposed those freelance manipulators of the supernatural, the shamans, but shamanism was no more to be extirpated from the Natchez chiefdom than superstition can be eliminated from modern society. Any Natchez who had been struck by a bolt of lightning and lived to tell about it was thought to have gained thereby the power to cure disease. Shamans were, however, neutralized by being given only minor official duties. It was their job, for example, to bless the tobacco pills that were swallowed before strangulation.

The Natchez had a very clear concept of the afterworld, and it appeared most attractive to them. They therefore went willingly to their deaths, either as companions to their deceased Great Sun or as warriors. "They believe in the immortality of the soul, and when they leave this world they go, they say, to live in another, there to be recompensed or punished," reported Le Petit.

The rewards to which they look forward consist principally in feasting, and their chastisement in the privation of every pleasure. Thus they think that those who have been the faithful observers of their laws will be conducted into a region of pleasures, where all kinds of exquisite viands will be furnished them in abundance, that their delightful and tranquil days will flow on in the midst of festivals, dances, and women; in short, they will revel in all imaginable pleasures.

But those who had violated the laws or the traditions had a different sort of world to look forward to, one where they

will be cast upon lands unfruitful and entirely covered with water, where they will not have any kind of corn, but will be exposed entirely naked to the sharp bites of mosquitoes, that all Nations will make war upon them, that they will never eat meat, and have no nourishment but the flesh of crocodiles, spoiled fish, and shellfish.

CASTE AND CLASS

Among the ranked Northwest Coast Indians, each man occupied a class by himself, but the Natchez recognized distinct hereditary classes. At the top, of course, was the Great Sun himself, who was the eldest son of White Woman (descent was matrilineal). His next younger brother was designated Little Sun, and he also held the post of Great War Chief. All the remaining brothers bore the titles of Suns. Beneath the topmost Suns were the Nobles, then the Honored People—and finally, at the bottom, the Stinkards. The Natchez system has sometimes been regarded as a caste system, but if so, it was an exceptional one. A caste system rigidly isolates all groups in the society into a hereditary hierarchy; the remarkable fact about the Natchez system was that it fostered movement from one class to another. Every member of the three noble classes had to marry a Stinkard, after which any remaining Stinkards who had not been able to make a match in the nobility married among themselves. Furthermore, any male offspring of a Natchez marriage almost always belonged to a different class from his father. A Sun was the product of a Stinkard father and a Sun mother. To be born a Noble, one's mother had to be a Noble and therefore married to a Stinkard. Since a male had to marry a Stinkard woman, his son fell a notch in rank, being a mere Noble instead of a Sun like his father.

To us, familiar with the rules of succession to European thrones, this complex system might seem preposterous. Even though the Great Sun was supreme, with each generation his male line regressed one step. His son became a Sun who was forced to marry a Stinkard woman—and so their male offspring, the Great Sun's grandson, dropped down to the Noble class. When it came time for this Noble grandson to marry, he also had to choose a Stinkard woman, and so the great-grandson was born a mere Honored. Finally, the great-great-grandson of the Great Sun was reduced to the class of a lowly Stinkard. This male line could bounce back to the nobility if the Stinkard great-great-grandson managed to marry a Sun woman; but never again could any male descendant of a Great Sun become another Great Sun. In the female line, White Woman was the mother of the Great Sun. Her eldest daughter, the sister of the reigning Great Sun, succeeded to the title of White Woman at her death. This daughter's eldest son would therefore become the next Great Sun, and the eldest daughter of the next White Woman. In that way the title of Great Sun remained in the female line—while with each generation the male line of the Great Sun sank lower.

As in the Northwest Coast chiefdoms, the noble classes were set apart by sumptuary laws and customs. Within each Natchez village, the location, the size, and the richness of furnishings of the dwellings reflected differences in class. Children of both sexes and of all classes were entitled to tattoo a simple mark across the face. If they rose in rank later on they could add to it other tattoos, such as sun symbols and serpents. The entire body of a person of very high rank or of a distinguished warrior thus became covered with a bewildering array of patterns. In the matter of dress, only men belonging to the higher classes could wear breechclouts dyed black; all other men wore white ones. Only Sun women were permitted to adorn their hair with diadems made from the feathers of swans.

For all the rigidity of the marriage rules and the class system, social mobility was far greater among the Natchez than among the Northwest Coast Indians. The broadest avenue for advancement lay in warfare. Through his warlike exploits, a Stinkard might become an Honored; and if he lifted himself out of the Stinkard class, then his wife rose with him. As soon as a Stinkard performed his first great deed in war and was advanced to the class of Honored men, he received a new name and new tattoo marks. To make the jump from Honored to Noble, though, was much more difficult: The warrior had either to take twenty scalps or to obtain ten captives. The early French reports are not clear on whether it was possible for a warrior to move up more than a single notch in his lifetime; it would appear that it was not.

When we consider the details of this Natchez class system, something is obviously amiss. First of all, the numbers of Nobles and Honored People would burgeon in successive generations while the Stinkard class would be steadily depleted because of the drain of furnishing marriage partners for the nobility. Calculations have been made, based on the assumptions that the population totaled 4,000, that it included sixteen Suns, and that each Sun and Noble male had two wives. By the ninth generation, the nobility would have become more numerous than Stinkards, and eventually the Stinkards would have disappeared altogether. Second, the system appears to have contradicted the realities of political power, at least so far as the Suns were concerned. Assume that Suns married to Stinkards produced an equal number of female Suns and male Nobles. If these then married Stinkards and also produced an equal number of sons and daughters, there would be twice as many Nobles as Suns in that generation, three times as many Nobles as Suns in the subsequent generation, and so on. The Suns, who controlled the political system, would thus be sanctioning an arrangement guaranteed to put their descendants out of power.

Various attempts, most of them unsatisfactory, have been made to elucidate these paradoxes. One such explanation is that conquests by the Natchez of neighboring peoples would have added to the Stinkard class, thus replacing those lost by marriage to the nobility. But although this explanation might account for the replenishment of Stinkards, it does not account for the multiplication of Nobles and Honored People in relation to the number of Suns. A clue to a different sort of explanation is found in the small number of Suns, recorded as only seventeen in 1700. Since great care was taken to assure that Sun females and the Great Sun never met violent death, the descendants of Suns should already have multiplied into a sizable class—but obviously they had not. From recent re-evaluation of early reports about the Natchez marriage system, it now appears that the Suns were not so much a class as a royal family which ruled for only three generations, after which its members fell to the rank of Noble. It also appears that the daughters of Noble men became Stinkards and not Honored women—which would explain one way in which the Stinkard class was replenished. The only Honored women, it is now believed, were those who were married to Honored men. And like the knights of Europe, the Honored men did not constitute a social class but rather a group to whom titles had been granted by the nobility—just as the Suns themselves constituted a level of rank rather than a social class. As with British knighthood, the rank of Honored could not be inherited by one's offspring, who were thus born into the Stinkard class. This reinterpretation shows how the complex Natchez system could have perpetuated itself—had it been allowed to do so.‡

Exactly thirty years after the first missionary visited them in 1699, the Natchez made their final desperate attempt to fight back against the encroaching French. They attacked a trading post and massacred about two hundred Whites. Retaliation was brutal; within two years the French and their Choctaw allies had utterly crushed the Natchez. Most of the Natchez were slaughtered, and about four hundred survivors (including the Great Sun) were sold into slavery in the West Indies. A few managed to escape and take refuge with the Chickasaw, Creek, and Cherokee. The sacred fire that had been intended to burn as long as the sun shone was forever extinguished. Remarkably, in 1940 two old people of Natchez ancestry were discovered living among the Cherokee, and they still spoke the old language.‡ When they were gone, the last remnant of the Natchez culture had vanished. Though Natchez blood still flows here and there in the veins of some Chickasaw, Creek, or Cherokee, the one surviving memorial of that culture is the name of a city beside the Mississippi River.

X

Aztec: Total Power

THE RISE TO RESPECTABILITY

The people of Mexico who made Cortés so avaricious with their wealth in gold, who horrified him by their human sacrifices and impressed him by their military domination of much of Middle America, are known variously as the Aztec, as the Tenochca, and as Colhua–Mexica. Their names changed as their fortunes rapidly expanded. All that is known for certain about their origins is that they were a branch of the Uto–Aztecan peoples, related to the impoverished Great Basin Shoshone and to the Hopi. At first they called themselves after what they maintained was their northern homeland, a probably mythical place called Aztlán.* After they had won a foothold in central Mexico, they acquired the name Tenochca, in honor of the patriarch who founded their capital city of Tenochtitlán, on the sites of what is now Mexico City. After becoming allied by marriage with a respected and ancient lineage, the Colhuacán (pronounced Kool-wah-KHAN), they came to be known as Colhua. That was the name the people of the West Indies kept repeating to Columbus when he asked who lived to the west of the islands. In their final

---

* In the Nahuatl language, every consonant is usually sounded. Pronunciations that might give difficulty are indicated, with accent marks to show where the stress should be.

years, just before their conquest by Cortés, they became known as Colhua–Mexica (that is, descendants-of-Colhuacán and rulers-of-Mexico). The origin of the word "Mexica" has been much disputed, but several authorities agree that it probably meant "the navel of the moon."

The history of the Aztec is an epic of social evolution —from band to tribe to chiefdom, and finally into a state, all in a period lasting only three or four centuries. Much of this evolution is documented in the written records of the Aztec themselves. (As in any dictatorship, the Aztec were determined to have their view of history prevail. Most of these books were destroyed by the Spaniards, who considered them heathenish, but enough have survived to provide a broad picture of Aztec life.) The Aztec began their history as lowly hunters following the breakdown of the Classic civilizations of central Mexico and the final collapse in the twelfth century of the mighty Toltec of Tula (on a site about forty miles north of Mexico City). A period of chaos followed as various groups sought to stake out territories for themselves. Five important new states were established by the middle of the twelfth century. The most illustrious of these was Colhuacán, whose rulers were descended directly from the royal line of Tula. At about the same time many bands and tribes invaded the area in search of land, and among them were the people who said they had left Aztlán and wandered about, guided by the image of their chief god, Huitzilopóchtli ("Hummingbird-on-the-Left," pronounced Wheat-zeal-oh-POTCH-tlee), both a war god and a representative of the sun.

The lowly Aztec could not at first find a place in crowded central Mexico, but eventually they were taken on as serfs and mercenary soldiers by the lordly Colhuacán. Their populations increased after they began to steal wives from their neighbors. When they went to the Colhuacán and boldly asked for a princess as a wife for their chief, their request was, surprisingly, granted. They no doubt thought they were paying a unique compliment to the Colhuacán when in 1323 they sacrificed her, in the belief that she would then become a war goddess. The horrified Colhuacán expelled the Aztec from their lands. And so the Aztec, no longer a band of hunters but a people acquainted with the practice of agriculture through their service to the Colhuacán, set out once again.

They paused on the southwestern edge of a chain of shallow lakes surrounding what is now Mexico City. Here, on an uninhabited island, the Aztec, who viewed themselves as a chosen people who would one day found a mighty city, saw an ancient prophecy fulfilled: An eagle sitting upon a cactus and devouring a snake marked the site of their future capital. By about 1345 they had already made remarkable progress in draining the swamps; the islands were filled in and connected; the lands were brought under cultivation; and a start had been made in building Tenochtitlán, one of the most magnificent cities ever erected on any continent. At this time the Aztec's social and political organization was still basically tribal, with a few of the more complex characteristics of the chiefdom. But theirs was a culture that appropriated freely from others, and they seized on every opportunity to learn and to change.

By 1428 the Aztec were ready. They totally crushed their rivals and became the mightiest state in Mexico. They immediately took steps to give themselves the grandeur they believed was their destiny. They first burned the books of the conquered groups, as a penalty for failing to take due notice of the people of Tenochtitlán. And they instituted a policy of war to obtain both tribute and captives for sacrifices. By terror and by diplomacy, the peoples of central Mexico were soon forced to accept the fiction that these Aztec or Tenochca, these Colhua, these Mexica—whatever you called them—were the only true heirs of the great Toltec tradition.

By 1502 the Aztec had conquered most of the peoples as far south as Guatemala and as far north as the deserts of Chihuahua; they dominated much of Mexico from the Gulf to the Pacific Ocean. This was also the time of a cultural flowering. New aqueducts carried water from the mainland to the island capital; giant causeways were built to span the lakes. The fabulous Great Temple (on the site of the Zócalo and the National

Palace in present-day Mexico City) was erected—and dedicated by the sacrifice of at least twenty thousand captives. The crafts and literature were encouraged, and many new schools were established. The philosopher–king Moctezuma II assumed power; in his time the blaze of Aztec culture lighted up all of Mexico—until that blaze was extinguished by Cortés. (*Montezuma*, the usual spelling, is inaccurate; a precise English rendering would be *Motecuhzoma*, but *Moctezuma* is one accepted by most specialists.)

THE VALLEY OF MEXICO

The heartland of the Aztec, and of several earlier great civilizations, is the central region known as the Valley of Mexico. Actually it is not a valley at all, but a 3,000-square-mile basin in the highlands, completely surrounded by mountains. Because this basin has no outlet, water flowing into it from the mountains during the dry winter season once formed five shallow lakes, which merged into a single large one during the wet summer season. In 1608 the Spaniards began constructing a canal to divert the water out of the lakes and channel it to the Gulf of Mexico; the waters were almost completely drained by a tunnel built about 1900. All that remain of them today are the shallow Lake Xochimilco (Show-she-MEEL-ko) to the southeast of Mexico City and the puddle known as Lake Texcoco (Tesh-KO-ko) to the northeast. As a consequence of this drainage, the modern Mexico City is sinking back into the soft earth beneath it.

Most of the valley is arid, and the summer rains fall in an erratic pattern. Complicating the problem even more is the evaporation of the water in the lakes; it has left behind a residue of salt, as has happened also at Great Salt Lake in Utah. To control the Valley of Mexico, the Aztec obviously first had to control the water resource. They were able to flourish on the marshy islands by using a unique method of cultivation known as the chinampa system. The Aztec did not invent it—it may be as much as two thousand years old—but they developed it intensively to feed their growing populations. Chinampas are narrow strips of land—about three hundred feet long and between fifteen and thirty feet wide—almost completely surrounded by canals. They produce several crops a year and remain amazingly fertile, generation after generation. They once were extremely widespread in the valley, but today they are reduced to only a few areas, one of them the "floating gardens" of Xochimilco, now a tourist attraction just outside Mexico City.

Chinampa farming in Aztec times probably used much the same methods as now. The farmers reach their chinampas on flat-bottomed canoes, from which they do the work of cultivation. Before each new planting the farmer scoops the rich mud from the bottom of the canals, loads it on his canoe, then spreads it on the surface of the chinampa. As crop after crop is grown, the height of the chinampa gradually rises. The farmer then lowers it once again by excavating the mud from the top and by using it to build a new chinampa elsewhere. Each chinampa produces about seven crops a year—usually two of maize, and five others chosen from among beans, chili peppers, tomatoes, amaranth, and vegetables introduced from Europe, such as lettuce, carrots, cabbages, beets, and onions.

Chinampa production enabled the Aztec to erect a fabulous capital city. When Cortés reached Tenochtitlán, it was still growing rapidly, and probably had a population of from 200,000 to 300,000 people—several times that of London in the same period.‡ All the wondrous cities the Spaniards had seen on the march from the Gulf of Mexico had not prepared them for the sight of Tenochtitlán rising out of the waters of Lake Texcoco. Cortés declared it to be "the most beautiful city in the world," comparing it to Venice. The perceptive and reliable chronicler of the Cortés expedition, Bernal Díaz del Castillo, conveys the astonishment of his first glimpse of the city in November 1519:

We saw so many cities and villages built in the water and other great towns on dry land and that straight and level Causeway going towards Mexico [the city of Tenochtitlán], we were amazed and said that it was like the enchantments they tell of in the legends of Amadis, on account of the great towers and buildings rising from the water, and all built of masonry. And some of our soldiers even asked whether the things we saw were not a dream. It is not to be wondered at that I here write it down in this manner, for there is so much to think over that I do not know how to describe it, seeing things that we did that had never been heard of or seen before, not even dreamed about.‡

He goes on to describe the palaces "wonderful to behold," constructed with exotic woods. He describes a walk through orchards and a garden, with its great variety of trees and flowers, each with its own sweet scent. But a note of sadness, over an Eden willfully destroyed, also pervades his description:

I say again that I stood looking at it and thought that never in the world would there be discovered other lands such as these, for at that time there was no Peru, nor any thought of it. Of all these wonders that I then beheld today all is overthrown and lost, nothing left standing.

THE CONQUEST BY CORTÉS

In 1507, just five years after Moctczuma became ruler, one of the fifty-two-year cycles that made up the complex Aztec calendar came to an end. For the Aztec, the end of every cycle was a time fraught with peril, but their fears in 1507 seemed well founded. During the next decade, portents of doom followed one another and brought increasing terror: Soothsayers reported that the omens for the next cycle were bad; a huge comet illuminated the sky; mysterious fires broke out in the Great Temple; the waters of the lakes flooded the capital city; strange sounds, as of crying in the night, were heard. Moctezuma ordered anyone having a dream about the fate of the empire to hasten to him, and he sent his soldiers to scour the city for people thus visited. The mighty ruler who had been able to command tribute from much of Mexico was now paying tribute to his own citizens for their dreams. But none of the dreams he paid for satisfied him, and so he massacred the dreamers.

The ancient books of the Toltec foretold the return from the east, someday, of the cast-out god Quetzalcóatl (Kate-zal-KO-atl), the "Plumed Serpent." Moctezuma concluded that the portents meant he was destined to preside over the destruction of Mexico. His fears were confirmed in 1519 when the young adventurer named Hernán Cortés landed near Vera Cruz with an army of 508 soldiers, 16 horses, and 14 pieces of artillery. A few months later Cortés headed westward for the interior, bent on conquering the millions of central Mexico. He was driven to such apparent foolhardiness not by a romantic spirit of adventure nor by a patriotic desire to win lands for his monarch, as some historians would have it, but by a simple lust for gold. At a time when every European dreamed of gold, many sought it in abandoned caves or by the practice of alchemy, and some would have sold their souls to the devil for it, Cortés frankly told one of the first Mexican nobles he met that he had come across the seas to their country because of a sickness: "The Spaniards are troubled with a disease of the heart for which gold is the specific remedy."‡

The details of the conquest have been told in full by Bernal Díaz del Castillo, by Cortés himself, and by William Prescott in his *Conquest of Mexico*. In brief, the mighty Aztec empire began to disintegrate almost as soon as Cortés landed. The original 508 Spanish soldiers were quickly reduced to about 400, but their ranks had been swelled by thousands of Indian allies who flocked to the banner of Cortés in the hope that he would free them from their Aztec oppressors. Cortés did not even have to fight his way into the capital city; he was invited in by Moctezuma, who put himself at the mercy of the conqueror.

A major battle did ultimately take place, and Cortés had to flee Tenochtitlán after Moctezuma died—whether at the hand of Cortés or of a disease, or as a victim of assassination by one of his own people, no one knows for certain. Within four months, his successor was dead of smallpox and had been succeeded by Cuauhtémoc (Kwow-TAY-mock), who led the fight against the Spaniards. Reinforced by fresh Spanish troops, and with tens of thousands of Indian allies, Cortés marched back to Tenochtitlán. The Aztec fought valiantly, from street to street and across the rooftops, while the canals flowed with the blood of their people. Altogether, as many as 120,000 of them died. But the hope of victory for the Aztec had passed. After eighty-five days of siege, with his soldiers massacred and his people starving, Cuauhtémoc surrendered on August 13, 1521. Cortés, true Spanish knight that he was, received this eleventh, last, and undoubtedly noblest of the Aztec kings with much pomp and flattering courtesy. He had him ignominiously hanged three years later. All that remains today of what was once the most magnificent city in the world is some sculpture and the rubble of its temples—"wonderful to behold"—that lie buried under the foundations of modern Mexico City. Shortly after the conquest, a native witness of the downfall of the city wrote the following poem in the language of the Aztec:

The waters are red as if stained,
And when we drink it is as if we drank salt water.
Meanwhile we laid low the adobe walls
And our heritage was a net of holes.
Shields protected it,
But even shields could not preserve its solitude! . . .
We have chewed salty couch grass,
Lumps of adobe, lizards, mice, the dust of the earth, worms.‡

THE AZTEC STATE

In their rise and precipitous decline, the Aztec displayed every characteristic of an orderly and well-administered state—yet that state was merely an illusion. During their extraordinary rapid rise, the Aztec had not rid themselves completely of some traits of the less complex band, tribe, and chiefdom. They were plagued by these remnants in the body politic, much as the human body is sometimes plagued by that useless remnant of an earlier stage in evolution, the vermiform appendix. Remnants of more simple kinds of institutions persisted in all parts of Aztec society.

The Aztec state differed in several important respects from the less complex chiefdom. The Northwest Coast chiefs and the Great Sun of the Natchez commanded great deference; but they also were severely limited. Although a chief was more powerful than anyone else in his society, he lacked the exclusive right to use force. Lineages might feud with each other; a group of warriors might set out independently to raid a neighboring chiefdom; a kinship group might inflict punishment on some offender. In a state, on the other hand, the use of force was reserved by the state itself—that is, to the ruler and his legally sanctioned delegates such as the police and the army. Feuding in a state is a crime that is punished severely, for its very existence means that someone besides the state is making use of force. As soon as a society separates one group of people—those empowered to administer through the use of force—from the rest of the population, it can separate them in other ways as well, and so political classes arise. The Natchez had classes, and individuals differed in rank in the Northwest Coast chiefdoms; but these were social classes and ranks that had little political significance. Number one hundred at the potlatch was equal to number ten before the law.

A clear difference existed between the Aztec state on the one hand and those of Babylon, Egypt, and Rome on the other. The latter were successful empires—that is, they incorporated diverse cultures and different ethnic groups into one political system. The Aztec, in contrast, were more like marauders than colonizers. In some ways they resembled the Assyrians of the ancient Middle East, who also rose rapidly and underwent a precipitous decline. Again and again, the Assyrians plundered the rich cities of the Levant, then retired into their stronghold after exacting promises of tribute. The Aztec armies similarly sallied forth to quell disturbances, to protect trade routes, to plunder, and to exact tribute—and they likewise failed to alter deeply the basic makeup of the societies they conquered. They could arrange a political marriage between someone from their own ruling line and the ruler of a subject people, and they often substituted their own gods for those of the conquered peoples. But they did not permanently incorporate the vanquished territories. Instead, they left behind them an unchanged social system and a lingering hatred, which Cortés was quick to exploit. The Aztec state displayed little of the talent the Roman one did for integrating others. They were, after all, still amateurs at statecraft, having come so very far in so short a time.

Another problem arose in the Aztec state, and it is one that becomes more acute in the even more complex industrial society. Unless Aztec individuals were exceptionally gifted or well-born, they could not participate in the state's important activities. There was room for only a few honored persons at public functions; the rest watched from afar and were jostled by crowds of other individuals, unhonored like themselves. In a state renowned for the high fashion of its rulers, the Aztec commoner went around threadbare. The more complex the society, the better is its capacity to enrich each member; but in practice it becomes increasingly difficult for individuals to receive rewards, either economic or political. They are reduced to the position of onlookers, bystanders, while all around them momentous decisions are being made by someone else. Their participation is vicarious; they can identify with nationally known athletes or with the people from the village who have made good in the big city. The lower-class Aztec probably did just that, and they obtained a feeling of participation from observing the pomp of Moctezuma's court at Tenochtitlán. In the society of the Aztec, as in modern ones, those whose work produced most of the wealth were denied its satisfactions. Such a condition could never exist in an Eskimo band, for all members of the Eskimo society are aware of the necessity for full participation. Individuals unable to participate because of age or ill health often ask a relative to kill them, or else they commit suicide.‡

CLASS AND CLAN

The class system of Tenochtitlán was of extraordinary complexity, in large part because it was combined with territory, settlement patterns, economic specialization, and kinship. Territorially, the city was divided into four quarters, the *campans* or "great neighborhoods," as the Spaniards called them. Each of the four campans was divided into several *calpulli* or "small neighborhoods," of which there were twenty in the entire city. The calpulli, in turn, consisted of smaller kinship units known as *tlaxilacalli* (tlash-eel-ah-KAHL-lee) or "streets." Finally, the tlaxilacalli were divided into individual family plots consisting of several chinampas. Such an arrangement was undoubtedly regimented, but it was an excellent way to govern a large population.

Imposed upon this territorial system was a class system. The hereditary nobility lived on their own lands, which were not part of the calpulli system. The overwhelming majority of the population belonged to the class of commoners who were organized into the twenty calpulli. The calpulli appear originally to have been clans founded by the first settlers of Tenochtitlán. All members of the same calpulli claimed descent from a common ancestor; each calpulli had its own temple, and the most important of them also maintained military schools for their youths. In warfare the men of the same calpulli served as a unit under their own leader. The members as a group paid tribute to the nobility, and they worked the lands that belonged to them. So each calpulli was at the same time a landholding corporation and a settlement group, as well as a real or fictitious kin group.

The calpulli clan system might appear to have been basically egalitarian, as were the clans in a tribe like the Iroquois, but that is not so. All people were ranked within their calpulli according to their closeness to the fictitious founder of the clan. So it was inevitable that in each calpulli there were certain ruling aristocratic families; after each death of a chief, the new chief came from the same family. Just as the entire calpulli paid tribute to the state, so the lesser ranking members of each calpulli paid tribute to the higher ranking members. Furthermore, some of the twenty calpulli were looked upon as better than others—and among the four campans into which the city was divided, certain neighborhoods were likewise considered better than others. A man who came from the most aristocratic family within the most important calpulli in the best of the four campans was therefore a person to be reckoned with.

A much lower social class consisted of the *mayequauh* (mah-YEE-kwow), or "right hands." These were laborers drawn from the conquered peoples. They were usually the original owners of the conquered lands and they were bound to it every bit as much as a Russian serf was under the czars: An Aztec inherited his "right hands" along with the land. Except in their obligations to the land, they were otherwise free, and they could even own property; but they did not enter into the calpulli system. Yet another class consisted of the new nobility (in addition to the hereditary nobility), created in response to the increasing Aztec conquests. Its members were the "Sons of the Eagle"—and membership was an avenue of advancement for the more ambitious members of the calpulli. Becoming a "Son of the Eagle" was a reward for service to the state, and such recognition both afforded social mobility to the worthy and prevented discontent. These "Sons" were equivalent to the Natchez Honored men—or to Britain's present-day Honors List, which allows an ambitious politician, actor, or brewer to put "Sir" before his name, but does not entitle him to pass that honor on to his son.

Finally, the professional merchants, the *pochteca*, had a special place in the class system because of their services to the state. These long-distance traders brought back from Central America and the North American Southwest exotic products for the delectation of the nobility—feathers of the quetzal bird, turquoise, jaguar skins, feather coats, cacao beans, precious metals—but they were more than mere traders. They served also as spies who reconnoitered foreign lands in advance of the Aztec armies, and they probably also formed a fifth column just before an invasion. As reward for such service, they were organized into their own calpulli and had their own deities, emblems, and ceremonies, much as a guild in medieval Europe had certain privileges of its own. They administered their own laws in their own courts, and they were governed by their own officers. As a further concession, they were permitted to pay tribute to the state in the form of trade goods rather than in products of the land.

The position of the pochteca among the Aztec just before Cortés was in some ways similar to that of the rising mercantile class in Europe in the Middle Ages. As in Europe, the pochteca were privileged persons who moved from one city–state to another with political immunity; Aztec armies protected their trade routes, and molesting a pochteca was often an excuse for war. Several commercial sanctuaries or "open ports" were established where traders from competing societies could meet freely and bargain. Furthermore, the nobles resisted the rising pochteca, as they also did in Europe. In the years just before the conquest, the Aztec nobility managed to curb the growing power of the pochteca. They were, for example, barred from becoming officers in the army; some were even put to death and had their property expropriated by the nobles. Had the Spanish conquest not intervened, though, they probably would have succeeded in becoming crystallized as a merchant middle class, as happened in Europe.

The person in the state who was in a class by himself was, of course, the ruler. The Spaniards, reared under an absolute monarch, were impressed by what they thought was Moctezuma's unlimited power. But what so impressed them was an illusion; the reverence paid to Moctezuma masked his lack of a solid base as a ruler. He was treated as a semidivine personage; even the highest nobles did not dare to look him in the face, and before entering his presence they would garb themselves in the meanest clothing. Moctezuma was borne in a litter on the shoulder of nobles. When he deigned to set foot on the ground, nobles rushed to cover the path ahead of him with cloth so that he would not have to touch the coarse earth. During mealtimes he was shielded from view by a screen while he chose from the several hundred dishes offered for his selection.

Bernal Díaz was awed by the luxury in which Moctezuma lived, and particularly by his palace, whose rooms were filled with "the great number of dancers kept by the Great Moctezuma for his amusement, and others who used stilts on their feet, and others who flew when they danced up in the air." The palace also had a royal zoo that housed animals from all over Middle America, and a private sideshow of freaks and monstrosities of nature, including people with every known physical deformity. The Spaniard was overcome with wonder when he contemplated the royal garden:

> We must not forget the gardens of flowers and sweet-scented trees, and the many kinds that there were of them, and the arrangement of them and the walks, and the ponds and tanks of fresh water where the water entered at one end and flowed out of the other; and the baths which he had there, and the variety of small birds that nested in the branches, and the medicinal and useful herbs that were in the gardens . . . There was as much to be seen in these gardens as there was everywhere else, and we could not tire of witnessing his great power.‡

WARRIORS AND PRIESTS

Two things kept the state going, as the Aztec saw it: the tribute in food and raw materials from the conquered people, and the staggering number of sacrificial victims. Both needs could be filled in only one way, by war, and no other society in North America ever arrived at so intense a pitch of militancy. Every man was expected to bear arms. Not even priests were exempt, although they were permitted to fight in their own units. Each of the city's four campans contained its own arsenal, which was always stocked and ready for immediate mobilization. War was extolled, and a man who died on the battlefield was considered fortunate indeed. As an Aztec song put it:

There is nothing like death in war,
nothing like the flowery death
so precious to Him who gives life:
far off I see it: my heart yearns for it.‡

Aztec wars were surrounded by a mystique that makes an Islamic holy war seem uninspired. The Aztec conceived of war as a re-enactment on earth of a titanic battle waged every day in the skies: the Sacred War of the Sun, which had to fight off evil forces to make its way across the sky.

The demand for tribute was rather less mystical, as is demonstrated by the Aztec records of tribute exacted from the conquered peoples. The Spaniards destroyed most of the Aztec books, but being practical men, they preserved the tribute lists from Moctezuma's archives as a guide to what they could extort from the Aztec provinces. These records reveal the incredible tribute that each year flowed into Tenochtitlán: fourteen million pounds of maize, eight million pounds each of beans and amaranth, two million cotton cloaks, quantities of shields, feathers, precious stones, and many other items. Some of this haul was undoubtedly for the express use of the nobles, and the food was necessary to feed the Aztec populace. Much of the tribute no doubt also went to pay the artisans and others who rendered service to the palace and to supply the pochteca with goods to barter for other luxury items.

Aztec religion was based on the machinelike repetition of enormously complex cyclic rituals. Their solar year was composed of eighteen months of twenty days each, with five highly dangerous days just before the new year began. Each month had special ceremonies in which every Aztec was obliged to participate; the ceremonies were closely tied·up with the primitive cycle of the agricultural year, the planting and watering and harvesting of various crops. In addition, the Aztec recognized an Almanac Year of 260 days, in which each day, week, and month was associated with a particular god or goddess. The days were further broken down into "hours" somewhat longer than our sixty minutes, and each of their thirteen daylight hours and nine night hours was assigned its own deity.

Aztec religion seems caught up in rhythms and cycles, but these are not much different from the "cyclic group rites" occurring in most of the world's complex societies and correlating with the cyclic rhythms of nature. Modern Americans, who live in an age of technology in which very few people farm—and even those relatively few farms are mechanized—still observe religious calendars that are a carryover from the annual cycle of agriculture as it was practiced in the Mediterranean world of antiquity. Americans who have inherited the religious traditions of the Mediterranean world still observe the birth of a messiah at the time of the winter solstice, when the sun seems farthest away from earth but is about to return; and in spring, when nature is renewed, they recall the resurrection of Jesus or the setting out of the Hebrews from Egypt to found a new nation.

Aztec religious rites were controlled by an elaborate hierarchy, similar in its rigid organization and power to the priestly hierarchies of ancient Egypt and Mesopotamia. As in these cultures also, the influence of shamans was insignificant. Instead, the Aztec relied almost exclusively on priests. Unlike shamans, priests exercise no supernatural powers of their own but are merely those people selected by their society to become experts in the performance of sacred ritual. Shamans are born and not made, but priests most assuredly are made by long and arduous training. Whenever shamanism appears in the state, it is seen as a threat to orthodoxy, and everything possible is done to suppress it. The Roman Catholic Church, right up through the time of the Reformation, expended considerable energy in denouncing "false prophets" and "heretics," who were really shamans impelled by an inner religious feeling rather than by orthodox training.

In Tenochtitlán alone, the Aztec supported five thousand priests, who maintained a tight grip on ritual, the calendar and astronomy, scholarship, and both secular and religious education. The cosmology the priests taught depicted humans as living on the verge of doomsday, and the world as barely escaping from one cataclysm after another. The end of each fifty-two-year cycle was particularly threatening because that was the time when the gods might withhold the privilege of continued life. The fires in all the temples were extinguished, and the citizens fasted, prayed, and mutilated themselves. As soon as the priests thought they detected a propitious omen in the skies, the breast of a living victim was slit open and a new fire was started in that victim's heart. From it all the fires in the temples, and afterward in the homes, were relighted. The world was believed safe, more or less, for another fifty-two years.

The anxiety associated with all the cycles, whether of long or short duration, was the possible death of the sun—of its being extinguished by a flood, by having the sky fall upon it, or by a great wind. The Aztec regarded themselves as the people chosen to protect the sun against such constant dangers—and they did it by valor, sobriety, and sexual continence. They also had to nourish it and keep the contending forces of the heavens in balance by offering up sacrifices in numbers almost beyond counting.

On their march inland toward the Aztec capital, the Spanish soldiers, as hardened a lot of adventurers as had ever been assembled under one banner, were shocked by the enormous numbers of human sacrifices they witnessed. Bernal Díaz reported on what he saw in just one city: "I remember that in the plaza . . . there were piles of human skulls so regularly arranged that one could count them, and I estimated them at more than a hundred thousand. I repeat again that there were more than a hundred thousand of them."‡ The traditional view has been that the Aztec sacrificed about twenty thousand victims a year; but the evidence for this is weak, and indeed the actual number may be considerably higher. Some early historians believed the twenty thousand victims to be merely the number sacrificed on a single occasion during the year. This view seems corroborated by the sacrifice to dedicate the main pyramid at Tenochtitlán; it reportedly needed from twenty thousand to eighty thousand victims. One scholar has recently placed the number of victims each year just before the arrival of Cortés at 250,000; others, though, consider this estimate very much too high.

The Spaniards quickly realized that the huge ceremonial pyramids that they saw everywhere were really altars for human sacrifice. At the top of each pyramid lay a huge stone with a depression to hold the heart and a rill for the blood to run off down the steps. The victim was held spread on his back while a priest made an incision under the rib cage and ripped out the heart. Most captives were sacrificed in this way, but there were variations, including gladiatorial sacrifice and the roasting of a victim until he was near death before tearing out his heart. Huge numbers of small children were sacrificed to the rain god Tlaloc; the Aztec believed that the more the children cried with terror, the greater the placation of that god would be.

Human sacrifice was also practiced elsewhere in Middle America, but no other people carried it to such an extreme as the Aztec. Various attempts have been made to explain why this was so. Some scholars have tried to justify the sacrifices by comparing them to the wars and inhuman acts that still ravage the world today, but such comparisons are beside the point. Psychologically-oriented anthropologists have suggested that the explanation was a bloodthirsty Aztec "personality"—likewise an insupportable view, for no one has ever proved that the personality of individuals accounts for a particular culture.

The problem can also be explained in its own terms rather than by resorting to psychology or to history. Once the Aztec religion initiated the practice of human sacrifice to forestall the cataclysms awaiting the people, it was trapped in a circle of events. Sacrificial victims could be obtained only through war, yet war could be waged successfully only by sacrificing victims; and to obtain those victims, the Aztec first had to go to war. The loop of necessity thus expanded to include increasingly greater sacrificial offerings. Bows and arrows, which had been important in the early phases of Aztec conquests, were largely replaced by the spear and the battle ax (usually an obsidian-bladed club). The reason for this switch may have been that it is difficult to take prisoners using the bow and arrow. Most Aztec battles seem to have been fought hand to hand, and the enemy either disarmed or beaten unconscious before being dragged away.

One anthropologist has recently attempted to explain Aztec sacrifice on the basis of cannibalism. His thesis is that central Mexico, unlike other areas in which complex societies evolved, lacked animals that might supply the diet with necessary protein and trace elements. In fact, the only animals domesticated in central Mexico before the Spaniards were the turkey and a small dog (probably the ancestor of the hairless chihuahua), which as a carnivore itself competed with humans for animal protein. Furthermore, most of the animals that might have supplied food, such as the small Mexican deer, had been very nearly killed off. These statements are not controversial; what is controversial is to suggest that the sacrifices were a conscious or unconscious excuse for cannibalism. Most scholars have chosen to ignore what happened to the victims after their hearts were torn out and their bodies tumbled down the steps of the temple pyramid. The early Spanish chronicles indicate that attendants then cut off the arms, legs, and head. The skull went onto the skull rack and three of the limbs were given to the victim's captor, who then gave a feast at which these were served, cooked in a stew of tomatoes and peppers.

Bernal Díaz reported sacrifices everywhere and cannibalism in many of the villages:

Moreover every day they sacrificed before our eyes three, four, or five Indians, whose hearts were offered to those idols and whose blood was plastered on the walls. The feet, arms, and legs of their victims were cut off and eaten, just as we eat beef from the butcher's in our country.

Despite many such reports of cannibalism, a number of specialists on the Aztec contest their reliability, and they contest also the extent to which cannibalism was practiced other than for its ritual use of obtaining the good qualities of the victims through devouring them.‡

Human sacrifice never occurs in societies below the level of the chiefdom, because in simple societies almost everyone has a relationship to everyone else through marriage alliances, sodalities, or economic partnerships. A Zuñi would not sacrifice Mr. X because it might turn out that Mr. X was married to his grandmother's sister's son's daughter. Nor would the Eskimo be so foolish as to sacrifice those kin and partners whom he might someday need to cooperate on a hunt or to help him avenge an insult. Only when societies become increasingly complex does the awareness of kinship fade; only then do humans become willing to sacrifice one of their own kind or an animal surrogate. Human sacrifice has appeared in complex societies around the world, but in Eurasia the practice seems to have centered in the Mediterranean world and surrounding areas. It was widespread in ancient Mesopotamia, Egypt, India, China, and Europe. The Roman Senate finally outlawed it in 97 B.C., but in the few centuries preceding the collapse of the Roman Empire it reached monumental proportions.

THE DEATH OF THE SUN

The cataclysm that had been foretold for so long finally came. In 1521 the sacred fires were forever extinguished, and Spanish priests began to baptize the Indians of Mexico—so many millions of them that priests are said to have used their own saliva because the supply of holy water was so limited. The collapse of the Aztec empire was total and final, and after the Spaniards killed the last Aztec ruler in 1524, they met almost no resistance. Historians have long wondered how only five hundred Spaniards managed to conquer a state that put brave and well-armored warriors into the field by the hundreds of thousands. But even the brief view of the Aztec social and political structure given in this chapter reveals that it was vulnerable to the sort of attack made by someone like Cortés. No single weakness led to the downfall; rather, the cause was the total kind of society the Aztec had erected. Using hindsight, we must wonder why the conquest took Cortés as long as two years. The Aztec defeat was inevitable because of the following factors:

LACK OF AZTEC SOCIOPOLITICAL INTEGRATION. The Aztec had not yet achieved an integrated empire, and vanquished neighbors were always ready to rise in rebellion. Even though the Aztec displayed much organizational ability in their class system, in the priesthood, and in the army, they were remarkably poor administrators of the conquered territories, exploiting them unmercifully for tribute and sacrificial victims without offering them the benefits of Aztec culture. Cortés stumbled into a land that was already on the verge of rebellion, and ready to turn against the oppressors.

POOR MILITARY TACTICS OF THE AZTEC. Marvelously organized, numbering warriors almost beyond counting, lavishly equipped with efficient weapons and quilted armor that the Spanish soldiers regarded as superior to their own, well trained and desiring immolation on the battlefield, the Aztec war machine nevertheless had many weaknesses. It could not sustain a campaign after the initial attack, because the absence of beasts of burden made it impossible to bring up supplies, and the hostility of the conquered people made it difficult to live off the country. Despite their class of professional soldiers, the Aztec had developed no strategy of war other than the surprise attack. They were ignorant of a common European tactic that would have afforded them immediate victory over the Spaniards: Divide an enemy's forces into smaller units; then destroy these piecemeal. Mass attack by the Aztec was of no use, because they could bring only a portion of their overwhelming numbers into contact with the small number of Spaniards at any one time. In contrast, the small Spanish army was a marvelously efficient instrument. Generations of Spaniards had been trained in battle in the Moorish Wars, as well as in other conflicts in Europe. And they had learned about non-European tactics through their conquests in Africa and in the West Indies.

PARALYSIS OF THE AZTEC. The Aztec world view conceived of numerous intermeshed cycles operating largely beyond human control. The Aztec were constantly fearful that the smooth meshing of the cycles might someday go awry. The portents of doom in the decade or so before the arrival of Cortés seemed to indicate that just such a thing was happening; and the inevitable result was paralysis. Another cause for paralysis was a too rigid organization. Every star in the heavens had its place, and so did every individual on earth. The educational system trained youths to obey orders without question, and their religious training also demanded unquestioning faith. When the war chiefs were killed or captured, no lower-echelon Aztec warrior would step forward from his assigned place to take over the leadership. An Aztec commoner who had been trained all his life to obey could not suddenly learn to command.

LIMITATIONS ON THE POWERS OF THE RULER. Moctezuma may have appeared divine and authoritarian, but he was limited in his powers, and one of these limitations proved disastrous for him. He lacked the power to make long-range decisions alone; instead, he was committed to extended discussions with his chief advisers, high priests, and war leaders. As the Spaniards slowly made their way across central Mexico toward Tenochtitlán, Moctezuma's authority to act alone and to make decisions went on dwindling. Finally, once the Spaniards reached the city, he was so numbed by conflicting advice that he calmly handed himself over to Cortés as a hostage.

AZTEC LACK OF FOLLOW-THROUGH IN VICTORY. After the death of Moctezuma and the uprising against the Spaniards by the people of Tenochtitlán, Cortés was forced to retreat from the city in a rout in which he lost three quarters of his men. Instead of following up their advantage and destroying the Spanish remnants, the Aztec behaved as they always had after a victory: They plundered the corpses and searched for wounded Spaniards to offer as sacrificial victims. That gave Cortés valuable time to regroup and to await the replacements that aided him in his decisive victory the following year. Cortés was really fighting a different kind of war. At the very end, the Aztec leaders expected to bargain with their conquerors about the amount of tribute the Aztec would have to pay. They were quite unprepared for total war—for the cannons that battered their homes, the ruthless destruction of their gods, their cherished beliefs, and their lives.

All the above observations are based solely on conditions within the Aztec state and in Mexico at the time. No attempt has been made to explain the collapse of the Aztec by recourse to outmoded arguments about the superiority of the Spaniards in leadership, armaments, morale, or "race." Cortés was a competent leader, but any other leader of average ability probably would have conquered the Aztec just as easily—not because of the superiority of the Europeans but because of the intrinsic social and political weaknesses of the Aztec culture itself.

Part Two

◙

The Long Migration

XI

The Peopling of
North America

THE NEW CONTINENT

Previous chapters have discussed some of the Indian
groups that the explorers and later settlers encountered.
From the very first the explorers wondered who these
people were and how they had arrived in North America in the first place. Because of the Indians' exotic
customs and their unusual dress—or lack of it—the
explorers wondered whether the Indians belonged to
the family of humankind. Pope Julius II solemnly declared that the Indians were descended from Adam and
Eve—but that did not halt the speculations about the
way in which they had reached the New World. One
popular theory held that the Indians were the children
of Babel condemned to a primitive existence because of
their sins. The belief that the Indians were descended
from Israelites had its vogue and then fell into disrepute,
although the Church of Jesus Christ of Latter-Day
Saints (Mormon) affirms it to this day. Cotton Mather,
the Puritan divine, attributed the Indians' arrival in
America, as he attributed so much else, to the devil who
willfully led them there to prevent their salvation. A
partial list of peoples proposed as the Indians' ancestors

—who had either migrated to North America intentionally or arrived there in ships that had blown off course—includes ancient Egyptians, Trojans, Greeks, Etruscans, Carthaginians, Tartars, Chinese, Asiatic Indians, Mandingos of Africa, Huns, ancient Irish, Welsh, and Norse.‡ No need exists, however, to account for the origin of the American Indian by miraculous intervention or by the arrival of wayward fleets of ships from the Old World. The real story of the peopling of North America is fantastic enough—one of the great sagas in human history.

As the land mass of the North American continent gradually acquired the contours we know today, the life it nurtured was also evolving. Alaska and Siberia, at their closest point, are now separated by fifty-six miles of fogbound, choppy water. Until about a million years ago the two continents were solidly joined by land, and a variety of animals crossed from one continent to another: the ancestors of horses, camels, opossums, wild dogs, weasels, as well as many kinds of birds. But a million years ago many groups of mammals familiar in North America today still had not made the crossing from Siberia to Alaska. Notably absent were human beings, who had already spread through much of Eurasia. At that time, a warping of the earth's crust around the Arctic caused the land connection to sink into the Bering and Chukchi seas. The two continents thus became effectively separated.

Up until the past few decades, no clear idea had been offered of how humans and such Asiatic mammals as moose, elk, musk ox, mountain sheep, bears, wolves, foxes, and bison could have reached North America. The explanation has been found in recent discoveries concerning the Pleistocene epoch, commonly called the Ice Age, which began perhaps three million years ago. The Pleistocene was ushered in by great climactic fluctuations; eventually, four successive ice sheets advanced and then retreated, and the most recent retreat is still going on. At their greatest thrust, the sheets buried about thirty-two percent of the land area of the globe.

The spreading ice meant drastic changes for all living things. Ancient forests were mowed down as if they had been clusters of matchsticks; the courses of rivers were altered, and some of them were so thoroughly dammed by ice packs that they turned into enormous lakes; huge basins, such as those now filled by the Great Lakes, were gouged out of the land.

The early humans had no fur to protect them against the cold climate; they lacked fangs, and their clawless hands were no match for such ice-age mammals as the sabertooth and the long-tusked mammoths and mastodon. Humans were opportunistic feeders on whatever they could find: seeds and roots, insects such as locusts and termites, lizards, and small mammals. Yet, as ice sheet succeeded ice sheet, humans continued to evolve and to spread across the steppes of Asia. The large and complex human brain enabled them to outwit prey, to withstand cold with the help of clothing and of fire, and to produce weapons that overcame the size, speed, and fangs of large mammals.

The Pleistocene saw first the emergence, and then the triumph, of the human species. By the middle of the most recent advance of the ice, which began some 65,000 years ago and lasted until about 13,000 years ago, *Homo sapiens* had become firmly established in Siberia. Our species had become an accomplished manufacturer of tools and weapons, a builder of semisubterranean shelters, a tailor of clothing made from animal hides, a wonderer about the supernatural. The development of a technology to hunt the large mammals of the ice age probably resulted in a spurt in human populations throughout Eurasia. Since a lone hunter could not kill one of the huge beasts unaided, cooperation must have become even more important than formerly, and sociopolitical organizations must have become more complex. For all this, though, humans still had not cultivated any plant or domesticated any animal except possibly the dog; they had not yet invented the bow and arrow or the boat. Nor had they yet reached North America.

OVER THE LAND BRIDGE

Homo sapiens was able to reach the New World because the ice sheets locked up, in the form of glacial ice, immense amounts of the planet's water supply and in that way lowered the level of the sea. Geologists do not agree about the exact depths to which the sea fell at various times in the Pleistocene, but during the last advance of the ice it probably dropped between 150 and 300 feet. A lowering of the sea by 300 feet would have allowed a land bridge to emerge that was 1,000 miles wide, wider even than the north–south span of present-day Alaska. A lowering by only 150 feet would have exposed a land bridge nearly a third as wide. The land bridge endured, off and on, for some tens of thousands of years until a sudden rise in temperature throughout the world, a little more than 10,000 years ago, accelerated the melting of the ice and poured water back into the sea. The land bridge was soon inundated, and it has been under water to this day.‡

Since the bridge was exposed whenever the ice sheets were at the maximum, we might think that at these times the land bridge must have been impassable. But that is not so. During part of the last glacial advance, when the ice extended as far south as what are now the Ohio, the Missouri, and the Columbia rivers, most of Alaska and western Canada escaped the ice, and so did much of Siberia. No one can explain this fact for certain, but it appears to have been caused by low precipitation around Bering Strait at that time; with little rain and snowfall, the ice would not have been sufficient to cover more than the mountain ranges. Siberia and Alaska would thus have been linked by dry land during a large part of the Late Pleistocene. The width of the land bridge varied in rhythm with the advances and retreats of the ice, becoming more exposed as glaciation increased, becoming narrower and even disappearing altogether during the interglacial melts when the sea rose again. In effect, the connection between Siberia and Alaska was a slowly opening and closing drawbridge.

When the land bridge was exposed, it blocked off the

cold Arctic waters, allowing the warm Pacific air to temper the northern climate. Much of the land bridge was a rolling plain that glistened with lakes and ponds; large grazing mammals found pasturage on its vegetation, a luxuriant growth of tall grasses or a tangle of dwarf birch, willows, alders, heaths, and mosses such as exists today on the tundra of northern Canada. These conditions were exceedingly favorable for the herds of large ice-age mammals that, in search of food and living space, crossed from one continent to another. A wealth of mammals, many of them now extinct, reached North America: large camels resembling the two-humped kind still found in Asia, ground sloths, a bison that stood seven feet high at the hump and had horns measuring up to six feet from tip to tip; a beast somewhat similar to a large moose, several kinds of musk ox, and mammoths. Also crossing to North America was the horse, an animal that had evolved in North America and then spread to Eurasia before becoming extinct in the western hemisphere; it later became extinct for a second time, and none were found on this continent until the sixteenth century, when they were brought across the Atlantic by the Spanish explorers.

The portal that admitted humans to the New World is now known to have been the Bering land bridge. They did not cross via the Aleutian Islands. Though on a map this chain appears to thrust out a connecting link to Asia, the great depth of the water west of the island of Attu rules it out, and so does the fact that the Aleutians, unlike most of Alaska, were heavily glaciated. Nor does any evidence exist that other primates (monkey, ape, or Neanderthal) in the direct line of human evolution ever crossed the land bridge before *Homo sapiens* did so. Humans crossed on dry land over a bridge exposed by the fall of the sea—not, as was once believed, braving the swirling snows or picking their way from iceberg to iceberg. (Of course, those latecomers who arrived more recently than about 10,000 years ago could at times have crossed the fifty-six-mile gap of Bering Strait on the winter ice; still more recent migrants, the Aleut and the Eskimo, made the crossing in

The probable outlines of the Bering land bridge are shown during the last ice age when the sea fell below present levels. The water locked up as ice in the glaciers allowed a bridge to emerge that was sometimes wider than Alaska itself.

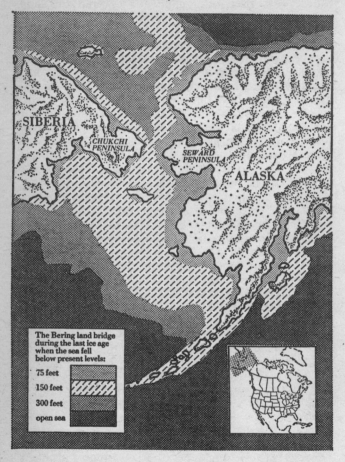

boats.) Nor can we read into this migration from one continent to another any sermon on the innate adventurousness of the human spirit; humans crossed to Alaska quite as unwittingly as the mammals they hunted for food.‡

No one knows for certain when the very first humans crossed the Bering land bridge, and the prospects of uncovering precise evidence in the future are not good. The sea has risen once more and covered the land bridge, and in some places nearly a hundred feet of sediments have drifted to its bottoms, burying the evidence still deeper. It is certain, though, that humans have been in North America for a very long time indeed. About 11,000 years ago the migrants from Asia had already reached land's end; unmistakable signs of human occupancy have been found dating from that time in Fell's Cave at the southern tip of South America. The actual crossing, of course, must have been earlier, for it would have taken thousands of years for the trickle of generation after generation to span that distance from Siberia. Many other sites in both North and South America suggest that the arrival of at least some bands of humans took place considerably earlier than these calculations would indicate.

Anthropologists disagree about how long humans have lived in North America. Hopes have been raised from time to time that clear evidence had been found of extremely early occupation by human groups. One such—the Calico site near San Bernardino, California—received considerable publicity several years ago because arguments for its great antiquity had the support of Louis S. B. Leakey, whose efforts at Olduvai Gorge in East Africa have pushed back the dates for the earliest humans by a few million years. Nevertheless, specialists in New World prehistory have not found any convincing evidence for the existence of the hearths, charcoal, or human-made tools that supposedly dated back more than 50,000 years.‡ (The dating of archeological sites is a most difficult art; a brief outline of the various techniques is given in the Notes and Sources on pages 322–27.) In 1977 yet another site was dated as being probably in excess of 40,000 years: a collection of mammoth bones found with what appear to be stone tools on Santa Rosa Island, once connected to southern California. And at Lewisville, Texas, an archeological site containing hearths, the burned bones of extinct mammals, a hammer, a chopper, and some flakes left from the manufacture of tools has been given dates ranging from 37,000 to more than 40,000 years ago. The controversy over Lewisville hinges on whether the charcoal samples used to obtain the radiocarbon dates were from human-made fires or from fires started accidentally by lightning or spontaneous combustion. Many archeologists, though, continue to regard this site as one of the most important and exciting yet discovered in the unearthing of prehistoric America.

As for the skeletal remains of the humans themselves, hard evidence is difficult to find, given the many obstacles to fossilization and the small size of their populations. The earliest remains that are almost unanimously agreed upon consist of a skull and a leg bone found at Laguna Beach, California, and dated by radiocarbon methods at 17,150 years in age. General agreement also seems to exist about the age—23,600 years—given to some remains found at Los Angeles. Considerable dispute, though, centers about human remains from the San Diego, California, area which have been given dates ranging from 28,000 to 70,000 years in age, on the basis of a controversial new technique using amino acids.‡

Proving that humans reached North America more than 40,000 years ago is difficult because archeologists have often refused to admit as evidence any but very sophisticated tools, rejecting simpler kinds of artifacts. Signs have been discovered that may point to an earlier human presence: carbon from possible campfires, various pieces of stone that appear to be crude scrapers and choppers, and tiny flakes that seem to mark some sites as tool workshops. But archeologists often disagree about this evidence. Some insist that the stones may not be artifacts at all but only the accidental work of nature, such as stones smashing against each other in a stream; the so-called hearths may be from lightning-caused fires. Nevertheless, such hints of the first dawn of human life in the New World have been found in so many places that more and more respected archeologists have come to believe that humans crossed into North America considerably more than 20,000 years ago and possibly more than 40,000 years ago.

The approximate times during which the crossing was made can be narrowed down somewhat because the land bridge was above water only at certain periods: between about 50,000 and 40,000 years ago, from 36,000 to 32,000 years ago, and again from 28,000 to 13,000 years ago. Humans who crossed this bridge, however, were confronted by an additional obstacle, which would have served to narrow down the dates still further: a mile-high wall of ice that blocked the way southward through Canada. At times, though, the blockage was not complete—namely around 45,000 years ago, again between 36,000 and 32,000, and between 28,000 and 20,000 years ago, as well as from about 13,000 years ago down to the present. Migrations southward took place at least during the two more recent intervals, and possibly during all four.

The remains of the Paleo-Indians (as the prehistoric hunters up to about 7,000 years ago are called) are always associated with the bones of the mammals that flourished at the end of the last ice age. All of these now-extinct species—early horses, big-horned bison, camel, mammoth, and mastodon, among others—shared several characteristics that were to be important for human success on the new continent. They all fed on grass; they traveled in herds over open country and so were visible at great distances; and each supplied a large amount of food in a single package. Their many hooves also left plainly marked trails that led to water and to protected valleys, to salt licks and over mountain passes. The White explorers later relied on the trails across North America left by millions of bison; Daniel Boone followed a bison trail in laying out his Wilderness Road across the Cumberland Gap, and many railroad beds through the mountains followed routes pioneered by bison.

Early humans in North America probably also followed such trails, which would have led to their crossing of the Bering Strait land bridge in the first place. The route of the ancestors of the Indians is not as yet known for certain, but it probably followed the northern foothills of the Alaskan ranges before turning southward. The foothill route offered the advantages of being drier than the mucky lowland tundra and of affording high points for the sighting of game—which might explain why most early sites so far discovered in Alaska and northwestern Canada are located on the flanks of mountains. (Some of the bands also appear to have crossed the land bridge in the Seward Peninsula area, then followed the Yukon River upstream.) With no competition from other humans and with an abundant food source, their populations must have increased. A buildup of population pressure would have forced bands on the fringes into new areas; when these bands then increased in numbers, additional expansions into new territories would have taken place. At various times an ice-free corridor to the interior of the continent opened up around the Mackenzie valley. The Mackenzie, in turn, led to the eastern flank of the Rocky Mountains and to the Great Plains. Travel southward from Alaska along the Pacific Coast is highly improbable. Boats had not yet been invented, for one thing; moreover, the coastline, with its few beaches and its deep fjords, somewhat like those of Norway, would have made travel on foot very difficult, and in many places impossible.

Today the North American plains are an arid tableland, broken only by eroded badlands and low hills. But toward the end of the last ice age they were threaded with rivers and dotted with lakes and marshes; tall grasses grew luxuriantly, and on them fed large mammals such as the world had perhaps never seen before. If the migrants traveled southward along the mountain flanks, they would have had the best of two environments: the grasslands of the plains with their herds, and the sheltered valleys of the foothills. No special knowledge told these people to head southward. In fact, their ancestors had traveled generally northward and eastward to reach the Bering land bridge from Siberia. And they had no reason at all to expand until their populations increased, because with their limited technology they could not have harvested sufficient resources to provide for large populations in any one place. Some bands branched off to the east by following river valleys, and to the west through passes in the

Rocky Mountains that had not been glaciated; some moved southward until eventually their descendants reached the tip of South America. Not all of the traffic, of course, was one way from Asia to North America. Some indications exist of the flow of cultural elements in the opposite direction as well.‡

THE EARLIEST BIG-GAME HUNTERS

From the time that humans arrived in the New World until after the melt of the ice perhaps 7,000 years ago, two basic ways of life have been documented: big-game hunting in the Great Plains and eastern forests, and the collecting of wild plants and small game, primarily west of the Rocky Mountains. The period from roughly 13,000 to 8,500 years ago was one in which skilled hunters developed a variety of tool kits that seem uniquely American in their development. (Claims are made from time to time that these artifacts resemble those found in northeastern Siberia, but any similarity appears to be largely accidental and is not considered significant.)‡ Of these two orientations toward obtaining food, that of hunting big game appears to have been the more widespread, although possibly this may be because much more information about it has been unearthed.

Another possible distortion of the archeological record should also be mentioned at this point. The emphasis on big-game hunting may result from an unconscious bias in interpretation on the part of male archeologists. Big game assuredly was hunted; the unearthing of quantities of large spear points shows that. Nevertheless, previous to the development of agriculture, human groups probably obtained their food by foraging for both wild plants and animals, as do almost all the hunting–gathering cultures that survive today. And contrary to what most people have learned, the surviving groups show that hunting by males accounts for only a relatively small proportion of the food supply. The mainstay of hunter–gatherer subsistence is the female gatherer of wild plants, who is sometimes a

fisher and hunter of small animals as well. What has
been true of the so-called hunting societies around the
world in historic times was probably true also of the
Paleo-Indians. The stone spear points used by male
hunters were easily preserved in the archeological record, but the simple wooden sticks used by females for
digging out roots had very little chance of being fos-
silized. In short, the Paleo-Indian emphasis on big-game
hunting may have been just what the record indicates,
but if so it was probably a temporary phenomenon
during the glacial melt. More reasonably, female gathering must have provided vast amounts of food, but indications of these efforts were rarely preserved as fossils.

Possibly the oldest known site of the big-game
hunters is one discovered in 1936 in the Sandia ("Water-
melon") Mountains near Albuquerque. Archeologists
from the University of New Mexico crawled into a cave
for several hundred yards and discovered the claw of
an extinct ground sloth, evidence that the cave had been
occupied for many thousands of years before the modern Pueblo Indians used it. As the archeologists dug
downward into the rocky debris they found layers showing that generation after generation of Paleo-Indians
had lived here and left traces atop the rubble of the one
before. The bottommost layer revealed bones of mammoths and bison that had been shattered as if to extract
the marrow, along with charcoal deposits from fires,
flint tools, and spear points. These Sandia points, as
they have come to be known, were crudely chipped,
but they are very distinctive: Most of them have a
rounded shoulder on one side of the base, which probably made it easier to attach the point to the shaft.
Claims have been made that Sandia points date from
25,000 years ago, and inconclusive radiocarbon tests
have been interpreted as supporting so early a date, but
nowadays most archeologists believe that Sandia points
go back no more than about 12,000 years. Sandia points
are well documented from only a few other places,
mostly close to Sandia cave itself, although claims have
been made for other sites in Oregon and Ontario.‡

Another very early Paleo-Indian culture, only very

recently unearthed and therefore still controversial, is the Meadowcroft site in western Pennsylvania. It was occupied as early as 16,000 years ago, and possibly even 6,000 years before that. The people there both hunted (the largest mammal remains identified so far belong to the elk) and gathered wild plants (some forty edible varieties have already been found). But the oldest Paleo-Indian hunting culture about which most archeologists agree, and which is known in considerably greater detail, is the Llano (also called the Clovis because it was first discovered near Clovis, New Mexico). The primary indicator of the Llano is its distinctive spear point, the Clovis Fluted. It is thin, usually between three and four inches long, and about a third as wide. It was rather crudely made, with only scant retouching of the edges of smoothing of the base; it had a flute, a narrow channel that extended part way from the base to the point. Clovis Fluted points, and assemblages of other artifacts usually associated with them, have been found at numerous camps or butchering sites, many of which date from about 12,000 years ago. These Clovis points have also been found in every one of the forty-eight contiguous states, southward to the tip of South America, northward to Alberta, and eastward to Nova Scotia.

So uniform was the Llano culture across the continent, particularly east of the Rockies, that a site in Massachusetts is scarcely distinguishable from another in, say, Colorado. A large inventory of stone tools has been discovered, including bone awls, needles, rubbing stones, scrapers, knives, and gravers. A shell engraved with the figure of a mammoth has also been unearthed, indicating an artistic skill comparable to that of the stone-age inhabitants of Europe who painted animal figures on cave walls. Practically every find of Clovis points has been associated with the bones of mammoths, although occasionally bones of horses and big-horned bison are found as well. The large number of immature mammoths at several sites indicates that the hunters were skilled in separating young animals from the formidable adults in the rest of the herd. And it is clear, too, that these Llano peoples must have cooperated in the hunt, for a single mammoth excavated in Arizona had eight fluted points embedded in it.‡

The next major culture after the Llano was the better-known Folsom, named after the community in New Mexico where it was first unearthed. The accidental discovery of Folsom spear points in 1925, by a cowpuncher searching for lost cattle, was an important event: It offered the first major support to those archeologists who had been ridiculed for their claims that humans had been in North America for more than 10,000 years. Nineteen points were found here, most of them embedded in remains of the big-horned bison. Numerous Folsom points have since been discovered elsewhere, and they all date from between 9,000 and 11,000 years ago. Even to the untutored eye of the amateur, these are beautifully fashioned. First, a piece of flint about three inches long was flaked to the approximate shape. Then a few flakes, which sometimes reached from the base very nearly to the tip, were chipped away on each face to make long grooves. Finally, the maker retouched the edges by removing tiny chips, after which the base was ground smooth. Considerable dispute has centered around the reason for the elaborate fluting on Folsom points. Some archeologists believe that it made attachment to the lance easier; others, that it lightened the weight of the point so that it could be thrown farther. A third hypothesis is that it was for the same purpose as the grooves on a bayonet—to cause the blood to flow more freely from the wound. The suggestion that fluting made attachment to the lance easier seems the most probable one. The evidence for this is that the lower edges of the points are usually dulled, as though the maker wanted to be sure a sharp edge did not cut through the taut sinews used to haft the point to the shaft.

A culture known as the Plainview, which flourished for a time after the Folsom, shows still further improvements in hunting technique. The Plainview points much resemble the Folsom points in their basic outlines, though they lack the fluting. The remains of a thousand big-horned bison were unearthed near Plainview, Texas.

These animals represented the mass slaughter of a herd that obviously had been stampeded over a bluff into the valley. The animals at the bottom were found to have no points in them; they must have been at the head of the herd, killed by the fall and the weight of the other bison on top of them. But the bison that were at the rear and that fell on top of the heap had probably only been stunned. These were the ones that had been dispatched by the flint points found embedded in their bones.

The position of Plainview in the chronology of the Paleo-Indian hunters is not yet agreed upon, but it does seem clear that most of the sites so far discovered were butchering stations rather than settlements. This would imply the existence of nomadic populations oriented toward hunting. Very little is known about these people aside from the tools they used to kill the bison and to prepare the skins; in addition, only a few paint palettes, beads, and decorated stone disks (probably used as ornaments) have been found. But the discovery of the Plainview sites is important in one respect: It reveals the great antiquity in North America, as in the Old World, of hunting bison by driving the herd over a cliff, a method that was still being used by the Plains Indians early in the last century. The Lewis and Clark expedition, for example, reported more than one hundred bison carcasses left to decay after such a stampede. The Plainview people effectively dispel the romantic illusion that all the ancestors of the Indians were conservationists who killed only as much as they could eat. The stampede as a method of hunting meant the slaughter of many more animals than were needed for food.

Plainview and a number of other cultures after Folsom are believed to have been transitional to the next major culture based on a hunting economy. First associated by archeologists with Yuma County, Colorado, and Eden Valley, Wyoming, where many spear points typical of it were discovered, this culture is now usually given the name Plano; most of the known sites date between 7,000 and 9,500 years ago. This was a time of increasingly arid climate on the North American continent, as the luxuriant carpet of grasses grew sparse. Mammoths, horses, and camels were dying out or were already gone, and even the big-horned bison had begun giving way to the species that survives today. The prey animal in which the largest number of Plano points have been found is still the big-horned bison, but at some sites the remains of modern bison, pronghorn antelope, and even deer also occur.

THE GREAT EXTINCTION

The bones of ice-age mammals, and the variety of weapons and tools used to kill and butcher them, have left an impressive record, all the way from Alaska to Cape Horn, of the Paleo-Indians' ability to exploit their environment. It was the climate—the very thing that had brought it into existence in the first place—that caused the hunting economy to dwindle and finally, about 7,000 years ago, to disappear. At the end of the last ice age the climate in interior North America was generally cool and moist, with numerous shallow lakes bordered by luxuriant vegetation. Under these conditions, ideal for hunting, lived the people who made the Llano and Folsom points, and the same conditions prevailed for most of the Plano people also. When the ice began its rapid melt about 10,000 years ago, the climate started to change in major ways: Temperatures rose and the cloud cover diminished; the water that lay over much of the land began increasingly to evaporate. With the northward retreat of the cold air masses, precipitation probably was reduced as well. Slowly at first, and then at an accelerating rate, the plant cover thinned out, and the great herds declined drastically. The end of the limitless abundance is marked by the last of the Paleo-Indian sites based on big-game hunting, dating to some 7,000 years ago. From then on, the hunting of large mammals was limited largely to a few wet areas in the plains, where it was based solely on the modern species of bison, and of course in the Sub-Arctic, where moose and caribou are still hunted today.

STAGES AND CULTURES	APPROX. DATES	PRIMARY GAME HUNTED	PROJECTILE POINTS
PLANO	9,500 TO 7,000 YEARS AGO	Pronghorn Antelope, Modern Bison, Big-Horned Bison	
PLAINVIEW	10,000 TO 7,500 YEARS AGO	Big-Horned Bison	
FOLSOM	11,000 TO 9,000 YEARS AGO	Big-Horned Bison	
LLANO	15,000 (?) TO 11,000 YEARS AGO	Mammoth	
SANDIA	25,000 (?) TO 12,000 YEARS AGO	Mammoth, Camel, Big-Horned Bison, Horse	
PRE-PROJECTILE STAGES	40,000 (?) TO 20,000 (?) YEARS AGO	Mammoth, Dire Wolf, Horse, Sabertooth	No Undisputed Projectile Points — SCRAPERS

The last ice age closed dramatically with the melting of huge blocks of ice, pouring out freshets of water that swelled into torrents—and it closed also with one of the greatest extinctions of mammals the planet has ever known. Beginning about 12,000 years ago, and continuing over the next 6,000 years, this dying out of mammals in North America was of nearly the same magnitude as that of the dinosaurs some 65,000,000 years earlier. Some of the better-known mammals and the approximate dates of their disappearance are: woolly mammoth, 10,000 years ago; various forms of tapir and ground sloth, 9,500 years ago; giant ground sloth and big-horned bison, 8,500 years ago; horse, camel, giant armadillo, and Columbia mammoth, about 7,500 years ago. The La Brea tar pits at Los Angeles, California, strikingly demonstrate the range of this extinction. The remains of thirty-five kinds of mammals that lived 15,000 years ago have been unearthed there; 9,000 years later, not one of them still survived in North America.

It might be supposed that these extinctions were due simply to severe changes in climate at the end of the last ice age. But the explanation is likely to be more complicated than that. All the mammals that became extinct had already survived previous expansions and retreats of the ice, with their attendant climate changes, during the Pleistocene. Although a few species became extinct in other parts of the world as well, the major extinctions occurred in North America. The camel and the horse died out there, but both survived in Eurasia despite the melting of the ice; tapirs and ground sloths disappeared from North America, but both endured in South America. Something was obviously different about the conditions in North America, and that difference was apparent only at the end of the last ice age: humans equipped with fire and a sophisticated hunting technology.

The extinction of ice-age mammals was less severe in Africa and in Eurasia, possibly because humans and mammals had been together on those continents for several million years and the mammals had had time to adapt. Also, Africa had already gone through its great extinction some 50,000 years ago, when twenty-six groups of large mammals disappeared—a time when a human culture that specialized in hunting with large stone tools had spread over that continent. South America suffered no equivalent extinction, possibly because the human populations there were not large enough to cause a significant decrease in the mammal populations.

Climatic change must have placed the mammals of North America under great stress; but the final tipping of the balance toward extinction may have been the toll taken by the Paleo-Indians' hunting economy.

Paul S. Martin of the University of Arizona has attributed the extinction of large mammals in North America at this time to hunting "overkill." He has made the following hypothetical calculation. Suppose that a band of about one hundred Paleo-Indians set out southward from Edmonton, Alberta, at an average annual speed of between seven and eight miles per year—and that the band doubled in population every twenty years. Also, suppose that just one person in a family of four managed to kill a thousand-pound mammal every week. Martin calculates that if all these conditions were met, the band could have destroyed the entire big-game population between Edmonton and the Gulf of Mexico in only about 300 years.

Three things are wrong with Martin's hypothesis, however. First, the band's population probably could not have continued to double every twenty years, simply because of the limitations of both hunting technology and social institutions at the time. Second, from what is known of the surviving hunter–gatherers around the world, it is clear that most hunts end in failure; that some able-bodied males even in the midst of the abundant game of Africa have not killed a large mammal in decades; and that the killing of a thousand pounds of meat every week, on an average, by a quarter of all men, women, and children is practically impossible. Finally, an average speed of seven to eight miles per year might seem reasonable—but only so long as the people were migrating through a single environmental zone. It would, though, require centuries to move only a few miles from one zone to another because of new plants and animals that would be encountered, demanding new strategies of hunting and gathering, new kinds of tools and weapons to be developed, and experiments with unfamiliar raw materials. It seems almost inconceivable that bands would have been able to pass through radically different environmental zones, ranging from the frozen tundra to steaming rain forests, between the Bering Strait and Tierra del Fuego, in only a thousand years, as Martin contends.‡

Relatively small numbers of humans might, though, have tipped the balance toward extinction as a result of certain ecological laws that govern animal populations. Every species of animal requires a minimum population to survive. The fifty breeding pairs of heath hens that survived for a time on Martha's Vineyard, off Cape Cod, were below the critical minimum for their species and it was owing to the inability of this small population to breed successfully that in 1932 the species became extinct. In Siberia it has been found that because of complex ecological relationships, the optimum number of reindeer making up a herd is between three and four hundred. Should the herd drop below that, it might soon die out. The extinction of the ice-age mammals undoubtedly began with enormous losses in their populations because of the changing climate. The Paleo-Indian hunters would then have had to kill comparatively few of the mammals to reduce their numbers beneath the critical minimum necessary for survival. If so, the descendants of the Paleo-Indians were made to pay a cruelly heavy penalty for the overhunting. When the horse that became extinct in the New World returned some 7,000 years later, it carried the Spanish cavalry who struck terror into the Indians of Mexico and the Southeast.

As the great herds began to disappear like the melting ice, the Paleo-Indians moved into deserts and coastal regions where they experimented with harvesting the continent's incredible variety of small mammals, birds, fishes, and plants. The hunting cultures of the ice age, which had spread from the Pacific to the Atlantic, and nearly from pole to pole, gave way to a variety of local cultures. These Archaic people, as they are called, specialized in nothing, but made a versatile attempt at everything. Throughout a remarkable diversity of environments—the rich pine woods of the Southeast, the cold northern forests, the arid West—the Archaic people invented fish spears, snares for trapping rodents and birds, darts for bringing down small game, and containers for storing roots. Manos (round milling stones, somewhat in the shape of rolling pins, that are held in the hands) and metates (the base stones on which the manos are rolled) for grinding seeds and roots became increasingly common as time went on. Their appearance was a clear indication that the Archaic people were finding new uses for plant foods, including their tougher parts. Settlement patterns changed also, as humans colonized the seacoasts and rivers where they obtained fish, shellfish, and small game, as well as plants. Life became considerably more sedentary, and the numbers of people seem to have increased markedly. New ways of exploiting different environments fostered the budding off of new cultures and the growth of new institutions for making them effective.

To modern Americans, possessors of an advanced technology, it may not appear very important whether people kill a large mammal or a variety of smaller animals for food—any more than it matters whether one orders steak or chicken for dinner. But at earlier stages in cultural development the differences may have been crucial. The food of collectors comes in smaller packages than that of the big-game hunters; different methods of hunting, transporting, distributing, and preparing the food have to be developed. Instead of merely cutting off steaks from a single mammoth, new techniques of butchering, skinning, utilization, and storage must be devised. Instead of spear points, a new technology of snares and weirs has to be developed for capturing small land animals and fishes.

It would be an extreme oversimplification to visualize a continent full of Paleo-Indian hunters who, when their prey animals declined, promptly switched over to the Archaic way of living. In the archeological record, the big-game hunters overshadow the other, far different Archaic economies that must have been developing. When with the melting of the ice, the climate began to change, bringing with its changes in plant and animal life, the Archaic cultures had already emerged sufficiently to take advantage of the new conditions.

THE DESERT CULTURE AND THE
EASTERN ARCHAIC

After the melting of the ice, the Archaic way of life, already continent-wide, took two forms: the Eastern Archaic and the Desert culture of the West. From the deserts and the Great Basin westward to the Pacific, the land was largely arid and devoid of the large mammals that had enabled the specialized hunting cultures to arise. The Desert culture was instead oriented toward plants—the collecting of small seeds and roots for food, the use of plant fibers for baskets and footwear. Wherever it existed, the Desert culture possessed certain hallmarks. Most characteristic are the baskets for transporting and storing grain, and the manos and metates used for grinding. At Danger Cave, Utah, the typical pattern of the Desert culture appears to have prevailed as much as 9,500 years ago, at about the same time as the Llano and Folsom cultures were flourishing on the Great Plains.‡

Using nets, snares, and grinding stones, the Desert people exploited every possible food resource in their inhospitable land. The discovery of a number of caves they occupied in Nevada, Utah, Arizona, and Oregon has given a clear picture of their tools and their way of life. The caves are small and were only intermittently occupied, indicating that the people lived in small groups and wandered much of the year in search of food. For thousands of years after the Desert culture emerged, scarcely any changes took place in the basic pattern of food collecting. And at some places in California and the Great Basin, the Desert way of life persisted virtually unchanged until the arrival of the Whites. It was, however, this Desert culture, with its emphasis on plants, that later provided the substratum upon which the agricultural cultures of the Pueblo and of the Mexican states were erected.

Because the Eastern Archaic culture was not primarily dependent on a single food source, plants, it is less easily defined than the Desert culture. Many archeologists see it simply as a long period of time during which local environments were skillfully exploited in a multitude of ways. More than ten thousand Eastern Archaic sites are already known, and their common denominator is that in each one humans came to terms with what the habitat offered, skillfully utilizing all resources without destroying the environment. Archaic peoples used antlers and bones to manufacture fishhooks, spears, and harpoon heads; some learned to beat copper into ornaments; they shaped a variety of projectile points for various kinds of game. More than 7,000 years ago, the Archaic people were already developing extensive trade networks. Shells from the Florida coast were traded far to the north, and copper collected from rich outcrops around Lake Superior found its way, in the form of crude weapons and tools, to places as distant as New England and the Southeast.

One of the oldest Eastern Archaic sites, dating back more than 9,000 years, is the Modoc Rock Shelter, a cave in the bluffs on the Illinois side of the Mississippi River southeast of St. Louis. The bottommost, and therefore the oldest, layers of artifacts and refuse in the cave reveal a simple culture, quite different from that of the ice-age hunters who lived at about the same time. The Modoc Shelter contains no bones of mammoth or big-horned bison; instead, the people who lived there hunted deer, elk, raccoon, and opossum. Hunters of mammoth and bison had to be prepared to follow migrating herds, but most of the mammals hunted by the inhabitants of Modoc tended to remain in the same locality. So the Modoc hunters had a year-round food supply without having to wander very far from their shelter in the bluffs. And the river provided a wealth of other food: fishes, turtles, snails, and mussels.

Since grinding stones are virtually absent from the bottom layers at Modoc, the primary food source in the early Archaic must still have consisted of small animals —and probably the softer parts of plants as well. By about 8,200 years ago, when the mano and the metate began to appear, plant foods were being increasingly relied upon. Deer, still a mainstay of the diet, was now being hunted more efficiently, using light spears hurled by an atlatl (spear thrower). The variety of tools began to widen: Bone was used to make awls, and flint to manufacture drills; ornaments were made of shell and pendants of worked stone. The food base had broadened to include migrant ducks and geese, which must have abounded in the ponds and along the reedy riverbanks, much as they still do today. The bones of dogs appear, showing that they had become domesticated companions of humans, and possibly a source of food as well.‡

The Koster site, similarly located in southern Illinois and which is still being excavated, is filling in some of the gaps about the Eastern Archaic missing from Modoc. That the Archaic peoples developed a sedentary way of life earlier than previously thought is indicated by postholes in a level dating from about 8,500 years ago—evidence of the presence of timber uprights, even though no structural pattern is yet apparent. Levels occupied from about 7,000 years ago onward, though, show posthole patterns that clearly indicate the construction of dwellings. Also found at Koster, and dating from about 8,500 years ago, are the remains of three dogs, each of them buried in an individual grave. And, as at Modoc, a diversity of foodstuffs was harvested, including large numbers of fish only an inch long, suggesting that these people cooperated in groups to harvest this resource from local ponds.

The Eastern Archaic emerges as an Arcadian time in the history of North America, during which humans utilized resources to the fullest, yet still lived in harmony with their environment. In fact, a specialist in the archeology of eastern North America has lauded the Archaic people for what he calls their "primary forest efficiency"—their adaptation to many environments in which only the surplus food resources were cropped as they became seasonably available. The range of those resources was quite remarkable. By the time explorers reached the Great Lakes area, the descendants of the Archaic people were using 275 species of plants for medicine, 130 for food, 31 as magical charms, 27 for smoking, 25 as dyes, 18 in beverages and for flavoring, and 52 others for miscellaneous purposes.‡ No animal or particular group of animals was singled out for exploitation; the Eastern Archaic peoples practiced what is today known as multiple-use conservation.

BEGINNINGS OF AGRICULTURE

Agriculture developed in the Near East perhaps 10,000 years ago, but it did not begin in the New World until a few thousand years later. Its rise in the New World was unquestionably independent of the Near East, just as it was in China and in Southeast Asia. The first crops cultivated in the Near East, and later on in Europe, were wheat, barley, and rye—plants that did not exist in primeval North America. New World agriculture was not only different from that practiced in Europe; it was also more extensive. At the time of the Europeans' discovery of North America, the American Indians already cultivated a wider variety of plants than did the Europeans. The intimate connection between the Indians and the plants they domesticated is demonstrated by maize. Old World wheat or rye can survive as a weed, but New World maize is never found in the wild; every maize plant that grows anywhere today is of a domesticated variety. Its domestication has been so complete that maize would promptly become extinct were humans to stop growing it, since it does not possess any way for its seeds, the kernels, to be dispersed.

Grown throughout the area bounded by southern Canada and Chile, maize was the Indians' most widespread and important crop. Because it was the foundation upon which the complex cultures of the New World were built, it has been important for anthropologists to discover the steps by which it was domesticated. Many fruitless searches were made in Central and South America, and many hypotheses were put forth, only to be discredited. Then in 1960, the exploration of caves in the Tehuacán valley, south of Mexico City, finally answered the questions of how, when, and where maize had been domesticated in the New World. Digging down into the rubble, the archeologists unearthed twenty-eight levels of human occupancy, a complete record of human history from about 12,000 years ago until approximately 1521, when Cortés conquered Mexico. No other archeological region in the world has ever afforded so clear a picture of the rise of a civilization step by step.

Between about 12,000 and 9,200 years ago, the Tehuacán caves were occupied by nomadic families, gatherers of wild plants and hunters of such small animals as rabbits and birds. Then a gradual shift in emphasis took place: Plants were used increasingly as food. Between 8,700 and 7,000 years ago, the people still relied upon wild varieties of chili peppers and beans, but they had also begun to grow domesticated squash and avocados. By about 7,200 years ago wild maize appeared. Each ear was no larger than the filter tip on a cigarette and the plant itself was probably no more conspicuous than many kinds of weeds that grow today along roadsides and in abandoned fields. But maize had the potential, with human aid, for growing larger and for evolving into a plant with long rows of seeds on large cobs. The domestication of beans, also about 6,000 years ago, was particularly significant because of certain biochemical aspects of human nutrition. Like other grains, corn is high in protein; but the human body can metabolize this protein only in the presence of the amino-acid lysine, in which corn is deficient. Beans, however, have a high lysine content—and thus the two foods eaten together provide a much more nutritious diet than either one alone.

Permanent settlements had been established, laying the groundwork for more complex cultures, by nearly 5,400 years ago. At that time, about a quarter of the food consumed by the cave inhabitants came from domesticated plants. By 3,500 years ago, evidence appears of village life, pottery, elaborate religious rituals, and the intricate social organization that all these things imply. And by 2,000 years ago, large-scale irrigation works were being constructed; tomatoes and peanuts had been added to the long list of food plants, and turkeys had likewise been domesticated; occupations had become specialized, notably in religion, art, and government; evidence appears of a far-flung trade. All of these elements culminated about 1,000 years ago as part of the high culture of the Mixtec, who ruled until they were conquered by the Aztec shortly before the arrival of Cortés. And so the story of Tehuacán demonstrates the gradual evolution over 12,000 years of small, nomadic bands of hunters and gatherers into a complex state based on agriculture.‡

Using oversimplified data from the Near East, social scientists in the past spoke glibly of an "agricultural revolution," a time during which human populations suddenly soared, cities were founded, and the many trappings of civilization made their appearance. More recent archeological discoveries from the Near East cast doubt on this view, and the discovery of the thousands of years that were needed for agriculture to develop at Tehuacán have shown it to be incorrect. The food-production revolution turns out to be a slow evolution, a long period of experimentation rather than a sudden explosion. Although indications that plants were being domesticated appear at Tehuacán as early as 8,700 years ago, signs of settled village life do not appear until about 3,500 years later, pottery not until 5,000 years later, and a population spurt not until 5,500 years after the initial domestication of plants. In fact, it was not until about 2,500 years ago that what might be called a high civilization arose.‡

TRANSOCEANIC CONTACTS?

The Tehuacán caves demonstrate the way in which cultures gradually evolve as new ideas and techniques emerge. The archeological records thus refutes those who are quick to attribute cultural changes in North America to new migrations of people, by way either of the Bering Strait or of voyages across the oceans. Some archeologists have pointed to several innovations in the Archaic that they believe had been imported from Asia. Agriculture was supposedly one such importation, but Tehuacán now offers indisputable evidence to the contrary. Similarly, the building of earthen burial mounds was long attributed to Asia, but now most archeologists are convinced that the mounds were a logical outgrowth of the Archaic's increasing concern with burial and the afterlife.

Some resemblances cannot be denied; but many of them can be explained by two well-known scientific principles. One, which perhaps can be more clearly understood in biological than anthropological terms, is convergence: the tendency in species of plants or animals from widely separated parts of the world to look alike, not necessarily because they are related, but rather because they have evolved similar adaptations to similar environments. For example, cacti are widespread in the deserts of the New World, but they never grew in Africa until they were introduced there accidentally in modern times. Native to the African deserts, instead, are the euphorbias—taxonomically an entirely different group of plants, but also spiny, succulent, adapted to arid conditions, and often looking enough like cacti to confuse even some horticulturists. Convergence occurs in cultures also. Two human societies not related and far distant from each other, but in environments offering the same potentials and subject to the same limitations, may arrive at the same way of doing things. In the forests of the Amazon, where wood and plant poisons are available, Indians developed the blowgun; living in much the same sort of environment, with wood and plant poisons similarly available, the Semang of Malaysia did the same.

The second scientific principle is concerned with limited possibilities. Only a limited number of sounds can be made by the human vocal apparatus. In the aboriginal California language known as Yuki, the sound *ko* means "go" and *kom* means "come." No other similarities between Yuki and English have been found, and it would be absurd to imagine that the two languages are closely related. To take another example, human sex organs can be depicted in only a limited number of ways, so that fertility symbols tend to be universal. Menstruation can be surrounded with whatever mystery the human mind may concoct about it, but the number of possibilities soon runs out. Similarities, therefore, will—given the laws of probability—almost inevitably appear in widely separated societies that have never been in contact.

A decade or so ago, it appeared certain to some archeologists that pottery was one cultural item that had diffused to North America from Asia. At that time, the earliest known pottery in the New World was from the area around Valdivia on the coast of Ecuador, and dated to about 5,000 years ago. Its unusual designs and decorations had not been found anywhere else in the world except in sites associated with the Jomon culture on the southernmost island of Japan, where pottery was being manufactured at approximately the same time. Furthermore, no shards of cruder pottery had been found in Ecuador before the sudden appearance of that similar to the sophisticated Jomonware. So it was conjectured that a Japanese fishing vessel must have been caught offshore in a storm and carried by the prevailing currents the eight thousand miles to Ecuador, where the Japanese had found apt pupils ready to learn pottery techniques. Earlier pottery, bearing no resemblance to Jomonware, has now been found at Valdivia, thus effectively putting an end to the fanciful hypothesis of the Japanese voyage.‡

Probably most of the resemblances between Asian and American Indian cultures can be attributed to the principles of convergence or of limited possibilities. But some resemblances still remain that cannot be so easily accounted for. The laws of probability must be stretched to the breaking point to explain how Asians and Mexican Indians could have worked out, independently and by accident, exactly the same complicated rules for the game known in the Old World as parchisi and in the New as patolli. Nor does chance entirely explain how a bundle of panpipes from the Solomon Islands of the Pacific not only came to look like one from the New World, but also how the two societies hit upon tuning their instruments to the same pitch and using the same scale. An atlatl from the North American plains is exactly the same in design as some spear throwers found among Australian aborigines. Quite an impressive list of similar cultural items could be drawn up, including stone clubs from California and New Zealand, and similar bells from Arizona and China. Other cultural items that do not seem to have an accidental similarity, or to be easily explained as having been invented independently in both hemispheres, are certain animal deities, a cycle of seven days, the umbrella as a sign of power, the myth of a deluge, and the concept of zero.‡

The importance to be attached to such similarities is nevertheless uncertain. The essential point is not whether contacts took place between Asia and the New World across the Atlantic or the Pacific, but rather to what extent they influenced the native cultures of North America. Infinitesimally small numbers of Asians probably did drift across the Pacific from time to time and were cast ashore in the New World. That such a thing is possible was demonstrated in 1815 after a Japanese junk that had set out from Osaka lost its mast and rudder. It drifted for seventeen months before the three men left alive in it reached Santa Barbara, California. Such fortuitous arrivals, though, could not have taken place until seaworthy ships were invented in the Old World—and by that time, the major configurations of the New World cultures would already have taken shape. Some specialists in Asian prehistory assert that the Chinese by 2,600 years ago had vessels able to reach islands of the Pacific and return. Yet, although New Zealand is much closer to Asia than the Americas are, it was not to be settled until a mere seven hundred years ago—and then by Polynesians rather than Chinese.

So the first argument against the importance of transoceanic contacts is that they would have occurred too late to have much influence on the native cultures that had already emerged in North America. A second argument is that it really is unimportant, when looking at the evolution of cultures, whether or not temple mounds and parchisi reached the New World from across the Pacific. Of much more concern are the ways in which already evolving cultures utilized, modified, or even rejected innovations from outside. The example of the Eskimo is instructive as a demonstration of the improbability that elements from one culture will be transferred to another unless the latter is ripe to receive them. Between about A.D. 985 and the end of the fourteenth century, the Norse planted colonies in Greenland, where they must have been in close contact with the Eskimo— but so far as the Eskimo culture was concerned, it was the same as though they never arrived. A few words of Old Norse and Old Icelandic found their way into the Greenland Eskimo dialect, and a few tools were made of metal. Otherwise, no survivals of this earlier occupation were to be found when the second wave of European colonists arrived.

A third argument in favor of the independent evolution of the American Indian cultures is this: If prehistoric contact did indeed take place across the oceans, then it had remarkably little effect on anything in the New World so important as agriculture. Out of the many thousands of plants that are grown on the planet for food or fiber, only four are shared by the Old World and the New: cotton, the gourd, the coconut, and the sweet potato. Coconuts are adapted for dispersal by ocean currents over distances of at least a few thousand miles; they remain buoyant and viable after many months in sea water. Similarly, the gourd is easily transported by ocean currents. The Old and the New World species of cotton are different—and furthermore, they were domesticated at about the same time, at least 5,000 years ago, in both Mexico and the Indus valley of Pakistan.

Thus the only possible evidence in support of the notion that a prehistoric agricultural exchange took place across the oceans is the sweet potato. At the time of the Europeans' discovery of the New World, it was widely cultivated in tropical America and apparently also on some Pacific islands. Great controversy has surrounded the question of how and when the plant crossed the ocean. The sweet potato sometimes flowers and sets seed, which could have been carried on floating logs or in the guts of birds. Peruvians, who had seaworthy vessels, might possibly have carried the plant to Polynesia in recent prehistoric times. And there is also the possibility that the sweet potato might have been independently domesticated from similar wild species in the Americas and in the western Pacific.‡

The final argument against important transoceanic contacts is that numerous sophisticated inventions undoubtedly originated in the New World. They include many aspects of plant domestication and horticulture, the hammock, the tobacco pipe, an intricate system used for ventilating and cooling ceremonial chambers, the enema, the hollow rubber ball, the toboggan, and numerous other objects and ideas that were brought back to the Old World after Columbus. If Indians could invent these, could they not also, quite independently, have invented other things that were also known in the Old World?

In itself, the question of whether or not contacts took place is a relatively trivial one. Whether a boatload of Phoenician, Irish, Polynesian, or Japanese sailors did or did not at one time or another land on the shores of the New World is not of much importance to the evolution of North American cultures. The real question is whether such landings were frequent enough, or sufficiently influential, to modify the culture of the western hemisphere. A fair-minded person must inevitably conclude, after reading the papers presented at a symposium on the subject held by the Society for American Archeology, that such contacts as may have taken place were remarkably unproductive of important cultural influence. We might expect that those who did make any such contact would recognize the importance of one another's crops. Judging by the remarkable speed with which the exchange of crops between the New World and the Old took place after Columbus, we would expect their value to have been recognized long before. Yet no clear evidence exists for the introduction of a single animal or plant from either direction before the arrival of Columbus. Thus, any pre-Columbian contacts that may have taken place may be assumed to have had no more lasting effect on other aspects of culture.‡

The end of the Archaic period is marked by cultural innovations of every kind. In view of the foregoing, it would be intellectually reckless to attribute that flowering to the importation of ideas from Asia or elsewhere. The numerous specializations that arose among the various Indian groups must have been indigenous, not merely a reflection of alien technologies cast up on the North American shore. In the words of one archeologist, the Archaic culture itself possessed a great "reservoir of innovators."

THE FLOWERING OF DIVERSITY

During the 3,000 years that preceded the arrival of Europeans in North America, the fabric of Indian culture grew increasingly rich and varied. For every site that is known from the Archaic, scores of more recent ones have been found, and these differ considerably among themselves. Cultures in many parts of the continent were becoming more diverse and specialized.

Until recently, most archeologists regarded the agricultural cultures in the southwestern deserts that arose after the Archaic as no more than variations on a single theme.‡ The uniformity they pictured, though, is now known to be illusory. Several major specializations arose that were quite distinct. For example, in the vicinity of Phoenix, Arizona, centered on the Gila and Salt rivers and their tributaries, were the Hohokam ("those who have vanished," in the present-day Pima Indian language). Numerous differences can be found among cultures of the southwestern deserts, but what makes the Hohokam noteworthy is the development of irrigation works. The earliest of these at Snaketown, south of Phoenix, dates from some 2,000 years ago. Rather than merely incorporating agriculture into an existing pattern of collecting seeds, as did other desert peoples, the Hohokam had attempted to control their environment. They built dams that redirected the flow of water into irrigation canals, some of them thirty feet wide in places and extending for more than twenty-five miles.

Much mystery still surrounds the Hohokam culture.

Once viewed as indigenous, it is now fairly certain that it was brought into the region by migrant groups from Mexico as early as 2,250 years ago. No antecedents existed locally for its particular constellation of traits, among which were established villages, water control, pottery, shell carving, stone sculpture, skill in textiles, and varieties of maize and other crops new to the region. The Hohokam appear to have been receptive to new ideas, and especially to those brought by migrants from Mexico. They built flat-topped pyramids and ball courts, where they used rubber balls imported from Central America; and they are believed to have relied on astronomy to calculate planting dates. The Hohokam may also have been the first to use the technique of etching with acid in their remarkable designs on marine shells. But around A.D. 1100 their distinctive way of life disappeared, and the descendants of the Hohokam survive today as the Pima and Papago Indians of southern Arizona, only pale shadows of the once-great culture that had existed in this area.‡

Whereas Hohokam may be considered a northern outpost of Mexican culture, one that emerged about A.D. 300 from the Desert Archaic foundation was clearly indigenous. This, the culture of the Anasazi ("the ancient ones," in the language of the Navajo, who later occupied much of their territory), is still the best known of all prehistoric southwestern cultures. The cliff dwellings at Mesa Verde in Colorado, Chaco Canyon in New Mexico, and Canyon de Chelly in Arizona are among the hundreds of Anasazi ruins to be found in these states as well as in southern Utah. The culture of the Anasazi was influenced by those in the southeastern United States; the type of maize they grew was southeastern, and so was the pottery they made. Their architecture, however, is distinctively their own, and unique among all the southwestern cultures. Built at Pueblo Bonito in Chaco Canyon, for example, was a huge apartment house five stories tall and containing eight hundred rooms. The Anasazi made use of irrigation (although not so extensively as the Hohokam), and their skills in weaving, basketry, pottery, and masonry

NORTHWEST COAST: STATUS AND WEALTH

The abundance of the sea off the
Northwest Coast was harvested by fishermen
and harpooners in seagoing canoes.
This Haida carving, made in the last half
of the nineteenth century, shows a
canoe filled with oarsmen. The Haida
alone carved from argillite slate,
which is comparatively soft while being
carved, but which soon hardens
after exposure to the air.

Above: The complexity of Northwest Coast art can be seen in this shaman's rattle, which shows a large raven with a human reclining on its back. The human is sucking on a frog's tongue to draw out a poison that the shamans believe to be of aid in working spells.

Right: Totem poles at the abandoned Kwakiutl village of Alert Bay, British Columbia, boast of real and fictitious events in family histories.

NATCHEZ: PEOPLE OF THE SUN

The Great Sun of the Natchez, who is being carried to the harvest festival by a relay of litter-bearers, was sketched by the French explorer Du Pratz in the early 1700's.

AZTEC: TOTAL POWER

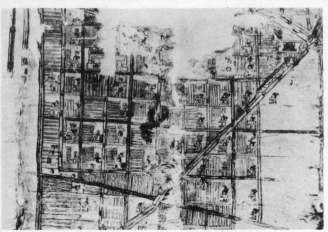

Chinampa system is shown on an Aztec map—part of which has been damaged—of Tenochtitlán. Each house appears to have had six to eight plots associated with it, and the main canals are indicated.

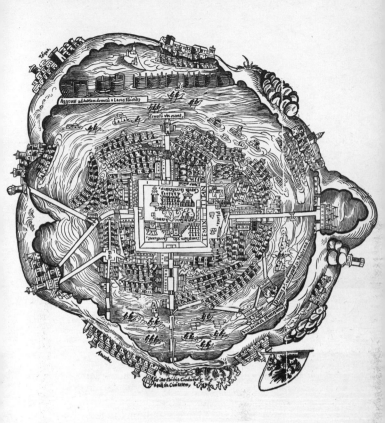

Map of Tenochtitlán, published in 1524 to
illustrate Cortés' dispatches, clearly depicts much
of the city planning and architecture of the capital
city of the Aztec. Note the central temples
and great pyramid, the large number of private
dwellings, the causeways connecting the
city to the mainland, the busy commerce of Lake
Texcoco, and even the outlying cities.

Aztec calendar stone, thirteen feet in
diameter and weighing more than twenty tons,
was made from a huge block of stone quarried
on the mainland and dragged across the
causeway to Tenochtitlán. It symbolizes the entire
Aztec universe and the history of the world,
and would require many pages to explain
in detail. In the center is the sun, set within the
symbols for the previous eras, the dates of
which are given in hieroglyphs on the
four arms around the sun. The twenty day names
encircle the central symbols, and beyond them
are the sun's rays and various star symbols.
The two great fire serpents that form the outer rim
probably were intended to symbolize time.

The ritual of human sacrifice demanded stone
vessels for the storing and burning of hearts. Such
vessels were gouged out of lava rock, then
lavishly decorated or sculptured to refer to the gods
for whom the sacrifices were made. This
one represents the ocelot.

THE LONG MIGRATION

Mummy Cave at Canyon de Chelly National Monument in Arizona shows the sweep of Pueblo settlement from the early pit houses at right to the multistoried dwellings at left. The site was abandoned before the end of the thirteenth century and the area evacuated.

Plan of Pueblo village is clearly revealed at the Tuoynyi ruin in Frijoles Canyon near Los Alamos, New Mexico. Note the central plaza and the circular ceremonial chamber, or kiva.

The Mississippian culture, which spread across
the Southeast and was still extant when the Spaniards
arrived, produced outstanding art, as demonstrated
by this gorget cut from the shell of a giant conch. The
figure on the left may be a panther or a bear; the
one on the right is undoubtedly an eagle.

Pictograph writing: Even those Indians who
did not develop a written literature, as did the Aztec
and the Maya of Mexico, used several kinds of notation
and memory devices. This wooden box was used
by the Ojibwa Indians of the western Great Lakes to
store ceremonial eagle feathers. Pictograph designs
on the cover served as reminders of the songs to be sung
at the ceremonies. They could not be read by the
uninitiated, any more than Chinese can be read
by an American without instruction.

SOCIETIES UNDER STRESS

The End of the Trail: The encounter between
an Indian and a White bureaucrat is bitterly satirized
in these early twentieth-century carvings by a
Salish Indian of the Northwest Coast. The artist said
that the figures tell the story, all too typical, of
the starving "Suppliant Indian" who goes to the "Indian
Agent" for help. The agent looks very severe as
he reprimands him with a long lecture on how
he should have saved his money. Reluctantly, the
agent gives the Indian some paper scrip that
entitles him to flour and potatoes.

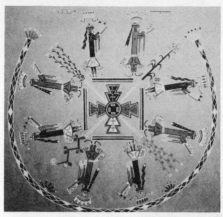

Borrowed Cultures: Left: Navajo sand painting
used in the Hail Chant, one of the many Navajo
ceremonials, illustrates a complex mythology.
It shows the figures of Rainbow Boy and Rainbow Girl
at their different positions as they walk around the
central lake, which has cloud symbols on four sides.
Four holy plants grow out of the central lake. Lightning
and rainbow symbols are at the open eastern
portion of the encircling rainbow rope. This is but
a small indication of the intricate mythology
contained in this one painting.

Right: Navajo Kachina Maiden reveals the
Navajo as seen through the eyes of the Hopi, a
neighboring Pueblo tribe in Arizona. Note
the satirical touches of the heavily rouged cheeks;
the hair elaborately combed into a bun; the
abundance of jewelry around the neck, on the belt,
and on the hands; as well as the typical Navajo
blouse, skirt, leggings, and footwear.

Left: The Hopes of the Oppressed: The Ghost Dance shirt was worn during the last desperate attempt by the Plains Indians to forestall the White conquest of their culture, as well as of their lands and lives. This Sioux shirt shows the mystic designs that were supposed to deflect White bullets. Each man painted his own shirt after having a vision of the particular designs that would protect him.

Below: The frozen body of a Sioux leader lies on the field at Wounded Knee. He was one of some three hundred Sioux men, women, and children waiting to surrender, who were massacred in 1890 by the United States Army cavalry.

Primeval custom of sharing endures
today, as seen at a Rosebud Sioux funeral
in which the deceased's belongings are
spread out for neighbors to share.
Similarly, the poor Indians of the late
nineteenth century, starved into
submission by Whites, shared the little
they had before starving together.

architecture were equaled by few Indians north of Mexico. With surplus food and relative stability, they developed an exceedingly rich ceremonial and artistic life. The pomp of their religious festivals can be inferred from the size of their dance courts or plazas. The dances surviving to this day among the Pueblo Indians of Arizona and New Mexico, impressive as they are, must be only the faded relic of the Anasazi's exuberant religious life.

The Anasazi culture came to an abrupt end about A.D. 1300. The populous villages were evacuated, and their inhabitants migrated to their present locations, pueblos situated on mesa tops in Arizona and New Mexico, and near the Rio Grande River around Santa Fe and Albuquerque. Many explanations have been offered for this sudden exodus. Archeologists have variously attributed it to warfare between the pueblos, to raids by the Ute and Apache Indians who were filtering into the Southwest from the North about that time, and to a great drought that lasted for twenty-five years at the end of the thirteenth century. These explanations no doubt have some truth in them—and there is an indication of warfare in the design of the later pueblos, which include such ingenious safeguards as removable ladders. But consideration must also be given to changes in the environment. The river channels on which the Indians depended for water in raising their crops apparently cut deeper into the land, so that the irrigation ditches were eventually left high and dry. The Indians did not know the principles of the siphon and the pump, and so they could not lift the water to the level of the fields. The loss of these lands for agriculture was probably aggravated by the increasing unreliability of the rainfall.‡

THE EASTERN WOODLANDS

At approximately the same time as the southwestern cultures were emerging out of the Desert culture, some 3,500 years ago, the Eastern Archaic was marked by two developments: the manufacture of crude pottery and an increased attention to burial observances. Archeologists have given the name of Woodland to this new cultural pattern, which reached its fullest development between 2,800 and 1,200 years ago in the area that now includes southern Ohio, northern Kentucky, and the adjacent corner of West Virginia. This regional flowering, known as the Adena culture, was typified by a cluster of burial mounds containing the bodies of eminent personages, and of those presumed to have been their retainers, along with elaborate funeral offerings. One mound rose atop another as new burials were made and fresh earth was added, until some of them rose to a height of seventy feet. A complex of several mounds usually was surrounded by an earthen wall as much as five hundred feet in diameter. The sheer size of the mounds and their richly ornamented contents point to a complex religious life and also to political organization at the level of a chiefdom.

The Adena culture is the more remarkable in that, for all its artistic richness and political complexity, including marked social classes and the large size of its population, it appears to have developed in the near-absence of agriculture. The Adena sites have yielded remains of squashes, pumpkins, and sunflowers, but no maize; rather, the subsistence pattern is the typically Archaic one of hunting and gathering. To the simpler hunting-and-gathering peoples around them, the Adena people must have represented the apogee of Woodland life, much as ancient Rome would have represented to Gaul the fulfillment of the Pax Romana.

The Adena was but a prelude to another culture— the most remarkable, influential, and extensive to have arisen north of Mexico since the Archaic. It is referred to as the Hopewell, named after the owner of a farm in Ross County, Ohio, where large earthworks, a village site, and burial mounds were found. Centered in southern Ohio and Illinois, it eventually dominated much of the Adena area itself and extended its influence as far away as Minnesota, New York, Florida, and Louisiana. Hopewell had already appeared by nearly 2,350 years ago, and in some places it and Adena existed side by side until A.D. 300.

The Hopewell fused elements of the Adena, the

Archaic, and other Woodland patterns of life. Thus it cannot technically be identified as a culture—that is, as a society with its own social, political, and technological ways of doing things. Rather, the Hopewell people were an amalgam of many societies whose customs varied greatly, but who were bound together by two things: a cult of the dead and a trade bond. Enormous quantities of grave objects went into the cult of the dead, and to procure them, a network of trade linked widely separated areas of the continent.

In every way, the Hopewell people did things on a much grander scale than the Adena; their burial mounds were considerably larger, and their tomb offerings much richer. The surrounding earthworks extended for miles in patterns of octagons, squares, and circles; one earthwork enclosure in Ohio surrounds an area of four square miles. (In the nineteenth century, many Whites considered these constructions beyond the capability of the American Indians and instead ascribed them to a mythical, vanished people they called the Mound Builders.) The burial offerings were munificent; one site alone yielded 48,000 fresh-water pearls. The exotic raw materials in which they traded were fashioned by Hopewell artisans into some of the most finely wrought objects ever to appear in the Americas. Copper from around Lake Superior and mica from the Appalachians were worked into delicate ornaments; obsidian from the Rocky Mountains was used to make elaborate ceremonial knives; alligator teeth and large conch shells from Florida and the Gulf of Mexico went into necklaces or into richly decorated clothing; several kinds of stone, from quarries in Minnesota and Wisconsin, were carved into tobacco pipes that had the shapes of animals.

The Hopewell people, though, were more than a bigger and wealthier Adena. From the extent of the earthworks, it would appear that a tremendous labor force must have been recruited—which in turn implies a large sedentary population and also a strong central authority to coordinate these activities. The existence of such an authority appears to be confirmed by the burials of important personages, and also by the vast tribute in goods rendered to the Hopewell people by their simpler Woodland neighbors. Further, a cult of the dead implies a permanent priesthood. And that so much ceremonial art, of a uniformly high order of excellence, was produced indicates that a specialized artisan class must have been subsidized by the priesthood.

Some archeologists have attributed the origins of the Hopewell cult, and in particular the burial mounds, to diffusion from the Vera Cruz area of Mexico. But in North America the tradition of heaping mounds of earth above the dead goes back three thousand years, and the earliest of these mounds are found in Ohio and Illinois, not in areas closer to Mexico. Furthermore, these earliest mounds were rounded, whereas those in Mexico were built in a pyramidal shape. Lavish mortuary rites and the burial of valued objects along with the dead also have precursors in the Eastern Archaic cultures and need not have been derived from Mexico.

By about A.D. 400, the Hopewell cult was in decline everywhere. The cause was once thought to be a decrease in population, but archeologists now know that the populations at the Hopewell sites during their last century were actually higher than for several centuries before. The most probable explanation for the decline is that Hopewell's social and political institutions could not carry the load of these increasing numbers. Institutions that had developed at a time when there were fewer people probably were inadequate for coping with new problems stemming from growing numbers and increasing complexity. One new problem must have been the onset of a period of warfare and raiding in eastern North America. At a typical site dating from near the end of the Hopewell period, seventy-eight percent of the males buried there appear to have met a violent death. After about A.D. 500 the Hopewell people no longer built ceremonial centers in open valleys, but instead sought out hilltops that could be defended.

Even then, however, the cult of the dead could not be successfully protected against raiders. The unsettled conditions of war also made it more and more difficult to obtain the goods that had gone into the elaborate burials. With the rupture of the trade bond that had been the unifying feature of the Hopewell cult, the cult itself was doomed. A few burial mounds stocked with meager offerings were built as late as A.D. 750, but these were the last. After that date the once powerful Hopewell had ceased to exist.‡

THE MISSISSIPPIAN

The Woodland Indians again settled back into much the same pattern as had prevailed in Archaic times, with one major exception: Along the Mississippi and other river systems of the South, a way of life emerged about A.D. 700 that was equal to the Hopewell in its richness. This was the Mississippian, the immediate precursor of the sophisticated southeastern chiefdoms—the Choctaw, Chickasaw, Natchez, and others—that had so impressed de Soto and other early explorers. Although the focus of the Mississippian was from the mouth of the Missouri River southward to Louisiana and from Tennessee westward to Arkansas, its influence extended as far as the Great Plains in one direction and what is now New York in the other.

Numerous questions about the Mississippian are still unanswered, even though it emerged no more than eight hundred years before the European discovery of North America and even though an abundance of sites have been uncovered. Archeologists do not agree, for one thing, about its origin. Some attribute it to the migration of ideas from the Yucatan peninsula of Mexico. It is indeed true that the sophisticated art of the Mississippian—pottery, textiles, and ornaments worked from shell, wood, copper, and stone—often resembles that of Middle America. But its roots can be found in Adena and Hopewell sites. Current thinking treats the Mississippian as an indigenous culture, an outgrowth of the Hopewell cults in the south, blended with certain Mexican elements.

The most imposing characteristic of the Mississippian is the pyramidal mound, built not to cover a burial but as a foundation for a temple or a chief's house. Some groups of mounds were carefully laid out around a central plaza; others consisted of a loose string of conical mounds. Dwellings were often near the ceremonial structures, but not always; occasionally they were placed at some distance away. Some of the centers were very small, comprising only two or three mounds, whereas the Cahokia site at East St. Louis, Illinois, contained more than eighty-five mounds and a village area that extended for six miles along the Mississippi. One of the largest Cahokia mounds was about one hundred feet high, and its base covered sixteen acres, several times more than the Great Pyramid of Egypt. The labor involved is awesome even in these days of bulldozers, but it is astounding to think of what it meant for the Mississippian people, who had neither wheeled vehicles nor beasts of burden. The mounds were constructed entirely by human laborers who carried every clod of earth in baskets. Several specialists have attempted to estimate the number of laborers and the span of years involved in building the Cahokia site; they agree only that it must have required thousands or tens of thousands of people working for a few hundred years. No shortage of muscle power existed, for the Mississippian population was extremely dense. At least 383 villages bordered the Mississippi River in the short distance of about seven hundred miles between the entrances of the Ohio and the Red rivers. And thousands of other villages were built up and down the Mississippi, on its tributary streams, and along other river systems.‡

In this brief survey of the archeological roots of the Indian cultures encountered by the explorers, many questions about their rise, diversification, and fall have necessarily been left open. At their various stages of evolution, the Indian cultures were presented with only a limited number of possibilities. The members of certain kinds of societies—the small band, the large band, the tribe, the chiefdom, the state, and variations of these—tended to make characteristic choices concerning religion, law, government, and art more often than they made different choices. Such choices were not, of course, consciously made, nor was a vote taken by the group. For a particular society, they either worked or they did not work. But often they were the only adaptive choices the members of the societies could make.

XII

The Generations of Adam

THE MISSING SKELETONS

Butchering sites of Paleo-Indians have been found; their projectile points and other weapons and tools have been unearthed, and so have the bones of the various animals they preyed on. Tens of thousands of artifacts have been discovered—but few of the bones from the hands that made them. The anthropologist needs to know more about the early inhabitants of North America than the spear points they made or the animals they hunted. Did they look primitive, with heavy brow ridges and underslung jaw, or did they resemble the modern Indian? Similarly, does biological information about contemporary native Americans correspond with the archeological record?

Skulls and skeletons of Paleo-Indians are scarce, partly because the human populations were small. Also, early humans in the New World may not have practiced ritual burial, although they often did in the Old, and the skeletons may have simply decayed. It is further possible, though, that numbers of Paleo-Indian skeletons have been located, but have been ignored and even destroyed because of a misconception: the belief that the early skeletons would have a primitive appearance and reveal a people with heavy brow ridges, stooped posture, and gangling arms. In other words, anthropologists were expecting to find a caricature of Neanderthal. Accordingly, while these anthropologists were adhering to the notion that only what appears primitive is old, many skeletons of early humans in North America could have been overlooked because they were assumed to be those of modern Indians.

THE EVIDENCE OF THE SKULLS

The previous chapter mentioned the possibility that the skeletal remains at Los Angeles, Laguna Beach, and San Diego are of tremendous antiquity. Even those conservative archeologists who for one reason or another reject the possibility nevertheless usually accept the dates for fossils found at the Marmes site in eastern Washington, and at the Midland site in western Texas, both of which may be as much as 13,000 years old. At the Midland site, a female skull was found in 1953, in a layer beneath one containing stone tools of the Folsom people and remains of the big-horned bison they hunted. The Midland woman is therefore older than the Folsom culture, which flourished in that area about 10,000 years ago. Several attempts have been made to fix a date for the Midland woman by radiocarbon and other techniques, but the various methods do not agree; the estimates range from 10,000 up to 20,000 years in age.

As the fragmented skull of Midland woman was painstakingly put back together again, several interesting facts emerged. She had delicate features; her brow ridges were light; her teeth and jaw were small. There is nothing "primitive" about her; she is just what would be expected of a *Homo sapiens* ancestor of the modern Indian. Those anthropologists who were looking for some robust, beetle-browed Neanderthal were simply looking for the wrong kind of human. Dressed in modern clothing, Paleo-Indians of the Midland type would hardly differ from the cross section of humanity to be seen on a New York City street. Nor could any of the skulls so far discovered be mistaken for those of the Neanderthal. All are unmistakably modern and of the same subspecies as ourselves.

The skulls confirm the general range of dates given by archeologists for the arrival of humans in the New World. Since no skulls so far found resemble the Neanderthal type, it would appear that humans did not begin moving into North America much before 40,000 years ago, when *Homo sapiens* had already evolved. So even though the number of skulls available for study is meager, a tentative conclusion emerges: Humans are comparative newcomers in the New World; they have been here for perhaps 40,000 years out of the approximately 3,000,000 years of human existence on the planet.

The same skulls also offer evidence that the ancestors of the Indians came from Asia, and that they did so no later than about 15,000 years ago. Some skulls unearthed recently in parts of China have been dated to about the same period of prehistory as the North American skulls. Any of these Chinese skulls placed in a collection of early North American ones would not be noticeably different. Like those of American Indians, they are only slightly Mongoloid—which means that neither group belongs to the Classic Mongoloid type that arose about 15,000 years ago, apparently as an adaptation to a cold environment. The ancestors of the American Indian must therefore have arrived in North America before the emergence of the Classic Mongoloids. (On the other hand, the earliest Aleut skull to be discovered, dating to about 4,000 years ago, is clearly Classic Mongoloid, and so are the oldest known Eskimo skulls.) Presumably both the early Chinese and the the American Indians represented a general Mongoloid type that was later overrun by the Classic Mongoloid that was adapted for cold climates; the older type appears to have survived only through migration to the New World or by isolation in remote parts of Asia. The Chinese skulls indicate that varieties of modern humans akin to the American Indian lived in eastern Asia during the late Pleistocene, and that they became the reservoir out of which the first Americans overflowed across the Bering land bridge.

THE NATIVE AMERICANS

The American Indians are one of the most homogeneous populations on earth. Probably no human population has ever expanded over such a large area and remained so uniform; the only exceptions are the late-arriving Eskimo, Aleut, and Athapaskans. Having invaded a new continent and found no other humans with whom to interbreed, the early arrivals in America were to become one of the world's major isolated populations. The blood types of the native Americans indicate as much. Again with the exception of the Eskimo, the Aleut, some populations in southwestern Canada, and the Navajo and Apache, the Indians are remarkably homogeneous throughout the entire New World. Unlike cultural traits and unlike such biological variables as skin color, blood types are an objective means of identifying human groups. Not only is blood type a matter of heredity—one that neither diet, health, nor climate can modify—it would also appear that the blood types of large populations remain stable over very long periods of time. A people with O blood type predominating will not suddenly produce large numbers of offspring with type B unless there has been an infusion of genetic material from outside the group.

The American Indians are unique in the frequencies of their particular blood types and in other physical traits. For example, the incidence of red–green color blindness and hair on the middle segments of the fingers is very low. American Indians almost never become bald or have gray hair, even in extreme old age, and their skin tans readily. They have a high frequency of arches rather than whorls in their fingerprints. Unimportant as these and other characteristics may seem, they provide the conclusive evidence that sets the American Indian apart from all other human populations.‡

Still, the various American Indian groups obviously differ from one another. As the early explorers traveled the length and breadth of North America, they encountered groups of Indians who differed greatly. For many people, the typical Indian is the brave portrayed on the buffalo nickel or riding across the plains in movie

Technicolor. But from the beginning, explorers reported Indians ranging in build from tall and thin to short and fat; in complexion from dark brown through red, yellow, and even pinkish with hair that might be straight or wavy, black or brown.

The divergence of a population into a number of distinct groups is explained by geneticists in four possible ways: mixture, mutation, random genetic drift, and natural selection. In the case of the Indians, mixture can be dismissed, because no other humans had ever lived previously in North America. Similarly, mutations—accidental changes in the genes that govern heredity—do not in themselves explain the diversity. Mutations are simply a source of something new in a population. Whether or not they will have important effects depends upon the third and fourth factors: random genetic drift and natural selection. Random genetic drift is an accidental change in the proportions of various genes in a population as a consequence of war, famine, migration, or anything else that may cause a fraction of an originally large population to become a new breeding unit. A small group of people is almost certain to differ genetically from the large population of which it was formerly a part. As members of this small population continue to produce new generations, the differences between it and the parent population will become accentuated still more.

To visualize how genetic drift works, suppose an original breeding population is represented by five hundred purple and five hundred green marbles. Then pick at random fifty marbles from the original thousand. The probability is that, with such a small sample, more of one color than another will be chosen—let us say thirty of the green to only twenty of the purple. Further suppose that this group of fifty marbles represents a small migrant group that has split off from the original breeding population. Obviously, the migrant group even at the outset will be different in its makeup: sixty percent green instead of only fifty percent. Then suppose that the marbles in this splinter population reproduce; the preponderance of green will probably become even more marked in the second generation. In fact, once the composition of the first-generation group has favored the green marbles, the chances are that the number of purple marbles will decrease with each random selection. The migrants, as represented by the marbles, will then be completely different from the original population: Instead of being only fifty percent green, they will all or nearly all be green. This example gives only a simplified picture of the much more complex changes that occur in splinter populations of humans. A breeding population as small as that postulated in the marbles example is not unknown among humans. The breeding populations of some Eskimo and Great Basin Shoshone groups number no more than a few dozen, and such small numbers were probably very much the rule during most of the human tenure in North America.

The effect of a mutation appearing in a small breeding population is dramatic, as compared to what it would be in a large population. A mutation in the large population of North America today will not spread rapidly, but neither is it likely to be lost; it will usually maintain a low frequency in such a huge gene pool. But in a very small population, a mutation may easily be lost through chance—as, for example, if the three people who carry it are killed in a skirmish. On the other hand, the same mutation would spread rapidly through a small breeding population if a large proportion of the people who do not have it were killed.

But the major cause for diversity in populations is natural selection—the fact that organisms possessing beneficial characteristics survive in relatively larger numbers and leave more offspring than do organisms of the same species that do not possess those traits. A disease, for example, is selective because it favors the individuals who possess an immunity to it. But for the early migrants the greatest natural-selection filter of all was the North American continent itself—ten million square miles of tundra, forest, grassland, and desert, all with their own climates and environmental stresses. Each Indian population was exposed to the pressures of natural selection in its particular habitat, and was influenced accordingly.

So genetic theory also is in agreement with the evidence unearthed by archeologists. The vastness and the variety of North America are sufficient to account for the diversity in the color, build, and stature of the Indian; this diversity is primarily the result of natural selection working upon small populations that had felt the effect of random genetic drift. No need exists to postulate subsequent invasion by large numbers of diverse peoples from across the Pacific or the Atlantic.

HALF A THOUSAND TONGUES

The science of linguistics has also helped to retrace the long trail the ancestors of the Indians followed through North America. Early explorers of the New World found a Babel of tongues. About 2,200 languages were spoken in North and South America—more than in all of Europe and Asia at the time.‡ Despite what some early explorers and European scholars believed, there never was an "American Indian" language—meaning, presumably, a single common tongue with local dialects. Dialects were spoken in plenty—that is, mutually intelligible variations of a mother tongue—but the Indians also spoke numerous distinct languages, as different from one another as English is from Chinese. About 550 of these distinct languages were found north of Mexico, and nearly every one comprised numerous dialects. (A survey made some three decades ago revealed that 149 native languages were still spoken north of the Rio Grande and, south of it, so were a majority of the original 350 languages of Mexico.)

A second misconception has likewise been corrected —that no language deserved the name if it was not a written one. In North America, written language developed only in Mexico, yet most Indian groups were able to hand down a rich oral tradition of poetry, oratory, and drama. A number of Indian groups did develop pictographs and other mnemonic devices for recalling important events. Wampum, which Whites nowadays often suppose to be the Indian form of money, was originally such a memory device. Beads from white and purple shells were woven into belts by both the Iroquois and the Algonkian tribes of the Northeast (from whose language the word itself comes). The designs recorded treaties and agreements, other important events, and public accounts. Among the Iroquois, one sachem was in charge of keeping the wampum belts and of remembering what the symbols meant, so that he could interpret them when the occasion arose. But this original purpose was corrupted by Europeans, who used the beads as a sort of money and then flooded the market with imitations manufactured in Europe.

Scholars who based their studies on the reports of the early explorers once thought that clues to the beginnings of human speech might be found in the preliterate cultures of the Indian. But further study of American Indian languages has clearly revealed that these are no more primitive than European languages, nor are they in general any more limited in their vocabularies. A typical dictionary of the English language for use by those with an education beyond the high-school level contains about 45,000 words; Shakespeare, in the rich imagery of all of his plays and poems, used only about 24,000 words, and the King James Bible uses about 7,000. The number of words recorded in the Nahuatl language of Mexico is 27,000; in Maya, 20,000; in Dakota, 19,000—and undoubtedly linguists have overlooked many of the nuances that make our dictionaries so bulky. Darwin considered barely human the speech of the natives of Tierra del Fuego, at the southern tip of South America—but a study of one of these people, the Yahgan, has revealed a vocabulary of at least 30,000 words.

Where did these and the other American Indian languages come from? Claims have been made at one time or another that they were closely related to Hebrew, Welsh, ancient Egyptian, and Chinese. No such links have ever been discovered. Logic would, of course, dictate that the languages crossed the Bering land bridge along with their speakers. But a time span of approximately 25,000 years is more than sufficient for the languages spoken in the New World to have evolved to such a point that resemblances to those now spoken in Asia either cannot be detected or are without significance. Resemblances do exist, but they may be attributable to the fact that humans everywhere, regardless of the language they speak, employ only a limited number of sounds combined in a limited number of ways. The Athapaskan languages, among others spoken in the New World, are tonal—that is, a rise or fall, or even a leveling, in the pitch of a syllable can alter its meaning. Chinese and other languages in eastern Asia are also tonal. Is this significant? Possibly, but the chances are that it is not—since very few other resemblances have been found between these widely-separated languages, and also since tonal languages are spoken elsewhere in the world, including Africa.

Languages do, of course, change somewhat over a period of time. English has gone through some striking alterations since *Beowulf*, and even since *Hamlet*. These changes provide linguists with written evidence; but even in the absence of such evidence, it would still be possible to piece together the history of English by studying its rules, its structure, and its relation to other languages. For example, the German noun *Tanz* means "dance," and *Trank* means "drink." An examination of many other German words beginning with *T* reveals that they are replaced in English by the letter *d*. Similarly, the German *D* is replaced in English by *th*, as in *Donner*, "thunder," or in *Danke*, "thank you." The science of historical linguistics has been able to demonstrate that the words *foot*, *pes*, *pous*, and *Fuss*—English, Latin, Greek, and German for the same thing—are derived from an ancestral word common to them all.

American Indian languages can be analyzed in much the same way. Languages are quite regular and consistent in their changes, and rarely will a sound change in one word only. Rather, that sound will change in the same way in all words where it appears. Linguistic rules such as this have been applied to the Algonkian Indian language family, whose speakers are still found from the Atlantic to the Pacific. By comparing a considerable number of words from the various Algonkian languages, and by studying the changes that took place from one language to another, linguists have reconstructed a Proto-Algonkian language that at least closely approximates the ancestor of the modern Algonkian language family. For example, a linguistic analysis of the sound shifts that produced the Fox *noohkomesa,* Ojibwa *nookkomiss,* Cree *noohkom,* and Menomini *noohkomeh* —all meaning "my grandmother"—has allowed linguists to postulate that the Proto-Algonkian ancestor of these was *noohkomehsa.*

Most of the developments that occur in a language are in its vocabulary. By inventing a new noun such as "radioactivity," the English vocabulary has been enriched but the language itself has not changed. And even though "belike" is now obsolete, the English language has not changed in any major way since the time when the word was in common use. The sounds of a language are much less subject to change than the vocabulary, and the over-all structure of the language— its grammar—usually changes very slowly. These principles apply equally to unwritten languages, even though the Europeans' sense of cultural superiority usually leads them to maintain that unwritten languages change more rapidly than written ones. As a matter of fact, during the past four centuries Spanish has changed much more than Nahuatl, the language of the Aztec state and of many Mexicans who still speak it today.

AT THE MERCY OF LANGUAGE?

Linguistically speaking, humans are not born free. We inherit a language whose rules of usage are already established; even more important, we inherit certain set forms of expression that may shackle our thoughts. Some linguists believe that a language may thus become a shaper of ideas rather than simply a tool for reporting them. The Americans' conventional words for directions, for example, sometimes limit their ability to read maps. It is an apt youngster indeed who can immediately grasp that the *Upper* Nile is in the *south* of Egypt and the *Lower* Nile is in the *north* of Egypt. Another example: English has only two demonstrative pronouns (*this* and *that,* together with their plurals) for referring either to something near or to something far away. The Tlingit Indians of the Northwest Coast can be much more specific. If they want to refer to an object very near and always present, they say *he*; by *ya* they mean an object also near and present, but a little farther away; by *yu* they refer to something still farther away, and by *we* to an object so far away as to be out of sight. So the question arises whether even the most outspoken members of American society can "speak their minds." Actually, for certain subjects they have very few channels into which their thoughts can flow.

The effect of culture upon language becomes clear from a comparison of the ways in which the English and Hopi languages refer to H_2O in its liquid state. English, like most other European languages, has only one word —*water*—which is the same regardless of the quantity of the substance or the use to which it is put. The Hopi of Arizona, on the other hand, use *pahe* to mean the large amounts of water present in natural lakes or rivers, and *keyi* for the small amounts in jugs and canteens. Speakers of English, on the other hand, make distinctions that speakers of Hopi do not. The speaker of English is careful to distinguish between a lake and a stream, between a waterfall and a geyser; but *pahe* makes no distinction among lakes, ponds, rivers, streams, waterfalls, and springs.

Hopi speakers know, of course, that a geyser, which spurts upward, and a waterfall, which plunges downward, are not the same, even though their vocabulary makes no such distinction. Similarly, a speaker of English knows that a canteen of water differs from a river. But the real point of this comparison is that neither the Hopi nor the speaker of English uses anywhere near the possible number of words that could be applied to water in all of its quantities, forms, physical states, and functions. Such words number in the hundreds and would hopelessly encumber the language. So, speakers prevent the language from becoming unwieldy by grouping different kinds of water into a small number of categories. Each culture defines the categories in terms of similarities detected; multitudes of ideas are channeled into a few categories that are considered important. Speakers of American English grow up in a culture in which it seems important to distinguish between oceans, lakes, rivers, fountains, and waterfalls—

but relatively unimportant to make the distinction between the water contained in a canteen lying in a canoe
and the body of water underneath the same canoe. In
each culture, experience has been categorized through
language in ways that offer commentaries on the differences and similarities between societies.

The possibility of a strong causal relationship between language and culture has been formulated into a
hypothesis by two American linguists, Edward Sapir
and Benjamin Lee Whorf. According to Sapir, humans
do not live in the midst of the whole world, but only in
a part of it, the part that language permits them to
know. They are, says Sapir, "very much at the mercy
of the particular language which has become the me-
dium of expression" for their group. The real world is
therefore "to a large extent unconsciously built up on
the language habits of the group . . . The worlds in
which different societies live are distinct worlds, not
merely the same world with different labels attached."‡
To Sapir and Whorf, language provides a different network of tracks for each society, which, as a result,
concentrates on only certain aspects of reality.

Every language can receive or transmit any message
from any other language. This is not, though, the same
thing as saying that every language can transmit the
same message with equal ease. A controversy has gone
on for several decades over whether people who speak
different languages therefore necessarily think differently and inhabit different conceptual worlds. The
Sapir–Whorf hypothesis maintains that the differences
between languages are much more than mere obstacles
to communication; they represent basic differences in
the "world view" of the various peoples and in what
they understand about their environment.

The Eskimo can draw upon an inventory of about
twenty very precise words for indicating subtle differences in a snowstorm. About the best a speaker of
English can manage is to distinguish wet snow, powdery
snow, sleet, hail, and ice. Similarly, to most speakers
of English, a seal is simply a seal, and they have only
that one word to describe it; whoever wants to say anything else about the seal, for example concerning its

sex or its color, will have to put an adjective before the word *seal*. But the Eskimo have a large choice of words with which to denote various aspects of sealdom, and which translates as "a young swimming seal," "a male harbor seal," "an old harbor seal," and so forth. A somewhat similar situation exists in English with the word *horse*. This animal may also be referred to as a *chestnut*, a *bay mare*, or a *stallion*, and by other words that one would not expect to find in the vocabulary of the horseless Eskimo.

The Eskimo are, of course, preoccupied with seals, a primary food source for them, whereas some speakers of English seem to be concerned with the exact particulars of the domesticated horse. The real question is: Do these different vocabularies force the Eskimo and the speaker of English to conceptualize and classify information in different ways? Can the Eskimo look at a horse and classify it in their own minds as a "bay mare"? Or, because they lack the words, are they forever blind to the fact that this kind of animal exists? The answer is that with a little practice an Eskimo can learn to tell apart the different kinds of horses, just as an American can learn about the various seals, even though their respective languages lack the necessary vocabularies. So vocabulary alone does not reveal, or set cultural limits to, the thinking of a people.

But does the totality of the language tell anything about the people who speak it? To answer that, look at the English verb *grab*. A speaker of English says, *I grab it, I grabbed it, I will grab it*, and so on. Only the context of the situation tells the listener what is being grabbed and how the grabbing is done. *I grab it* is a vague sentence, in all ways except one. Speakers of English are concerned with the tense of the verb—with specifying whether the grabbing is going on now, or took place at some time in the past, or will be a future event. Speakers of the English language are, in their culture as well, preoccupied with time: They take great interest in calendars and in record-keeping, diaries, history, almanacs, stock-market forecasts, astrological predictions, and knowing, throughout every minute of the waking day, the precise time.

No such statement as *I grab it* would be possible in Navajo. To the Navajo, tense is of little importance; but their language is considerably more discriminating in other ways. It conveys much more about the person denoted by the pronoun "I" in the sentence in question: for example, whether the "I" initiated an action by reaching out to grab an inanimate thing, or instead grabbed at a horse racing by. Nor would the Navajo be content merely with a verb meaning simply "to grab." Their verb would have to tell the listener whether the thing being grabbed is big or little, animate or inanimate. Finally, a Navajo could not say simply "it"; the thing being grabbed would have to be described much more precisely and put in a category. (If you get the feeling that Navajo is exceedingly difficult for speakers of many other languages, you are correct. During World War II, the United States armed forces sent secret radio messages in Navajo, with the Indians themselves serving as senders and receivers. There was no danger of being decoded—for the reason that a language, unlike a code, cannot be broken but must be learned.)

From this example and other linguistic observations concerning the Navajo, its speakers would appear to be exceptionally exact in their perception of the elements that make up their universe. But is this a true picture of the Navajo? Do they perceive their world any differently from a White American? Anthropological and psychological studies of the Navajo show that they do. They visualize themselves as living in an eternal and unchanging universe made up of physical, social, and supernatural forces, among which they try to maintain a balance. Any accidental failure to observe rules or rituals can disturb this balance and result in some misfortune. Navajo curing ceremonies, which include the well-known art of sandpainting, are designed to put the individual back into harmony with the universe. To the Navajo, the good life consists of maintaining intact all the complex relationships of the universe. And so we might expect them to speak a language that made the most exacting discriminations.

Several words of caution are necessary, though, about the Sapir–Whorf hypothesis. Whorf concentrated his studies on a comparison of the language and culture of the Hopi Indians with European languages and culture. Among other things, Whorf concluded that European cultures are preoccupied with time, Hopi culture hardly at all. Further, he observed that the tense system of English and most other European languages makes it easier to measure time than does the Hopi language, which has no equivalent of past, present, and future tenses. From this he postulated a causal relationship between language and culture. But one objection to Whorf's conclusions is that a three-tense system is not firmly established in English. No specific verb form exists for the future tense, and to convey it the speaker of English must use such auxiliaries as *will* and *shall*. Also, speakers of English frequently use the present tense to convey the future, as in *I'm taking the train tonight*.

A more important objection to Whorf's conclusions is that no causal connection has been found between a language's emphasis on tenses and a cultural emphasis on time. Timekeeping devices are undoubtedly a feature of modern European and European-derived cultures, while such devices were largely absent in the primeval Hopi culture. But a preoccupation with time-keeping has also been associated with peoples whose languages are as diverse as ancient Egyptian, Mayan, and Chinese. Actually, the Chinese contributed as much to the invention of the mechanical clock as the Europeans did; so it is reckless to attribute the Europeans' concern with time to the languages they speak. Nor can language be shown to have been a determining force in other areas of culture. It is not true of religion; speakers from the same Indo-European language family adhere to a variety of faiths, among them Protestantism, Catholicism, Judaism, and Hinduism. Nor is it true of economic institutions; industrial capitalism has flourished in both Japan and the United States, whose peoples speak unrelated languages.

The Sapir–Whorf hypothesis has served to emphasize the fact that language is an important part of the total culture. The hypothesis suggests that language is more than a way of communicating. It is a living system that is a part of the cultural equipment of a group, and it reveals the character of a culture at least as much as do spear points, kinship groups, or political institutions. Language alerts the perceptions of its speakers to certain things; it gives them ways to analyze and to categorize experience. Such perceptions are unconscious and outside the control of the speaker. The ultimate value of the Sapir–Whorf hypothesis is that it offers hints for detecting cultural differences and similarities among peoples, such as are the concern of this book.

Part Three

□

Societies Under Stress

XIII

The End of the Trail

FIRST ENCOUNTERS

Much has been written about the genocide practiced by Whites upon Indians through warfare and by the deliberate spread of disease; through physically removing large populations to desert wastes and psychologically breaking their spirit; through destroying the bison, to empty their stomachs; and through tearing apart their cultures, to empty their hearts of hope. It is not the purpose of this book to add to that vast literature. But in order to understand the total experience of the native American—and also to understand the chapters that follow, about what happens to cultures as they disintegrate—something must be said about the changing relations between Whites and Indians.

The expectations of the Spaniards for the New World were, at first, certainly high. One historian in the early 1500's declared that the discovery of America was the most important event since the coming of Jesus. Their expectations were also distorted by medieval legends and by fanciful notions that may unconsciously have influenced their attitudes toward the inhabitants of the New World. Columbus, and other explorers as well, fully expected to encounter the mythical beings depicted in medieval literature: giants, pygmies, dragons, bearded females, and other fabulous creatures. When Columbus landed in 1493 on the island of Hispaniola (that is, present-day Haiti and the Dominican Republic), he questioned the Indians about the monsters to be found there; and in 1522, Cortés sent back to Emperor Charles V not only booty but also samples of bones reputed to be those of giants. Given such notions, we should not be surprised that Cortés was commissioned to look in Mexico for certain strange beings with great flat ears, and for others having doglike faces—or that the Devil himself was reputedly living on an island in the Caribbean.‡

Aside from the Norse encounter with the Eskimo, the first report of an encounter with native Americans is by Columbus. He described the Taino branch of the Arawak Indians of the Caribbean as children of nature, "who invite you to share anything that they possess, and show as much love as if their hearts went with it." Indeed, Columbus was supposed to reciprocate such love, for when he left on his second voyage in 1493, he was specifically enjoined by Ferdinand and Isabella that the Indians should be "treated very well and lovingly." But in their haste to exploit the new abundance of the Americas, the Spaniards set the loving and sharing Arawak to labor in mines and on plantations. Whole Arawak villages disappeared as a result of slavery, disease, and warfare, as well as flight into the mountains. Even though Columbus had time and again asserted that the Arawak were the most kindly, peaceful, and generous people in the world, in 1496 he and his brother collected 1,500 of them for shipment back to Spain as slaves. Of these, the four available ships could carry only 500. So Columbus allowed Spanish settlers and officers to help themselves to as many of the remainder as they chose, after which those Indians still left over were told to flee. And flee they did, mothers even abandoning infants in their desperate fear of further cruelty. But at least these became free, if only for a while. The lot of the slaves shipped back to Spain was much worse. Many died en route. After landing at Seville, the survivors were put up for sale. One witness states that almost all of these died also, "for the country did not agree with them." Nevertheless, the slave trade in Indians continued. Given the treatment they received, it is no wonder that the native population of Haiti, for example, declined from an estimated 200,000 in 1492 to 29,000 only twenty-two years later.‡

The earliest responses of Indians and Whites to one another were inquisitive, yet wary, on both sides. Some Europeans at first were not certain that the Indians were truly human beings, and so King Ferdinand approved the importation of white women into the West Indies to prevent the Spaniards from mating with native women, "who are far from being rational creatures." But in 1537 the Pope proclaimed "that the Indians are truly men, and that they are not only capable of understanding the Catholic faith but, according to our information, they desire exceedingly to receive it." Even so, the debate continued between those supporting the papal bull and those who insisted that the Indians "should be treated as dumb brutes created for our service." The full intellectual resources of both sides were gathered at Valladolid, Spain, in 1550 to debate the issue, but neither side was able to convince the other.‡

Nor were the Indians certain what to make of the Whites. A Spanish chronicler reported that some Indians in the Caribbean islands drowned Whites they captured. They then stood guard over the corpses for weeks—to determine whether the dead were gods or were subject to putrefaction like other mortals. The contrasting attitudes of the Spaniards and the Indians point up the basic difference in expectations between the two cultures. The Whites treated the Indians like animals; the Indians suspected the Whites might be gods. Both were wrong, but the attitude of the Indians was more flattering.

Wherever the Whites penetrated, the Indian populations went into drastic decline. Probably no one will ever know for sure what the primeval population of the New World was. Not only has no agreement been reached about the total number, but the estimates cover such a wide range that no consensus appears possible. For North America (including Mexico and the Caribbean Islands) one conservative and long accepted figure was slightly over four million. Even most older archeologists, who had tended to underestimate the cultural achievements of the Indians, rarely thought in terms of a figure lower than two or three times that. In recent years, old evidence has been re-evaluated and new evidence has come to light, with the result that anthropologists have tended to raise these figures considerably. A recent attempt to estimate the total native population of Mexico just before the Spanish conquest, using a variety of techniques, gives a figure of somewhere between 30,000,000 and 37,000,000. And estimates of the Indian and Eskimo population from the Rio Grande River to the Arctic have been put at between 9,800,000 and 12,500,000.‡

Those archeologists opposed to such high figures argue that the Indians' technology could not support so great a population. They also have questioned whether such large numbers could possibly have been descended from what must have been the very small bands who crossed the Bering land bridge. But such an increase is indeed possible. One conservative calculation supposes that the total population of the bands that arrived in North America only 15,000 years ago was a mere four hundred adults of reproductive age. If this small number reproduced a new generation every twenty years, and if the population grew annually at the rate of a mere 1.4 percent (which is considerably less than the worldwide rate of population growth today), then ten million descendants would be alive now. Of course, very many more than four hundred adult migrants no doubt crossed from Asia, and they almost certainly did so longer ago than 15,000 years, thus giving more time to increase their numbers. Moreover, in the rich environment of the New World, where they encountered no competition from other humans, they must have increased at a rate considerably higher than 1.4 percent.

The extent of the Europeans' destruction of Indian numbers and cultures is attested by the long roll of groups that have become extinct, and by the small total number of survivors, among whom a considerable proportion are of mixed blood. The Aleut, who inhabit the

Aleutian Islands of Alaska, numbered upward of 20,000 people before they came into contact with White trading ships. Today a few thousand survive, living in scattered villages at river mouths, and their decline continues. For the Indian populations in the area comprising the forty-nine continental United States, the low point was reached about 1900 when the total fell to some 235,000. Since then the Indians have made a remarkable comeback—in numbers, if not in social and economic gains. The 1970 census puts the Indian population of the forty-nine states at nearly 800,000—without taking into account several hundred thousand others, who live away from reservations in urban areas or who are of mixed blood and do not choose to be classified as Indians. In addition, a total of approximately 225,000 Indians and Eskimos have been registered by various Canadian agencies.‡

After the White conquerors, who brought about large numbers of Indian deaths either directly or through inciting one Indian group to fight another, the greatest cause of death was disease. This was primarily in the form of smallpox, measles, and typhus, which have been called "the shock troops of conquest." Cuba and Hispaniola, for example, early suffered a smallpox epidemic which a Spanish chronicler at the time stated did not leave a thousand Indians alive out of the hundreds of thousands that once populated these islands. In 1585 Sir Francis Drake carried a highly contagious fever, probably typhus, to Florida—with the result, according to the chronicles of his expedition, that "the wilde people died verie faste and said amongst themselves, it was the Inglisshe God that made them die so faste." And so it was with the Indians of North America wherever the Whites made contact. In 1616 a pestilence swept through New England that, in the words of Cotton Mather, "cleared the woods of those pernicious creatures to make room for better growth." The Indians were almost completely wiped out in the area around Plymouth Bay at just about the time the Pilgrims were making plans to sail to the New World. The diseases spread like forest fires into the interior, far ahead of

the advancing Whites. The Iroquois, for example, probably lost more than half of their population through
epidemics in the 1630's and 1640's.

The native inhabitants of North America—isolated
from the rest of the world for many thousands of years
—possessed no immunity to numerous Old World diseases, and they died by the millions. The natural immunity of a population against any disease is maintained
by the constant presence of the organisms that cause it.
Exposure to these organisms, generation after generation, builds up a degree of resistance in individuals, and
thus in the population as a whole, that prevents the
disease from being as virulent as it would be in a population without a long history of exposure. The Paleo-
Indians presumably carried very few diseases with them
into the New World, since whatever infectious microbes
they started out with would most likely have been killed
during the passage across the "cold filter" of the land
bridge. Furthermore, the migrants would have found no
other humans in the New World who might pass on
disease organisms to them. For tens of thousands of
years, the Indians must have existed virtually free of
Old World diseases. As one specialist in the history of
diseases has written: "When the isolation of the New
World was broken, when Columbus brought the two
halves of the planet together, the American Indian met
for the first time his most hideous enemy: not the white
man nor his black servant, but the invisible killers which
those men brought in their blood and breath."‡

In addition to murder, starvation, and disease, another
reason that the Indian populations plummeted so drastically can be found in the physical and emotional stress
to which they were exposed. The effects of stress on
human populations still are not completely understood,
but it is known beyond doubt that they are deleterious.
World War II provided clear evidence of this. About
25,000 American soldiers became prisoners of the
Japanese; they were much more inhumanely treated
than the American prisoners in European camps. The
Japanese abused them mentally and physically, and
sapped them of all human dignity; more than a third of

the Americans died in prison, as compared with less than one percent of American prisoners who died in European camps. Six years after their liberation from the Japanese camps, a study was made of what had become of a group of former prisoners. The death rate for these men was twice that of males who had not been imprisoned—but who were otherwise comparable in age, ethnic origins, stature, and so on—even though the causes of death were not related directly to imprisonment. Twice the number that would statistically have been expected had died of cancer, more than four times as many of gastrointestinal diseases, and nine times as many of tuberculosis. Mercilessly uprooted and driven from their lands, torn from their families, finally to be herded like cattle onto reservations, the American Indians must equally have been decimated as a result of stress.‡

THE NOBLE RED MAN AND
THE BLOODTHIRSTY SAVAGE

Two contrasting images of the Indian—as Noble Red Man and as Bloodthirsty Savage—have prevailed in the minds of Whites over the past five hundred years, and attitudes have tended to shift back and forth between the two images. Columbus brought home six Indians to show to Queen Isabella. Dressed in their full regalia and decorated with war paint, the five who survived the voyage quickly became the curiosities of Spain. In England, Sir Walter Raleigh brought Chief Manteo to visit Queen Elizabeth; she was so delighted with the Indian that she dubbed him Lord of Roanoke. An Indian craze took hold in Elizabethan England, and Shakespeare had the jester Trinculo complain about it in *The Tempest*: "When they will not give a doit [a small coin equal to about half a farthing] to relieve a lame beggar, they will lay out ten to see a dead Indian."

After their initial confusion over what to make of these inhabitants of the New World, certain philosophers—most of them French—entertained a romantic view. Europeans had often thought that somewhere in

the world must dwell a noble race, remnants of that
golden age before humankind became corrupted by
civilization. As reports of Indians filtered back to
Europe, a distinguished French philosopher of the late
sixteenth century, Michel de Montaigne, took the trouble
to talk with explorers, to read the travelers' chronicles,
and even to meet three Indians who had been brought
as curiosities to the Court of Versailles. He concluded
that the Noble Savage had at last been found, for the
Indian "hath no kind of traffic, no knowledge of letters,
no intelligence of numbers, no name of magistrate, nor
of politics, no use of service, of riches, or of poverty;
no contracts, no successions, no partitions, no occupation but idle, no apparel but natural, no manuring of
lands, no use of wine. The very words that import a
lie, falsehood, treason, covetousness, envy, detraction,
were not heard among them."‡ Montaigne presented an
idealized picture about the inhabitants of the New World
that foreshadowed the Noble Savage of Jean Jacques
Rousseau.

By the seventeenth century, many writers were taking
special plans to salute the Noble Red Man. The Jesuit
missionary Bressani, who served in Canada from 1645
to 1649, reported that the inhabitants "are hardly barbarous, save in name. There is no occasion to think of
them as half beasts, shaggy, black and hideous." He
goes on to comment on the Indians' tenacious memory,
their "marvelous faculty for remembering places, and
for describing them to one another." An Indian, Bressani states, can recall things that a White "could not
rehearse without writing." Another Jesuit enthusiastically corroborates him by stating that the Indians
"nearly all show more intelligence in their business,
speeches, courtesies, intercourse, tricks and subtleties,
than do the shrewdest citizens and merchants in
France."‡

The Noble Red Man captivated Europe, but for those
colonists who lived on the advancing frontier, the widespread opinion was that the Indians were of an inferior
race. That did not prevent colonists from believing, at
first, that the Indians might seek salvation, and that
civilization, European style, could be conferred as a

blessing upon them. Only a few years after the permanent settlement of Virginia, some fifty missionaries arrived to begin the massive task of converting the heathen. The Indians, for their part, did not respond with alacrity to the idea of adopting a culture that to them seemed in many ways so barbarous. Furthermore, they increasingly resented the encroachments by Whites upon their lands: In an uprising as early as 1622, the Indians of Virginia killed about 350 colonists. When the Pequots resisted the migration of settlers into the Connecticut valley in 1637, a party of Puritans surrounded the Pequot village and set fire to it. About five hundred Indians were either burned to death or shot while trying to escape; the Whites devoutly offered up thanks to God that they had lost only two men. The woods were then combed for any Pequots who had managed to survive, and these were sold into slavery. Cotton Mather was grateful to the Lord that "on this day we have sent six hundred heathen souls to hell."

The Puritans failed miserably in their dealings with the Indians of New England. Scarcely a glimmer of kindness illuminates black page after black page of cruelty and humiliation. Many reasons can be found to explain why the Puritans outdid even the Spanish and the French in cruelty. The Puritans insisted upon a higher standard of religious devotion than the Indians were able or willing to give. The Puritans lacked any way to integrate the Indians into their theocracy, for they did not indulge in wholesale baptisms (as they charged the Spanish and French with doing), nor were any Puritans specifically assigned to missionary tasks. The heart of the matter, though, is that conversion of the heathen was not one of the compelling motives—or justifications—for the Puritan settlement of New England, as it was for the Spaniards in the Southwest. The contempt with which Puritans regarded Indians is revealed in this order from the General Court of the Colony of Massachusetts Bay in 1644:

It was ordered that noe Indian shall come att any towne or howse of the English (without leave) uppon the Lords day, except to attend the publike meeteings; neither shall they come att any English howse uppon any other day in the weeke, but first shall knocke att the dore, and after leave given, to come in (and not otherwise) . . .‡

The desire of Whites to occupy Indian lands, and the constant rivalry between French and English traders for the furs gathered by the Indians, led to many skirmishes and several bloody wars, all of which involved Indians on both sides. The Whites were determined to fight it out—down to the last Indian. These battles culminated in the French and Indian War of 1763, which represented a disaster to many Indian groups in the northeastern part of the continent. Lord Jeffery Amherst, who commanded the British military forces in North America at the time, debated with his subordinates the relative advantages of hunting Indians down with dogs or infecting them with smallpox. Dogs were not available, so officers distributed among the Indians handkerchiefs and blankets from the smallpox hospital at Fort Pitt—possibly the first use in history of biological warfare. Clearly, a sharp turn away from the glorification of the Noble Savage had taken place.

The Indian came to be regarded as a stubborn animal that had refused the obvious blessings of White civilization. The idea of the Bloodthirsty Savage took hold, and the same relentless pattern was repeated—across Pennsylvania, Ohio, Virginia, and Kentucky, across the whole western frontier as the new United States came into being. Hugh Henry Brackenridge, a modest literary figure of the young nation, stood for the changed attitude when he wrote in 1782 of ". . . the animals, vulgarly called Indians." Rousseau's Noble Savage was laid to rest when John Adams stated in 1790: "I am not of Rousseau's Opinions. His Notions of the purity of Morals in savage nations and the earliest Ages of civilized Nations are mere Chimeras." Even that man of enlightened homilies, Benjamin Franklin, observed that rum should be regarded as an agent of Providence "to extirpate these savages in order to make room for the cultivators of the earth."

THE GREAT REMOVAL

Following the War of 1812, the United States had no further need to woo the Indians as potential allies against the British, and as a result the fortunes of the Indians declined rapidly. By 1848, twelve new states had been carved out of the Indians' lands, two major and many minor Indian wars had been fought, and group after group of Indians had been herded westward, on forced marches, across the Mississippi River. To Senator Thomas Hart Benton of Missouri, the justification for such actions was obvious: The Whites must supplant Indians because Whites used the land "according to the intentions of the Creator." Some spoke of the benefits to the Indians of removing them from contact with Whites, which would give them the time to assimilate at their own pace the blessings of civilization. A senator from Georgia, hoping to expedite the removal of Indians from his state to what was later to become Oklahoma, glowingly described that territory as a place "over which Flora has scattered her beauties with a wanton hand; and upon whose bosom innumerable wild animals display their amazing numbers."

Such statements do not mean that the Indians lacked defenders, but the degree of their indignation was in direct proportion to the speaker's distance from the Indian. On the frontier, the Indian was regarded as a besotted savage; along the eastern seaboard, where the Spaniards, Dutch, English, and later the Americans had long since exterminated almost all the Indians, philosophers and divines began to defend the Red Man. In response to Georgia's extirpation of its Indian population, Ralph Waldo Emerson protested: "The soul of man, the justice, the mercy that is the heart's heart in all men, from Maine to Georgia, does abhor this business." Jefferson, Monroe, and Adams, all of whom came from the eastern states, occasionally displayed some scruples about the treatment the Indian was receiving. Thomas Jefferson, though, shortly before his death stated that the White presence should be credited with assisting in the cultural evolution of the Indians:

Let a philosophic observer commence a journey from the savages of the Rocky Mountains, eastwardly towards our seacoast. These he would observe in the earliest stage of association living under no law but that of nature, subsisting and covering themselves with the flesh and skin of wild beasts. He would next find those on our frontiers in the pastoral state, raising domestic animals to supply the defects of hunting. Then succeed our own semi-barbarous citizens, the pioneers of the advance of civilization, and so in his progress he would meet the gradual shades of improving man until he would reach his, as yet, most improved state in our seaport towns. This, in fact, is equivalent to a survey, in time, of the progress of man from the infancy of creation to the present day.‡

President Andrew Jackson, though, had been reared on the frontier and was utterly insensitive to the treatment of the Indians. He denounced as an "absurdity" and a "farce" that the United States should bother even to negotiate treaties as if Indians were independent nations with a right to their lands. Completely in sympathy with the policy of removing the eastern Indians to west of the Mississippi, he exerted his influence to make Congress give legal sanction to what in our own time, under the Nuremberg Laws, would be branded as genocide. Congress dutifully passed the Removal Act of 1830, which gave the President the right to remove the eastern Indians. The entire venture was estimated to cost no more than $500,000—the expenses to be kept low by persuasion, promises, threats, and the bribery of Indian leaders. When U. S. Supreme Court Justice John Marshall ruled in favor of the Cherokee in a case with wide implications for protecting the Indians, Jackson is said to have remarked: "John Marshall has made his decision, now let him enforce it."

During the following ten years, most (but not all) of the Indians were cleared from the eastern states. The Chickasaw and Choctaw went resignedly, but others left only at bayonet point. The Seminole actively resisted and some retreated into the Florida swamps, where they stubbornly held off the United States Army. The Seminole Wars lasted from 1835 to 1842, costing the United States some 1,500 soldiers and about $20,000,000 (or forty times what Jackson had estimated it would cost to remove all the Indians). Many of the Oneida and the Seneca were moved westward, but fragments of Iroquois tribes managed to remain behind in western New York and many found sanctuary in Canada. The Sac and the Fox made a desperate stand in Illinois against overwhelming numbers of Whites, but ultimately their survivors also were forced to move, as were the Ottawa, Potawatomie, Wyandot, Shawnee, Kickapoo, Winnebago, Delaware, Peoria, Miami, and many others who are remembered now only in the name of some town, lake, county, or state, or as a footnote in the annals of a local historical society. All in all, an estimated seventy thousand Indians are believed to have been resettled west of the Mississippi, but the number may have been closer to one hundred thousand. No figures exist, though, on the numbers massacred before they could be persuaded to leave or on the tremendous losses suffered from disease, exposure, and starvation during the trip westward, in some cases a thousand miles, across a largely unsettled and inhospitable land.‡

Some of the Indians who were forced west of the Mississippi might with justification be regarded as "savages," but this could not be said of the Cherokee. Around 1790 the Cherokee Nation decided to adopt the ways of their White conquerors and to emulate their morals, their learning, and their arts. They did so in a remarkably brief period. In their homeland in the mountains where Georgia, Tennessee, and North Carolina meet, they established churches, mills, schools, and well-cultivated farms. Judging from descriptions of that time, the region was a paradise as compared with the bleak landscape that their White successors have made of Appalachia today. In 1826 a Cherokee reported to the Presbyterian Church that his people already possessed 22,000 cattle, 7,600 houses, 46,000 swine, 2,500 sheep, 762 looms, 1,488 spinning wheels, 2,948 plows, 10 sawmills, 31 grist mills, 62 blacksmith shops, and 18 schools. Just one of the Cherokee districts owned some 1,000 books. In 1821, after twelve years of hard work, a Cherokee named Sequoya (honored in the scientific names for both the redwood and the giant sequoia trees of California, three thousand miles from his homeland) perfected a method of syllabary notation in which English letters stood for Cherokee syllables; by 1828 the Cherokee were already publishing their own newspaper. At about the same time, they adopted a written constitution providing for an executive, a bicameral legislature, a supreme court, and a code of laws.

Before the passage of the Removal Act of 1830, a group of Cherokee chiefs went to the Senate committee that was studying this legislation to report on what they had already achieved in the short space of forty years. They expressed the hope that they would be permitted to enjoy in peace "the blessings of civilization and Christianity on the soil of their rightful inheritance." Instead, they were daily subjected to brutality by White neighbors, harassed by the government of Georgia, cajoled and bribed by federal agents to agree to removal, and denied even the basic protection of the United States government. Finally, in 1835, members of a minority faction—five hundred Cherokee out of a total of some twenty thousand—signed a treaty agreeing to the removal of the entire tribe. The Removal Act was carried out almost everywhere with a notable lack of mercy, but in the case of the Cherokee—civilized and Christianized as they were—is was particularly brutal.

After many threats, about five thousand finally consented to be marched westward. But another fifteen thousand clung to their neat farms, schools, and libraries. So General Winfield Scott set about systematically extirpating the rebellious ones. Squads of soldiers descended upon isolated Cherokee farms and at bayonet point marched the families off to what in our day would be known as concentration camps. Torn from their homes, the families had no time to prepare for the arduous trip ahead of them. No way existed for the Cherokee family to sell its property and possessions, and the local Whites fell upon the lands, looting, burning, and finally taking possession.

Some Cherokee managed to escape into the gorges and thick forests of the Great Smoky Mountains, where they became the nucleus of those living there today, but most were finally rounded up or killed. They then were set off on a thousand-mile march—called to this day "the trail of tears" by the Cherokee—that was one of the notable death marches in history. Ill clad, badly fed, lacking medical attention, and prodded on by soldiers wielding bayonets, the Indians suffered terrible losses. An estimate made at the time, that some four thousand Cherokee died en route, is almost certainly too low. At the very moment when these people were dying in droves, President Van Buren solemnly reported to Congress that the government's handling of the Indian problem had been "just and friendly throughout; its efforts for their civilization constant, and directed by the best feelings of humanity; its watchfulness in protecting them from individual frauds unremitting."

One man who examined the young United States with a perceptive eye and who wrote it all down in his *Democracy in America*, Alexis de Tocqueville, happened to be in Memphis when the thermometer hovered near zero. There he saw a ragged party of Choctaw, some of the thousands who had reluctantly agreed to be transported to the new lands in the western part of what was then the Arkansas Territory. Wrote Tocqueville:

It was then the middle of winter, and the cold was unusually severe; the snow had frozen hard upon the ground and the river was drifting huge masses of ice. The Indians had their families with them, and they brought in their train the wounded and the sick, with children newly born and old men upon the verge of death. They possessed neither tents nor wagons, but only their arms and some provisions. I saw them embark to pass the mighty river, and never will that solemn spectacle fade from my remembrance. No cry, no sob, was heard among the assembled crowd; all was silent. Their calamities were of ancient date, and they knew them to be irremediable.‡

Tocqueville was a discerning observer of the methods used to deal with the Indians, and he described with restrained outrage their treatment by government agents: ". . . half convinced and half compelled, they go to inhabit new deserts, where the importunate whites will not let them remain ten years in peace. In this manner do the Americans obtain, at a very low price, whole provinces, which the richest sovereigns of Europe could not purchase." Reporting that a mere 6,273 Indians still survived in the thirteen original states, he predicted accurately the fate of the Indians in their new homes across the Mississippi:

The countries to which the newcomers betake themselves are inhabited by other tribes, which receive them with jealous hostility. Hunger is in the rear, war awaits them, and misery besets them on all sides. To escape from so many enemies, they separate, and each individual endeavors to procure secretly the means of supporting his existence.

Long before the science of anthropology and the study of what today is politely called "culture change," Tocqueville understood that an entire culture might become unraveled like some ripped fabric:

The social tie, which distress had long since weakened, is then dissolved; they have no longer a country, and soon they will not be a people; their very families are obliterated; their common name is forgotten; their language perishes; and all traces of their origin disappear. Their nation has ceased to exist except in the recollections of the antiquaries of America and a few of the learned of Europe.

The great removal was not the panacea its advocates in Congress had promised it would be. The different game animals in the West required new skills in hunting. To make matters worse, the Plains Indians, who had been inveigled into giving up some of their lands to make room for the eastern Indians, were hostile toward the newcomers, asserting that they had driven away the bison. Clashes between various groups became increasingly common. The Chickasaw, who had agreed to removal, protested that they could not take up the land assigned to them because of their fear of the "wild tribes" already inhabiting it. The United States government no more honored its obligation to protect Indians in their new territory than it had honored any of its previous obligations toward them. In 1834 fewer than three thousand troops were available along the entire frontier to maintain order and to protect the newcomers against the Plains tribes. The result was that the very Indians whose removal had been ordered ostensibly to pacify and to civilize them were forced once more to take up their old warrior ways simply to defend themselves.

THE LAST STAND

The plight of the Indian west of the Mississippi River was only a sad, monotonous duplication of what had happened east of it—warfare, broken treaties, expropriation of land, rebellion, and ultimately defeat. No sooner were the eastern Indians dropped down on the plains than the United States discovered the natural resources of the West. Miners and settlers were on the move, emigrant trains rumbled across the plains, and once again the aim of the frontiersman was to get the Indian out of the way. A Kansas newspaper summarized the general feeling about Indians in the middle of the last century: "A set of miserable, dirty, lousy, blanketed, thieving, lying, sneaking, murdering, graceless, faithless, gut-eating skunks as the Lord ever permitted to infect the earth, and whose immediate and final extermination all men, except Indian agents and traders, should pray for." The "extermination" was hastened by epidemics that swept the West and sapped the Indians' power to resist. A mere hundred Mandan out of a population of sixteen hundred survived a smallpox epidemic; the same epidemic, spreading westward, reduced the total number of Blackfoot Indians by about half. The majority of Kiowa and Comanche Indians were victims of cholera. The Indians would have been crushed by Whites in any event, but diseases made the job easier.

Up to 1868, nearly four hundred treaties had been signed by the United States with various Indian groups, and scarcely one had remained unbroken. The Indians finally realized that these treaties were real-estate deals designed to separate them from their lands. In the last three decades of the nineteenth century, Indians and Whites skirmished and then fought openly, with barbarous ferocity on both sides. Group by group, the Indians rose in rebellion only to be crushed—the southern Plains tribes in 1874, the Sioux in 1876, the Nez Perce in 1877, the Cheyenne and Bannock in 1878, the Ute in 1879, and the Apache throughout much of the 1880's until Geronimo finally surrendered with his remnant band of thirty-six warriors. These wars represented the final spasms of a people who had long before been defeated logistically and psychologically. General William Tecumseh Sherman attributed the final victory of the United States Army to the railroads, which were able to transport his troops as far in one day as they had been able formerly to march in a month. General Philip Henry Sheridan, on the other hand, had urged the destruction of the bison herds, correctly predicting that when they disappeared the Indians would disappear along with them. By 1885 the bison were virtually extinct, and the Indians were starving to death on the plains.

One way or another, the Indian Wars finally ended. And with the enforced peace came an economic recession in the West, for the United States government had spent there about one million dollars for every Indian killed by 1870. For nearly three centuries the frontier had lived under both the myth and the reality of the scalping knife and the tomahawk, and now the Bloodthirsty Savage was nearly gone. The Whites were in full control of the Indian situation, and the remnants were shifted about again and again, as many as five or six times. All of which led the Sioux chief Spotted Trail, grown old and wise, to ask the question: "Why does not the Great White Father put his red children on wheels, so he can move them as he will?"‡

A concern for the plight of the Indian developed in the eastern states after the Civil War. The sincere efforts of humanitarians were immediately seized upon by opportunists who developed a plan to use the Indian as a means of plundering the public coffers. A well-intentioned movement had gained support to give the remnant Indian populations the dignity of private property, and the plan was widely promoted in the halls of Congress, in the press, and in the meetings of religious societies. As a result, Senator Henry L. Dawes of Massachusetts sponsored the Dawes Allotment Act of 1887; he hoped it might salvage something for the Indians, who, he feared, would otherwise lose everything to voracious Whites. When President Grover Cleveland signed the act, he stated that the "hunger and thirst of the white man for the Indian's land is almost equal to his hunger and thirst after righteousness." The act provided that after every Indian had been allotted land, any surplus would be put up for sale to the public.

The loopholes with which the Dawes Act was riddled made it an efficient instrument for separating the Indians from this land. The act permitted Indians to lease their allotments, and many did so, ignorant of the value of the property. Indians were persuaded to write wills leaving their lands to White "friends." After this ploy became widespread, a suspicious increase in the number of Indian deaths from undetermined causes was observed; in some cases murder was proved. The plunder was carried out with remarkable efficiency. The first lands to go were the richest—bottom lands in river valleys or fertile grasslands. Next went the slightly less desirable lands, such as those that had to be logged before producing a bountiful crop. Then the marginal lands were taken, and so on, until all that was left to the Indians was desert that no White considered worth the trouble to take. The Indians did what they had always done: They shared the little they had and went hungry together. Between 1887, when the Dawes Act was passed, and 1934, out of the 138 million acres that had been their meager allotment, all but 56 million acres had been appropriated by Whites. The Bureau of Indian Affairs examined these remaining lands and concluded that 14 million acres were "critically eroded," 17 million acres "severely eroded," and 25 million acres "slightly eroded." Of the 56 million acres of land the Indians managed to hang onto, not a single acre was judged by soil conservationists to be uneroded.

The victory over the Bloodthirsty Savage—reduced in numbers, deprived of lands, broken in spirit, isolated on wasteland reservations—was complete except for one final indignity. That was to eliminate the Indians' last recollection of their ancient traditions—in short, to exterminate the cultures along with the people. Not very many of the Indian traditions were left to eradicate, but zealous Whites found something. Orders went out from Washington that male Indians must cut their hair short, even though many Indians believed that long hair had supernatural significance. The Indians refused, and the battle was joined. Army reinforcements were sent to the reservations to carry out the order, and in some cases Indians had to be shackled before they submitted.‡

Most of those who attempted to Americanize the Indians concentrated on the children, who were often taken from their families and sent to boarding schools far from their homes. In the Southwest, for example, the children usually were kept at boarding school for eight years, during which time they were not permitted to see their parents, relatives, or friends. Anything Indian—dress, language, religious practices, even outlook on life (and how that was defined was up to the judgment of each governmental administrator)—was uncompromisingly prohibited. Ostensibly educated, literate in the English language, wearing store-bought clothes, and with their hair short and their emotionalism toned down, the boarding-school graduates were sent out either to make their way in a White world that did not want them or to return to a reservation to which they were now foreign. The Indians had simply failed to melt into the great American melting pot.

This is the point at which to halt the story of the changing relations between Whites and Indians, for to all intents and purposes the diverse cultures of the North American Indians had been irreparably altered by early in the twentieth century. The White conquest was nearly complete, and the Indians were being remade in the White's image or else safely bottled up on reservations. It is for other books to describe the plight of the Indian in American society today—the median family income of about $30 a week, the average age at death nearly thirty years younger than for Whites, an infant mortality rate about twice that of White neighbors. And of the Indian infants that survive, one study has shown that about 500 of every 1,700 die in their first year of "preventable diseases."‡

In concluding this litany of abuses heaped upon the Indian, the temptation exists to utter pieties and homilies, to express compassion, to point an accusing finger. But perhaps it is better to remind the reader of an earlier time when the New World was truly new to Europeans, when the Spaniards and the English felt that they had at last found the "new heavens and a new earth" prophesied in Isaiah (65:17), when their Indian hosts were so bewildered by these strangers who seemed to possess much yet understand little. Most Americans know the story of Pocahontas and Captain John Smith, but not a moving speech that was made to Smith by Pocahontas' father, Powhatan:

I have seen two generations of my people die. Not a man of the two generations is alive now but myself . . . Why will you take by force what you may have quietly by love? Why will you destroy us who supply you with food? What can you get by war? We can hide our provisions and run into the woods; then you will starve for wronging your friends. Why are you so jealous of us? We are unarmed and willing to give you what you ask, if you come in a friendly manner, and not with swords and guns, as if to make war upon an enemy.‡

Powhatan's questions were never answered. Indeed, even today, historians are hard put to explain the unnecessary brutality and lack of compassion, not to mention the ignoring of their own self-interest, on the part of Whites.

XIV
Borrowed Cultures

THE DEBT TO THE INDIAN

Whenever two cultures collide, something is bound to happen, and world history has shown that the responses cover a wide range. The change produced in one culture by its encounter with another is called "acculturation." Rarely is the exchange of culture traits an equal one, and never does one culture emerge entirely untouched. The encounter almost always results in an increased similarity between the two cultures, but with one of them left dominant. In some cases, assimilation proceeds so far that it is virtually complete except for a single element that separates one group from the rest—as, for example, the refusal of the otherwise assimilated Jews in pre-Hitler Germany to convert to Christianity. On the other hand, one culture may be overwhelmed physically, but not assimilated by the other. That is what most often happened to the American Indians.

Yet, culturally, the Indians have influenced their White conquerors. About half the states have Indian names, and so do thousands of cities, towns, rivers, lakes, and mountains. Americans drink hootch, meet in a caucus, bury the hatchet, give clambakes, run the gantlet, smoke the peace pipe, hold powwows, and enjoy Indian summer. The epithet "skunk" that the frontiersmen hurled so freely at the Indian itself derived from an Indian word, as are many others in the

English language. The march of settlers westward often followed the same trails that the Indians had used, and eventually these developed into today's network of concrete highways. Indians supplied Europeans with foods that were new to them, taught them to plant and hunt with Indian methods, guided them safely through a dangerous wilderness, and equipped them with tools and techniques that enabled them to survive. The plunder the Europeans were thus given the means to take, in gold and other treasures, built up the European nations and in part laid the groundwork for the industrial revolution.

More than fifty new foods first domesticated by Indians were carried back to the Old World, including the turkey, maize, white potato, pumpkin, squash, peppers, the so-called Jerusalem artichoke, tomato, avocado, chocolate, and several kinds of beans. (Potatoes and maize now rank second and third in total tonnage among the world's crops, behind rice but ahead of the earliest cultivated grain, wheat.) The European has turned for relief to drugs and pharmaceuticals the Indians discovered: tobacco, quinine, ephedrine, novocaine, curare, ipecac, and witch hazel. Moccasin-style shoes are patterned after Indian footwear; canoes, after their birchbark craft; toboggans, after their sleds; and apparel worn at ski resorts is copied from Eskimo clothing. We make use of other Indian inventions as well, including the snowshoe, hammock, poncho, parka, rubber ball, and even the syringe. The Constitution of the United States and those of several state governments were partly influenced by the democratic traditions of Indian societies.

The psychoanalyst Carl G. Jung once stated that he discerned an Indian component in the personality of some of his White American patients—which, if true, is a demonstration of how subtly the culture of the conquered can invade the very personalities of the conquerors. Some critics regard Jung's statement as psychological rubbish, but White Americans have probably always unconsciously accepted a proposition that they would vehemently deny if it were put to them directly.

This proposition is that for them the essence of America is not the motel-stripped, tamed, and ravaged land of today but the Indian's primeval one that offered Europeans an unscarred and harmonious world, in short a second chance and a New Jerusalem.‡

SQUAW MEN

One rarely mentioned aspect of the encounter between Indians and Whites was the appeal that the Indian societies held for generation after generation of Whites. No sooner did the first Europeans arrive in North America than a disproportionate number of them showed a preference for Indian society over their own. Within only a few years after Virginia was settled, more than forty male colonists had married Indian women, and several English women had married Indians. The colony of Virginia had only one reason for instituting severe penalties against going to live with Indians: Whites were doing just that, and in increasing numbers. In fact, the word "Indianize"—in its meaning "to adopt the ways of the Indians"—originated as far back as the seventeenth century, when Cotton Mather was led to inquire: "How much do our people Indianize?" They did so to a great extent. Throughout American history, thousands of Whites enthusiastically exchanged breeches for breechclouts.

Indianization impressed Michel Guillaume Jean de Crèvecoeur, who wrote in 1782 in his *Letters from an American Farmer*: "There must be in the Indians' social bond something singularly captivating, and far superior to be boasted of among us; for thousands of Europeans are Indians, and we have no examples of even one of those Aborigines having from choice become Europeans."‡ Crèvecoeur touched precisely the sore spot that so bewildered Whites: Why did transculturalization seem to operate only in one direction? Whites who had lived for a time with Indians almost never wanted to leave. But virtually none of the "civilized" Indians who had been given the opportunity to sample White society chose to become a part of it. And the White squaw men persisted in their defections, even though they were subjected to legal penalties and to great contempt from other Whites.

Numerous attempts have been made to explain Indianization. Some scholars have speculated that civilization forms merely a thin veneer over the basic bestiality of humans, who revert to savagery at the first opportunity. Yet Indian society, with its complicated relationships between a welter of households, its kin groups, moieties, sodalities, ranks, and classes, was even more structured than the White society of the time. Others have regarded Whites who gave up the blessings of civilization and Christianity as simply renegades and backsliders—or, in psychological terms, rebellious personalities. But explanations for why particular individuals chose to Indianize do not illuminate anything about why entire groups of people acted in that way.

Special aspects of Indian society made it possible for so many thousands of Whites to be incorporated into it. One thing that impressed the earliest explorers, almost without exception, was the hospitality with which Indians received them. The Indians later changed their attitude when they learned that the Whites posed a threat, but the initial contacts were idyllic. That was particularly true of those Indian societies at the band and tribal levels, although even the people in the chiefdoms of the Southeast and the West Indies at first warmly greeted the Spanish, French, and British. Hospitality and sharing were characteristic of Indian societies, almost without exception. Another pertinent way in which Indian society differed was in the matter of adoption. If a prisoner of war was not reserved for torture, he was usually adopted by a family to replace a lost husband or a dead child. The adopted person was thoroughly integrated into all aspects of the Indian society of which he had become a part. He had the same rights and obligations as any native-born member; he had new parents, new kin, new memberships in ceremonial societies, new allegiances. Such total adoption explains the complaint of the squaw men, typically stated by one of them: "When you marry an Indian, you marry her whole damn tribe!"

The pattern of Indianization had obviously been established among Indians themselves long before the Whites arrived; it required no major readjustment to adopt Whites, as in the past Indians had been adopted. So thoroughly were adoptees integrated into the complex social structure of the Indian society that even Whites who had originally gone unwillingly as captives of the Indians often refused to be ransomed. A White could become an extremely important person in Indian society. When an anthropologist analyzed thirty cases of captive Whites, fifteen men and fifteen women, he found an unusually high percentage of social success; three or four of the men had become chiefs and about the same number of women had become the wives of chiefs.‡

The Indians' willingness to receive squaw men is demonstrated by the numerous escaped slaves who joined Indian tribes. The Indians in the southern states learned slavery from the Whites, but they altered it somewhat to create a social role for the slave, who had been a nonperson among the Whites. Escaped slaves were not running away from "civilization" to return to "primitive" ways, as White apologists have stated, but rather were running into a society that was much more structured. They chose to be slaves under an Indian master who gave them something that the Whites did not: the opportunity to exist, even as a chattel, inside a set of social relationships. The slaves, in turn, were valuable to the Indian, for they brought skills learned from their White masters. Slaves among the Indians often had the opportunity to advance in status, and cases are on record of their rising to high office. For example, Osceola, the great Seminole leader, is believed to have been partly of African ancestry.

The question naturally arises why transculturalization did not work the other way. Why did not Indians enter White society, particularly in view of the numerous attempts made by Whites to "civilize" them? The answer is that the White settlers possessed no traditions comparable to the Indians' hospitality, sharing, adoption, and complete social integration. Indians who associated closely with Whites soon found themselves confronted by a social system in which—although they might on occasion be courteously and even kindly treated, or indeed be clothed and educated—tradition did not permit the adoption of an Indian as an equal member of the family. The Whites who educated Indians did so with the idea that these would return to their own people as missionaries and thus spread the gospel, not that they might become functioning members of White society.‡

ACCULTURATION WITHOUT ASSIMILATION

When two cultures meet, their relations do not inevitably result in total assimilation of one by the other. People can still cling to the old ways and retain a goodly number of their customs. In fact, the dominant culture may encourage them to do so for their quaintness and tourist appeal—as demonstrated during the Franco dictatorship in Spain, which encouraged regional dances and costumes yet demanded total conformity in religion and political association. Despite the Americanization movement, many immigrant groups managed to salvage something of the old country in their new homes in North America: the Friends of Italian Opera, the German beer hall, and the Saint Patrick's Day parade.

Along the border between the United States and Mexico two very different facets of European culture are divided by a political boundary, yet they have influenced each other while maintaining their own identities. The Spanish influence on the United States side of the border is seen in the names of cities (such as San Diego, Santa Fe, San Antonio, and El Paso) and of topographical features (arroyo, sierra); much of the architecture, including even government buildings, is Spanish-inspired; restaurants serving Mexican food are common, and many homes are furnished with Mexican pottery and textiles; most Americans in the area speak at least some Spanish. A similar situation prevails on the opposite side of the border, where American-made gadgets are very much in evidence, and where Mexicans go to restaurants that serve American-style food. Even uneducated Mexicans speak a good deal of English, and they pride themselves on knowing how to get along with the gringos.

Acculturation has taken place across the border, yet Mexicans and southwesterners are very different in the totality of their cultures. The interaction between the two groups has further been complicated by the presence of Indians on both sides of the border. Most of these Indians have learned to speak either Spanish or English or both, in addition to their native languages, and they have made adjustments to both cultures. The Pueblo Indians, in particular, have kept their social organization and religion intact, and they have salvaged a good deal of their material culture as well, through a form of passive resistance. Yet they seem, on the surface, to have accepted White ways. They speak both Spanish and English; their children are baptized by Roman Catholic priests, and the figures of saints are included in their ceremonials; they drive American automobiles and trucks; they eat Mexican-style food.

When today's surviving Indian societies are examined closely, it is seen how well some have worked out a compromise with their White conquerors—acculturation without assimilation. They use United States currency and banks, speak English to Whites, furnish their American-style homes with American-made goods, subscribe to American magazines, play baseball, and own television sets or radios that receive programs prepared by the dominant White society. They have accepted almost all of the material aspects of White American society. Nevertheless, at the Shawnee reservation in eastern Oklahoma, for example, one becomes aware that members of this tribe have managed to hold on to what is important to them out of their general defeat. By a steady intransigence, the Shawnee have maintained their own identity in the face of the White majority. Perhaps the Shawnee found this easier to do than some other Indian groups, since they had already become experienced in the problems of acculturation. Long before being herded onto reservations, long before their conquest by Whites, they had been migrants, thus coming into contact with other Indians of different languages and customs. The trail of the Shawnee, before

Whites finally placed them on a reservation in Oklahoma, leads from their earliest recorded home in Tennessee and South Carolina through Pennsylvania, Ohio, Indiana, Missouri, and Texas. In the face of constant exposure to outside influences, they apparently developed an anti-assimilation attitude. Although small in numbers, they survived culturally because they rejected oppressive aspects of the White culture at the same time that they accepted other aspects of less importance.

THE NAVAJO

In contrast to the Shawnee, the Navajo represent one of the world's best examples of the culture that tends to borrow rather than to reject. Far outnumbering any other group of Indians in the United States, they are also the fastest growing, having increased their population almost tenfold in the last century. Their reservation of more than 25,000 square miles, mostly in Arizona and New Mexico but also in southeastern Utah, much surpasses all others in size. Most of this vast area, though, is eroded and arid waste, not even capable of supporting sheep. And despite the tribe's aggressive business management—including even a computer to keep track of its oil, gas, and mineral leases—and its ownership of tourist facilities and small industries, the Navajo are among the poorest Indians in the United States.

From the time of their earliest appearance as a people, the Navajo have successfully borrowed from other cultures—the Pueblo, the Spaniards, the Mexicans, and White North Americans. They arrived in the Southwest from the north, probably less than several hundred years before the Spaniards, with only a simple cultural framework—but they could fit into it any aspects of other cultures that might be useful to them.‡ Furthermore, they were so impoverished culturally that they had nothing to lose and everything to gain by borrowing. Contacts between the sedentary Anasazi agriculturists and the seminomadic Navajo hunters took place along a broad front in Arizona and New Mexico. On their long trek southward, the Apachean people who were to become the Navajo had encountered many different Indian groups; now suddenly they were confronted with town-dwellers who had conquered the desert. To the sophisticated Anasazi, though, the Navajo must have seemed little better than barbarians.

The Anasazi and their descendants, the Pueblo Indians, were unlike the Whites in that they apparently did not undertake a program to "civilize" their new neighbors. They defended themselves against attacks by the Navajo, but they did not deliberately try to coerce the Navajo into accepting different ways. Left free, the Navajo could borrow whatever they considered useful in Pueblo culture. Had they been coerced, as Whites later attempted to do, then the Navajo might have reacted differently: They might have resisted all culture change.

Historical information about the Navajo does not appear until 1626. In a report written at that time, a Spanish priest distinguishes the Navajo as "Apaches del Nabaxu" from their relatives, the Apache who "live by the hunt." (*Navajo* is a Spanish corruption of the Pueblo word that means "big planted fields.") He goes on to describe the Navajo as "very skillful farmers" who had already learned how to store their surplus maize. After the Spaniards settled the Southwest, the Navajo began another burst of cultural borrowing—or, more accurately, stealing. By 1775, Spanish ranches and villages were so depleted of horses that the Spaniards had to send to Europe for an additional 1,500 of them. After the Pueblo Rebellion against the Spaniards had been put down in 1692, many Pueblo took refuge with their Navajo neighbors and taught them to make pottery. During this time the Navajo probably absorbed many Pueblo religious and social ideas and customs as well.

By the time the United States took possession of the Southwest in 1848, after the Mexican War, the Navajo had become the dominant military force in the area. Their population had grown from about four thousand in 1740 to more than fifteen thousand in 1848. The Navajo had also nearly completed their borrowing from the Pueblo, Spanish, and Mexican cultures. They had enlarged their agricultural inventory by growing wheat, melons, peaches, and other Old World crops in addition to their native maize and beans. Their architecture now included ceremonial hogans, and three other types of hogans as well. The role of the Navajo "singer" became important in those ceremonies that had borrowed sand paintings, prayer sticks, masks, and altars from the Pueblo Indians.

The victorious United States soldiers who occupied Santa Fe had little trouble with the Mexicans, but the Navajo stole several head of cattle from the herd of the commanding general himself, not to mention thousands of sheep and horses from settlers in the vicinity. The Americans launched numerous punitive expeditions against the Navajo, whom the army officers declared to be untrustworthy because the headmen signed treaty after treaty, all of which the Navajo soon broke. What the officers did not understand was that a Navajo headman's powers over his own group are limited and, over other groups, nonexistent. For their part, the Navajo headmen did not understand that a treaty obliged them to control every other Navajo group as well as their own. Finally, in 1863, Colonel Kit Carson was ordered to clear the country of Navajo Indians and to resettle any survivors at Fort Sumner in eastern New Mexico, where they could be "civilized." Carson's strategy was the same as that applied against the Plains Indians a little later: He destroyed the Navajo food base by systematically killing their livestock and by burning their fields.

Within less than a year, Carson had been eminently successful. A few Navajo bands managed to hold out in the remote mesas and canyons, but the people as a whole had been starved into submission. The survivors, begging for food, surrendered to the Whites. Ultimately, about 8,500 Navajo made what they still call the "Long Walk" to captivity at Fort Sumner, three hundred miles away. After they had been there for four years, they signed a peace treaty that entitled them to a reservation of about 3,500,000 acres, much less land than they had occupied previously. (This reservation has been enlarged from time to time to its present 16,000,000 acres, but its size has not kept pace with the growth of the

Navajo population from not quite 15,000 in 1868 to about 125,000 today.)

Although the Fort Sumner experience failed to Christianize the captive Navajo, it did succeed in altering their culture in one important respect: From that time on, the Navajo Indians ceased to be raiders. And now new elements were added to their culture. The first trading post opened on the new reservation in 1871, and by 1890 thirty-nine such posts had been established. The Navajo's experience with traders was much more congenial than it was with the government agents who tried to get them to cut their hair, or with the missionaries who gave them a vision of damnation when they already had fear enough of ghosts. The trader taught them the potentialities of a new kind of economic life. Silver-working, learned from Mexicans, was encouraged by the traders, and so was the weaving of blankets, which had been learned from the Pueblo about the year 1700. Through the trading post, and later through wage labor, the Navajo were drawn into the White American market economy. Pickup trucks have replaced the wagons that replaced the horses that in their turn replaced the dogs used for transport before the coming of the Spaniards. Male attire is now cowboy southwestern, although the Navajo women have been more conservative in retaining the velveteen blouse and calico skirt first worn at Fort Sumner. Factory-made utensils and tools have replaced the Navajo's pottery and baskets, their wooden and stone implements.

Today's Navajo are clearly different from the culturally impoverished wanderers who invaded the Southwest. Time after time, as the Navajo came into contact with Pueblo, Spaniard, Mexican, and White American, they borrowed from those cultures what they needed. Yet they remained Navajo—independent, proud, adjusting successfully to continual changes in their way of life. By no means are Navajo Indians simply imitation Whites. The Navajo learned the most from the Pueblo, who never tried to civilize them. In contrast, the brutal policy of Kit Carson and the humiliating experience at Fort Sumner basically affected Navajo culture in only one major respect: It caused them to switch from a partial dependence upon raiding to a market economy. The Navajo clearly illuminate a basic error made by Whites in their encounters with Indians, and also by Europeans in general with other native peoples around the world. Among the Navajo, the greatest and most durable culture change has come about as a result not of coercion, but of being offered a cultural model which they were free to accept or reject.‡

The same is true as well of certain other Indian societies. The potlatch, for example, became for some Northwest Coast Indians a symbol of defiance to White authority. The Canadian Indian Act of 1885 expressly forbade the potlatch and provided for imprisonment of up to six months for anyone who engaged in the practice. But among the Southern Kwakiutl, for one, the passage of the act was the signal for the golden age of potlatching to begin; outwitting the Indian agent and the Canadian police gave the traditional feast added zest. In 1952 a revised Indian Act rescinded the prohibition, and potlatching once again became legal in Canada. Only a handful of old men bothered to attend a potlatch given later that year—whereas if the law had remained in effect a large turnout might have been expected.‡

NAVAJO AND ZUÑI WAR VETERANS

The Navajo and the Zuñi share many cultural elements and live alongside one another in western New Mexico. Both are organized at the tribal level; the physical environment of their lands is much the same; their histories have been entwined for many centuries. Yet their cultures have remained distinct. This was vividly demonstrated by the different ways in which the Navajo and Zuñi responded to World War II, and also by the ways each of the groups treated its returned veterans. In the case of the Zuñi, 213 men went into the armed forces during the war years. Many more Zuñi were eligible to be drafted, but the council of high priests petitioned the draft board for deferment of men holding religious offices. When that was granted, the Zuñi priests then requested the exemption of almost all eligible males, for the priests claimed that every male belonged to a priesthood or else took part in an important ceremony. When the draft board agreed to defer only Zuñi "high priests serving for life," the Zuñi responded by creating new religious positions and reviving extinct ceremonies, some of which had not been performed for nearly forty years.

The Navajo displayed none of the reluctance of the Zuñi to go to war. Approximately 3,600 Navajo served, and about 15,000 more went away to work in war industries. An even greater number of Navajo would have entered the army, had it not been for an extremely high rejection rate because of illiteracy and poor health. Nor did Navajo officials attempt to obtain exemptions. On the contrary, delegates to the tribal council made speeches stating how pleased they were that their boys were going into the army. The departure of the Navajo men from their communities was even ritualized by the performance of the ceremony known as the Blessing Way.

At Zuñi, no fuss was made over the returned veterans; in fact, they were treated with great suspicion and subjected to gossip, rumor, and ridicule. When one Zuñi veteran wanted to establish a branch of the American Legion, a malicious rumor began to circulate that he was planning to use money from dues for his personal enrichment. The anxieties of the veterans resulted in a sharp increase in drunkenness and antisocial behavior. Within a few years, though, most of them had been reintegrated into Zuñi life; the thirty-three who refused to conform left the village. The veterans married, rejoined religious societies, and dutifully returned to work in the fields. On the other hand, the Navajo veterans were welcomed back by the performance of many ceremonials. Instead of harboring suspicion about the new knowledge the young men had obtained, the Navajo generally were proud that their boys had learned to speak English so well. And they displayed enthusiasm when, for example, the Veterans Administration offered to start an agricultural training program.

What differences existed in the two cultures that made the Navajo welcome the opportunity to serve in the war while the Zuñi remained steadfastly resistant both to service and to the veterans? Part of the answer can be found in the simple fact of different settlement patterns. The Navajo live on their reservation as scattered families that frequently shift residence, largely because of the needs of their livestock to browse. So when the Navajo veteran returned, he had only to adjust to his own family and to his neighbors. In contrast, the Zuñi village is compact. The Zuñi veteran returned not just to his own family but also to a tight web of households, lineages, clans, kivas, and societies in which he had to find his place once again. Because of the physical closeness of people in Zuñi, gossip could be brought into action immediately as an instrument of social control.

Second, the reactions of the two societies might have been predicted from the differing kinds of acculturation they had undergone. The Navajo had always freely borrowed cultural items, and World War II represented yet another opportunity for them to examine White ways close up. Some veterans were even encouraged to live off the reservation, among Whites, so they could bring back more of this valuable new information. In contrast, the Zuñi are examples of what has been called "antagonistic acculturation." They adopted the external trappings of the Whites without accepting White goals; in fact, most of the trappings were adopted so as better to resist White culture. Many Zuñi considered the incursions of White technology a threat to their religion, and they responded by becoming more secretive and more determined to maintain traditional ways. So the veterans, instead of being treated as returning heroes, were looked upon as threats, who might subtly introduce the new ways learned while living among Whites. When one Zuñi veteran appeared in a business suit, for example, he was ridiculed for trying to act like a White man.

The final explanation of the difference lies in the contrasting histories of the two cultures in the matter of warfare. Offensive warfare was an important feature of Navajo life until the internment at Fort Sumner in 1864, whereas for the Zuñi, warfare had been largely defensive; and they had been forced to give it up after the Spanish suppressed the Pueblo Rebellion in 1692. Also, the Navajo exalted the warrior for his individual exploits. Even in aboriginal times, on the other hand, the Zuñi warrior enjoyed little prestige because the people believed that his success depended largely on the prayers of the priests who stayed at home. The Zuñi veteran brought back no cultural booty, but only the danger of infecting his people with more White ways. He was entitled to no celebrations.‡

XV

The Hopes of the Oppressed

REVIVALISTIC MOVEMENTS

The members of a culture that is being swamped by another often react defensively, grappling physically with the outsiders and defending themselves culturally as well. The defensive cultural reactions have been given various labels by anthropologists: nativism, revivalism, revitalization, and messianism. Whatever it is called, the reaction amounts to a deliberate effort to salvage a new culture from the defeat or decay of an older one. This effort may be as fanciful as the attempt in Ireland at the end of the last century to revive a moribund Gaelic language in the face of British rule. For some minority groups in the United States, the defensive reaction to Americanization may consist of ethnic get-togethers at which foods from the old country are eaten, native costumes worn, folk dances performed, and the language of the homeland spoken.

The reactions of native peoples overpowered by White colonial empires have usually been much more extreme. Their lands appropriated, their social system ripped apart, their customs suppressed, and their holy places profaned, the natives were inevitably defeated by superior firepower and technology when they tried to resist physically. As hopelessness and apathy settled over these people, the ground was prepared for messianic movements promising the return of the good old days. North America in the wake of White contact has been the scene of many such movements, erupting and then dying down in one place after another, with bloodshed the almost inevitable outcome. These defeats produced further disillusionment in Indian groups and helped to spark the next messianic movement.

Once looked upon as no more than stubborn resistance by the heathen to the obvious blessings of White civilization, these movements have been shown by anthropological studies to have been more complicated than that. As the disintegration of their societies under military and cultural assault caused the Indians to yearn for a way of life that was fast disappearing, the situation became favorable to the rise of prophets who foresaw a return to the past and doom for the White intruders. In 1680 the Pueblo Indians expelled the Spaniards under the leadership of a prophet named Popé who had been living at Taos. Catholic priests were slaughtered in their missions and their bodies were left piled on church altars. About a fifth of the total Spanish population of 2,500 were killed outright, and the rest fled to El Paso. Virtually everything of Spanish manufacture or ownership—not only churches, houses, furniture, and art, but even swine and sheep—was destroyed. But when Popé attempted to become the unchallenged leader of all the Pueblo Indians, the movement collapsed. Their tribal organization was simply too fragile to survive for long in a more complex political system. The Pueblo confederation soon broke apart as the tribes began warring among themselves. In 1692 the Spaniards marched back and reconquered them.

The Pueblo Rebellion had been primarily a revolt against alien authority. The next major Indian uprising, which began in 1762, was clearly messianic. A Delaware Indian prophet appeared in Michigan, preaching a doctrine that he said had come to him in a vision; he called for an end to strife among Indians and for a holy war against Whites, to be carried on solely with bows and arrows. In thus rejecting all White culture, he of course rejected the white firearms that might have tipped the balance in his favor. After the prophet (whose name no one seems ever to have bothered to record) had inflamed the Indians around the Great Lakes, a much more practical man named Pontiac arose and became their leader. The result was an alliance of practically all the Indians from Lake Superior southward to the lower Mississippi River. In 1763 they made plans for a coordinated attack upon the English forts nearest to them. Pontiac's own plan to capture Detroit failed, but most of his allies were successful and the garrisons at many of the forts were massacred. But in the following year the English counterattacked and Pontiac was forced to sue for peace. Several years later, as he returned laden with gifts from a visit to his former enemies, he was murdered by an Indian whom they had bribed to dispose of him.

This unsuccessful attempt continued to fester like a wound for decades. Eventually, Chief Tecumseh of the Shawnee established the greatest Indian alliance ever to exist north of Mexico. He and his emissaries visited almost every band, tribe, and chiefdom from the headwaters of the Missouri River to Florida. Indians everywhere began arming themselves in readiness for attacking the Whites when the right moment came. At the same time the Shawnee Prophet, Tecumseh's brother, was repeating the promises of the Delaware Prophet to liberate the Indians and extirpate the Whites. In 1811 he launched a premature attack near the Tippecanoe River, a tributary of the Wabash; the Indians were repelled by troops commanded by General William Henry Harrison, who would later be elected President under the slogan "Tippecanoe and Tyler, Too." Tecumseh rallied his remaining forces to join the British in the War of 1812. In battle after battle, he fought bravely at the head of 2,500 warriors from the allied tribes—until they were finally defeated in 1813, once again by troops under General Harrison, at a battle in Ontario. Tecumseh was killed, but his followers spirited away his body, and for years thereafter the frontier was plagued by rumors of his imminent return. But the prophecy of his brother had been dramatically refuted by White bullets.

The story of the Shawnee Prophet was to have a sad and ironic sequel. He had a follower named Kenekuk, who became a prophet among the Kickapoo of Illinois. Kenekuk, instead of advocating war against the Whites, called upon his people to abjure killing, lying, the use of liquor, and all other sins; their reward, he said, would be the discovery of new green pastures where they could settle in peace. He and his people refused to leave Illinois until the government gave them green pastures in Kansas. It eventually did and there, in 1852, he died of smallpox. Heedless of possible infection, his band of faithful gathered around his body in the conviction that he would rise again on the third day. The cult was wiped out, almost down to the last follower, by the disease that had killed its leader.

DREAMERS

The Dreamers originated among the Indians who lived along the lower reaches of the Columbia River in Oregon and Washington. That cult, too, sought a recovery of the lost culture, but it differed from the previous revivalistic movements in that it had strong Roman Catholic overtones. Smohalla ("Preacher") was born about 1820 in the Rocky Mountains and was educated by Catholic missionaries. His teachings were largely influenced by Catholic doctrine; he also became known as a great shaman and worker of miraculous cures. But around 1860 he was challenged by another shaman, and their encounter left him bleeding and presumed dead on the banks of a river. Rising flood waters carried him downstream, a White farmer rescued him, and he eventually recovered. From there Smohalla wandered through the Southwest and into Mexico. Returning finally to his own people, he maintained that he had actually been dead and that the Great Spirit had conversed with him. The Great Spirit, Smohalla said, was disgusted that the Indians had forsaken their native religion for that of the Whites. Smohalla's miraculous return was sufficient proof for many Indians that the Great Spirit had chosen him as a messenger of revelation.

Because Smohalla went into frequent trances, he became known as the Dreamer, and the name was applied to his followers as well. Upon awakening from a trance, he would report to them whatever vision he had had. Out of these visions he pieced together a remarkable cosmogony: In the beginning, the Great Spirit created the earth, the animals, and all living things, including humankind. The first people he created were Indians, then Frenchmen, next priests, Americans, and finally Negroes—an order that pretty much represented Smohalla's opinion of humankind as he knew it. The earth therefore belonged to those first people, the Indians, who must take care not to defile it as the Whites had done. "You ask me to plow the ground!" said Smohalla. "Shall I take a knife and tear my mother's bosom? You ask me to cut grass and make hay and sell it and be rich like white men! But how dare I cut my mother's hair?" At a time when the official policy of the United States government was to force all Indians to become farmers, Smohalla's preaching posed a major obstacle.

In 1877, inspired by the teachings of Smohalla, Chief Joseph of the Nez Perce in Idaho rebelled. Before he was finally trapped only thirty miles short of refuge in Canada, he had consistently outwitted and outfought a superior United States Army across a thousand miles of Rocky Mountain terrain. This was also—at least on Chief Joseph's side—one of the most honorable of the Indian wars. He forbade his warriors to scalp or to torture, but the Whites massacred his women and children nevertheless. Finally, with most of his warriors dead, his people starving, freezing, and maimed, Chief Joseph walked toward the White generals, handed his rifle to them, and said: "I am tired of fighting . . . My people ask me for food, and I have none to give. It is cold, and we have no blankets, no wood. My people are starving to death. Where is my little daughter? I do not know . . . Hear me, my chiefs. I have fought; but from where the sun now stands, Joseph will fight no more forever."

Despite the promises contained in the surrender agreement, the United States Army did not permit the survivors to return to their lands. They were sent instead to the malarial bottomlands of the Indian Territory, where the six of Chief Joseph's children who had managed to survive the rebellion all died, along with most of his band. Chief Joseph and those few who remained alive were then shipped to a new reservation in northern Washington, fifteen hundred miles away. Despite Chief Joseph's defeat, and the defeat of several other Indian leaders who were inspired by Smohalla, the cult of the Dreamers survived for some time thereafter. It even had a minor resurgence in 1883, as a response by the increasingly frustrated Indians to the building of the Northern Pacific Railroad.

THE GHOST DANCE

The movement known as the Ghost Dance first appeared around 1870 among the Northern Paiute who lived on the California–Nevada border, soon after the Union Pacific Railroad completed its first transcontinental run. No doubt that event inspired the vision of the prophet Wodziwob, who declared that a big train was coming to bring back dead ancestors and would announce their arrival with a whistling sound. He proclaimed that a cataclysm would swallow up all the Whites, but miraculously leave behind their goods for the Indians who became his followers. A heaven on earth would then ensue, for the Great Spirit would return to live with the Indians. These miracles were to be hastened by ceremonial dancing around a pole and by singing the songs that Wodziwob had learned during a vision. The dances, having produced no effect, were eventually abandoned.‡

Two decades later the Ghost Dance erupted once more. Several disparate events had inspired it. One was the founding in 1830 of the Latter-Day Saints of Jesus Christ (Mormon) by Joseph Smith, who prophesied that a New Jerusalem would arise in the wilds, where all those with faith would gather, including certain tribes of Israel. To the Mormons, the Indians were the remnant of the Hebrew tribes who had fled Israel at the time of Jeremiah, about 2,500 years ago. The Mormons sent emissaries to the Indians, whom they renamed the Lamanites, inviting them to join the Mormon colonies and to be baptized. Joseph Smith was also supposed to have prophesied in 1843 that if he reached his eighty-fifth year—that is, if he lived until 1890—the messiah would appear in human form.

The teachings of the Mormons seem to have opened the way for a prophet in the tradition of Wodziwob. He appeared as the prophet Wovoka, whose father had been Wodziwob's assistant. Wovoka had led an obscure life until he fell into a trance during a solar eclipse. When he awoke, he reported that God had taken him by the hand and shown him all the dead Indians happy and young again. God then told Wovoka about a dance that the people must perform to generate the energy needed for bringing the dead Indians back to life. It was in 1890, that prophetic year for the Mormons, that Wovoka appeared and began preaching the Ghost Dance religion.

James Mooney, who is responsible for much of our information about Indian revivalistic and messianic movements, had no doubts about Wovoka's sincerity. After talking with the prophet at length in 1892, Mooney described him as a sleight-of-hand shaman but by no means a fraud. Wovoka never claimed to be the messiah awaited by the Mormons (although his followers did). He personally made no attempt to spread his teachings, and in fact he never even left Walker Lake, Nevada. But the dance was spread quickly, by Paiute missionaries and by other Indians who came to visit him. His teachings took hold among many of the Paiute and related Shoshonean groups—although not among the Indians in California and Oregon who had been made wary by the failure of Wodziwob and the first Ghost Dance in 1870. The Pueblo theocracy of course rejected it, and so did the Navajo.

Ethnographers have puzzled over why the Ghost Dance of 1890 made so little impression among the Navajo, since they had known defeat, starvation, disease, and forcible removal no less than the other Indian groups who enthusiastically adopted the dance. News of the movement had been carried to the Navajo by Paiute missionaries, and there is no doubt that they were familiar with all its teachings. To explain their total rejection, it has been suggested that the Navajo at the time were comparatively wealthy in livestock and no longer undergoing the stress of deprivation. But a more likely reason is to be found in Navajo religion. The news that dead ancestors were even now on their way to the reservation would not have been welcomed by the Navajo, who are fearful of ghosts. What to other Indians was welcome news would thus have seemed to the Navajo an imminent calamity.‡

As the Ghost Dance craze spread across the Rockies to the Plains tribes, it increasingly ran amok. Ironically, English, as the only language common to the various tribes, was the means by which Wovoka's teachings were communicated among the Indians. And—again, ironically—word of the new movement spread all the more quickly because those who carried it traveled on the Whites' railroads. The Cheyenne and the Arapaho in Oklahoma started dancing immediately. Of the other Plains tribes, the fervor reached its extreme among the Sioux, at that time the largest and most intransigent of them all. The indignities to which they had been forced to submit in a series of land grabs were so atrocious as to be almost unbelievable to one who reads of them today. When news of the Ghost Dance reached them, they were being systematically starved into submission by the White bureaucracy on the little that was left of their reservations in the Dakota Territory. And a spark to ignite the Sioux was the presence of Sitting Bull, a veteran of the battle of Little Bighorn in 1876.

The Sioux sent delegates to speak to Wovoka, whose advice was simply to work hard and to make peace with the Whites. By the time the messengers returned, though, Wovoka's message had become garbled and confused with earlier and more violent nativistic movements. The Sioux were told that dancing would not only bring back the ancestral dead and the herds of bison, but also exterminate the Whites. And, best of all, the Indians would be invulnerable to White guns, thanks to "ghost shirts," fancifully decorated with designs of arrows, stars, birds, and so on, that had the power to ward off bullets. The Ghost Dance took its most extreme form on the Rosebud Sioux reservation; from there it spread to the Pine Ridge Sioux and finally to Sitting

Bull's people at Standing Rock. The Sioux tribes now rose in a rebellion against the Whites that ended, in that fateful year of 1890, with the death of Sitting Bull and the massacre (unimpeded by ghost shirts) of about three hundred Indian men, women, and children at Wounded Knee. As swiftly as it had set the plains afire, the Ghost Dance had been extinguished.

Only a few months after the massacre, while the Sioux were still confused and embittered by their defeat, a deranged White man visited their reservations. He declared himself to be the messiah and predicted that the millennium would arrive that spring, when the star-pansy bloomed. When the star-pansies did bloom and the millennium did not come, the disillusionment of the Sioux was complete. Hope of a return to the old days was now supplanted by resignation in the face of whatever future trials the Whites had in store for them. When the Ghost Dance movement of 1890 died at Wounded Knee, something else died with it. The Ghost Dance was the last futile attempt by the American Indians to retrieve their fast-disappearing cultures.

ACCOMMODATION

Even before the Indians' hope of bringing back the old days had proved an illusion, a different response—peaceful adaptation to an alien White world—had taken root in firmer ground. Perhaps the earliest of the accommodation movements was begun in 1799 by a Seneca named Handsome Lake, whose teachings quickly spread from his own tribe to the rest of the Six Nations. Whites called his movement the "New Religion" of the Iroquois, but to them it is known as the "Old Way" and the name for its Code translates into English as "Good Word." So successful has it been that perhaps a quarter of the Iroquois on reservations in the United States and Canada now follow the Code.

Handsome Lake was regarded as a prophet at a period when the Iroquois fortunes seemed almost hopeless. The American Revolution had divided the allegiance of the Six Nations, causing them to fight among themselves; Jesuit missionaries had instigated migrations by some of their people to Canada; their population had been further diminished by warfare, disease, and alcoholism, and they had been deprived of most of their lands. By the time of Handsome Lake, though, they had already acknowledged the reality of the White conquest and were putting their dismembered culture back together. They had made peace with the new American republic, and they believed themselves to be protected by their solemn treaties with it. Thomas Jefferson had described the religion of Handsome Lake as "positive and effective," and the high esteem in which their prophet was held by Whites had given the Iroquois a new sense of security.

The Code of Handsome Lake is not Christian but contains borrowings from Christian teaching, particularly that of the Quakers, among whom Handsome Lake was brought up. Many Christian rituals and symbols had been combined with traditional Iroquois festivals and beliefs. The place of worship, for example, looks like a church but its known as a longhouse, thus recalling the traditional Iroquois dwelling and the hallmark of the League of the Iroquois. The Code itself is many things: an account of the career of Handsome Lake the prophet, a description of heaven and hell, a guide to the ceremonies to be performed in the longhouse, and a definition of the good way of life. It condemns alcoholism, theft, malicious gossip, witchcraft, adultery, wife-beating, and jealousy. Husbands and wives are to love each other and to treat their children with kindness; compassion is to be shown to those who are suffering; all are to revere the Great Spirit and His creation. Like the Judaic–Christian Bible, the Code of Handsome Lake is history and prophecy, commandment and prohibition—and above all a guide to conduct by which an Iroquois can live fruitfully in this world and happily in the next.‡

Unlike the Code of Handsome Lake, which is restricted to the Iroquois, the Native American Church is the primary native religion among scores of former bands, tribes, and chiefdoms in the United States. Based on a communal partaking of the hallucinogenic peyote, it is today the most vigorous of pan-Indian religions.

When one recalls the warfare between Indian groups in primeval times, its success appears all the more remarkable. The movement teaches accommodation to a White world, and at the same time becomes a nonviolent means of cultural emancipation. It can best be understood against the background of the Ghost Dance, that final and disastrous proof that Whites were in North America to stay. The Ghost Dance made its unfulfillable promises at a time when the Indians were ready to rebel. The teachings of the Native American Church spread at a time when the Indians were ready to admit defeat. No longer hopeful of fighting off the United States Army, they now had to wage a subtler war against the Whites' efforts to exterminate Indian cultures and substitute their own. The problem they had to solve was the same as for any messianic movement: how to coexist with an alien culture yet remain spiritually autonomous. The solution had been to borrow freely from White culture while salvaging what is considered important in Indian religious thought.

The Native American Church is definitely Christian in orientation, but what Indians call "the road of peyote" is quite independent of Christianity. For example, the church opposes attempts by Christian sects to impose their official canon on the Indians. As in most messianic movements among native peoples, the Judaic–Christian God is more acceptable than Jesus, who is associated with oppression by Christian Whites. Indians regard the eating of peyote as their own exclusive way of partaking of the Holy Spirit, much as certain Christians partake of the Eucharistic bread and wine. Peyote, a small cactus whose rounded top or "button" is cut off and eaten, contains stimulants related to strychnine and sedatives related to morphine. Since it is not habit-forming, it cannot be classified as a narcotic—much to the dismay of the United States Bureau of Indian Affairs, which has long attempted to stamp out its use.

In 1951 a group of anthropologists, in a statement concerning the government's efforts to have peyote declared illegal, said that they had partaken of the plant during the rites connected with its use, and had concluded that "it does not excite, stupefy or produce muscular incoordination; there is no hangover; and the habitual user does not develop an increased tolerance or dependence. As for the immorality that is supposed to accompany its use, since no orgies are known among any Indian tribes of North America, the charge has as much validity as the ancient Roman accusations of a similar nature against the early Christians."‡ The hallucinations are usually in the form of color visions, often described as elaborate and beautiful designs that change shape constantly much like those in a kaleidoscope. Sound sensations are somewhat less frequent: Users have described hearing the sun rise with a roar and fly across the sky to the accompanying sound of drums.

The recent history of the use of peyote is fairly well known. It grows wild in northern Mexico, where it had been eaten before the arrival of the Spaniards, but where its use increased as the Spanish regime became more and more oppressive. The first clear evidence of the use of peyote by Indians in the United States followed the visit of an Apache band to Mexico in 1770; but for the next seventy-five years or so its use north of the Rio Grande remained negligible. As the Plains culture disintegrated after the middle of the last century, the use of peyote spread northward. By the early years of this century it had reached the Great Lakes and the plains of Canada. It had also been carried east of the Mississippi River by Indians who had learned its use while living on reservations in Oklahoma.

The question arises as to why peyote spread in quite the way it did, why some Indians took it up enthusiastically while others rejected it. Peyote was checked in its spread west of the Great Basin by the presence there of jimsonweed, another hallucinogenic drug, to which potential users of peyote were already committed. The use of peyote became most firmly entrenched among the Plains Indians, a people who had long had the tradition of seeking the emotional experience of visions and who were searching for a way out of their despair at the end of the last century. In contrast, peyote was very slow to be adopted by most of the Pueblo Indians, although its use among them is increasing now. (At Taos, though, the most northeasterly of the pueblos and the

one that is closest both geographically and culturally
to the Plains tribes, peyote has been used since early
in this century.) For one thing, Pueblo culture has traditionally emphasized priestly ritual rather than individual religious experience. Further, the Pueblo Indians
did not suffer the great shocks of displacement, defeat,
and a changed way of life that the Plains tribes did.‡

MESSIAHS: INDIAN AND OTHERS

Several decades ago, miniature copies of a piece of
sculpture, dolefully called "The End of the Trail" and
depicting a fatigued Indian horseman, were commonly
seen in White American living rooms, apparently signi-
fying the final triumph over a vanishing Red man. Since
then, however, the Indians have not only refused to
vanish, but have, as we have seen, even managed to
salvage a part of their native cultures through revitalization and messianic movements. These have often been
well documented and they are of further interest to
anthropologists for the light they shed on such movements in general—how and why they originate, the
course they take, and the response of the dominant
culture.‡

Every messianic movement known to history has
arisen in a society under severe stress as a result of
contact with an alien culture, with accompanying military defeat, epidemic, and acculturation. The bewildered
search for ways of counteracting such stress may actually increase it, through raising anxiety over whether
the new solutions will be any better than the old. And
once doubts have arisen about the ancestral system itself, the stress may become unendurable. It is at this
point that the culture begins to break down—as manifested by widespread alcoholism, apathy, disregard of
kinship obligations and marriage rules, and intragroup
violence.

Such symptoms appear at precisely the time when the
culture is least able to cope with new problems, and so
the intensity of the stress increases still more. As this
cultural inadequacy becomes apparent even to the most
conservative of its members, the culture may deteriorate

to such an extent that it literally dies. The birth rate drops and the death rate rises; with no will to resist, its people are often fallen upon by predatory neighbors; the few survivors scatter, and the old ways disappear as these people die out or are absorbed by other groups. If, on the other hand, an acceptable revitalization or messianic movement arises, such a collapse may be forestalled or even averted.

Messianic movements around the world have almost always come into being following the emergence of a prophet who has had a vision. One thing about the leaders of such messianic movements must be emphasized: They certainly are not paranoics, as has so often been assumed. Paranoics may state that they are God, Jesus, the Great Spirit, or some other supernatural being. Prophets, on the other hand, never claim to be supernatural—only to have been in touch with supernatural powers. (Of course, after their death their disciples tend to deify them or at least to declare them saints.) A prophet typically bears a message from the supernatural that offers certain promises: the return of bison herds or of lost territory, a reign of peace and good will on earth. Whatever is promised, the prophet also offers a new sense of power, a revitalization of society. For these promises to be fulfilled, certain rituals must be followed: anything from dancing around a ghost pole to being immersed in water, usually along with numerous other duties that must be attended to day after day. And even as the prophet makes promises to the faithful, he also threatens punishment and catastrophe, the destruction of the world, or everlasting damnation. The old ways are declared dead; attention must be shifted to a new way or to some new conception of an old one. To spread the word of what he has learned through visions, the prophet gathers about himself a group of disciples and missionaries.

What is most impressive to the people around a typical prophet is that a personality change has taken place. Most often, prophets have lived in obscurity until they suddenly were noticed; almost all the American Indian prophets emerged following a period of spiritual apathy or after having been alcoholic. It is possible—though more research on this point is needed—that the sudden transformation in personality results from changes produced in the body under physical and emotional stress. Individuals do vary a great deal in their metabolic reaction to stress—which might explain why, when stress reaches a certain intensity in a culture, certain individuals feel called forth to become prophets whereas almost all others do not. In any event, the prophet emerges in a new cultural role, and his personality is liberated from the stress that called the response into being in the first place. Immune to the stress under which others still suffer, the prophet appears to his followers to be supernatural.

The disciples who gather around a prophet may also undergo revitalizing personality changes—as did Peter, to name one very familiar example. The prophet continues to exert spiritual leadership, but the disciples take upon themselves the practical tasks of organizing a campaign to establish the new movement. They convert large numbers of people, who in turn also undergo transformations of personality. If the messianic movement has been allowed by the dominant culture to survive up to this point, a vital step must now be taken. The prophet must emphasize that he is only the intermediary between the converts and the supernatural being whose good tidings he carries. Taking this step ensures the continuity of the new movement after the death of its founding prophet. The prophet then puts the converts and the supernatural beings into close touch with one another by calling for certain symbolic duties which the faithful must perform, such as a ritualistic eating of peyote or of bread and wine.

A new movement usually finds itself called upon to resist both an oppressive alien culture and the emergence of factions within its own ranks. A successful messianic movement will meet such resistance through any of several possible adaptations. Its teachings may change, as did those of the early Christians when they gradually gave up such Jewish rituals as circumcision. Or it may resort to political maneuvering and compromise. Most messianic movements, though, make the disastrous mistake of almost all movements among the pre-Christian Jews, as well as the majority of those among the American Indians: They choose to fight. Islam alone succeeded by force of arms, whereas the success of the early Christians was partly due to their choice of universal peace as their weapon.

Once the messianic movement has won a large following, a new culture begins to emerge from the ruins of the old; it influences not only religion but all aspects of social, political, and economic life as well. An organization with a secular and a sacerdotal hierarchy arises to perpetuate the new doctrine. The religion thus becomes routinized in a stable culture. All routinized religions today (including the Native American Church, Islam, Judaism, and Christianity) are successful descendants of what originated as messianic movements—that is, the vision of a new way of life for a culture under extreme stress.

THE PRESERVATION OF CULTURES

When Chief Black Hawk, the mighty leader of the combined forces of the Sac and the Fox, finally surrendered in 1832, he offered this grave warning:

The changes of fortune and vicissitudes of war made you my conqueror. When my last resources were exhausted, my warriors, worn down with long and toilsome marches, yielded, and I became your prisoner . . . I am now an obscure member of a nation that formerly honored and respected my opinions. The pathway to glory is rough, and gloomy hours obscure it. May the Great Spirit shed light on yours, and that you may never experience the humiliation that the power of the American government has reduced me to, is the wish of him who, in his native forests, was once as proud as you.‡

Black Hawk's warning to a young and confident nation was hardly noticed. But I quote these words at a time in which the society of the United States is being subjected to increased stress as the environment is befouled, resources are squandered, and the population continues to soar. The times are clearly out of joint when people are still suffering malnutrition and premature death in the mightiest nation ever seen on earth, when the Black American is still culturally disenfranchised after more than a century of legal and political freedom, when citizens have lost touch with an impersonal government.

The United States today is beset on all sides by difficulties and hard decisions. It should be no solace to hear that many of these problems are nothing new—that the Folsom people may have had to cope with at least a few of them and the Aztec assuredly with many —for a central assumption of this book has been that to examine the experience of humans throughout their 25,000 years on this continent is to hold up a mirror to the culture of Modern America. To understand the changes that have shaken religious orthodoxy in America today, it is illuminating to consider the nature of messianism and the evolution of religious practices along with different levels of social organization. To get at the causes of the discontent in America today, it is salutary to understand how complex a web binds the individual into the society; and here the experience of the Indians is likewise revealing. All through the inventory of culture—knowledge, belief, art, law, morals, and customs—much else of value can be learned by examining the cultures of the American Indian.

That their cultures have been allowed to die, and that the ancestors of many of us took part in the intentional eradication of these people, are matters against which both reason and our own sensibilities rebel. Americans have somehow found it easier to lament the extermination of the passenger pigeon, or the threatened extinction of the whooping crane and the ivory-billed woodpecker, than to consider seriously what it means to have destroyed native American cultures. Who mourns over losing the Pequot of Connecticut, the Beothuk of Newfoundland, the Mandan of the plains, the Mascouten of Wisconsin, the Yellowknife of Canada, the bands of Baja California—all of them now culturally, and in many cases physically, extinct? Who would recall the Delaware Indians had their name not been taken by a state? Until a moving book about him was published, few people ever knew, much less cared, that in 1916 Ishi, the last of the Yahi Indians of California, died at San Francisco in a museum of anthropology.‡ No crusade was undertaken to save the Yahi, nor was a dollar raised to preserve the cultures of the Kickapoo and Peoria Indians. Millions of dollars have been spent in excavating and transporting to museums the tools, weapons, and other artifacts of Indians long dead—but scarcely a penny to allow the ways of their living descendants to survive. Modern Americans are quick to prevent cruelty to animals, and sometimes even to humans, but no counterpart of the Humane Society or of the Sierra Club exists for the prevention of cruelty to entire cultures.

All over the world today, at an accelerating pace, simpler cultures are disappearing. The Tasmanians are already gone. The Yahgan of Tierra del Fuego, who were studied by Darwin, are virtually extinct; and every year sees fewer Seri in Mexico and fewer Negritos in the Philippines, fewer Aleuts in Alaska and Ainu in Japan, fewer Bushmen in South Africa and Polynesians in Hawaii. The Brazilians are today eradicating their Amazonian Indians with the same brutal gusto that North Americans displayed on their own frontier a century ago. And the same means by which the native American cultures were destroyed—military force, disruption, and uprooting, with attendant famine and disease—have recently been visited on the cultures of Vietnam.

Little is being done to preserve the numerous cultures that have so much to tell modern humans about themselves. Perhaps we, who for so long regarded ourselves as bringers of light to the shadowy recesses of North America, will finally admit that there is much about which the Indians can illuminate us. This was the message of Black Elk, a spokesman of the Oglala Sioux, who in 1886 joined a Wild West show so that he might journey to Chicago and New York, thereby to learn from the Whites and help his people. But he concluded:

I did not see anything to help my people. I could see that the Wasichus [that is, the Whites] did not care for each other the way our people did before the nation's hoop was broken. They would take everything from each other if they could, and so there were some who had more of everything than they could use, while crowds of people had nothing at all and maybe were starving. They had forgotten that the earth was their mother. This could not be better than the old ways of my people.‡

Many Indians today feel the same way. They are being seduced by an industrial society that offers them few values that Indians have traditionally cherished—most particularly, the conviction that human beings, not property, are central to society. Many Indians today are asking only for the opportunity to determine their own destinies and to recapture values that have proved their worth in the past. They ask for the right to decide how their land is to be used, how their children are to be educated, their customs perpetuated, and their reservations administered.

To do nothing now is to let our children lament that they never knew the magnificent diversity of humankind because our generation let disappear those cultures that might have taught it to them.

Notes and Sources

I: AN EXAMPLE FOR MODERN HUMANS

Much of the material in this chapter is based on the writings of Service (1975, 1971), Steward (1956, 1955), and White (particularly 1959, also 1969 and 1975).

Page 3   *The Journal of Christopher Columbus* (1960), New York: Clarkson N. Potter, p. 24.

Page 6   As outlined in *Ancient Society* (1877).

Page 7   A recent attempt, and one of the most ambitious, is by Ribiero (1968). It proposes a series of technological revolutions that cause societies to pass from Archaic to Regional and then to World Civilizations, with numerous steps in between. One problem with Ribiero's theory is that many of these revolutions actually turn out to be long evolutionary sequences.

Page 10   The Cheyenne example, as well as other examples of great importance to an understanding of cultural evolution, can be found in Meggers (1960).

Page 12   See my other arguments with Benedict on pages 92–94 and 130.
             The taxonomic classification of social organizations used in this book is based largely on the theories of Service and Steward.

II: GREAT BASIN SHOSHONE

In connection with the ethnological chapters that follow, several books will be helpful, both for their summaries of material and for their extensive bibliographies: Spencer, Jennings, *et al.* (1977), Garbarino (1976), Washburn (1975), Brandon (1974), Oswalt (1973), Driver (1969), and Josephy (1968). Excellent introductions to the literature by and about the American Indian are Turner (1974) and Sanders and Peek (1973).

313

Some classic sources for the Great Basin Shoshone specifically are two works by Steward (chapter 6 of 1955, and 1938), Stewart (1939), and Lowie (1924). An historical approach is Trenholm and Carley (1964); a valuable study of one particular group is Kelly (1964).

Page 18 *Roughing It* by Mark Twain, Harper & Brothers edition, 1871, pp. 131–132.

Page 19 *Native Races* by H. H. Bancroft, The History Press, 1886, p. 440.

Page 20 *The Descent of Man* by Charles Darwin, 1871, chapter 3.

Page 21 The biosocial view is nowadays becoming as fashionable as the culturalist view was in the 1950's and 1960's. Among the more important of such works are *Sociobiology* by E. O. Wilson (Cambridge Mass.: Harvard University Press, 1975) and *The Imperial Animal* by Lionel Tiger and Robin Fox (New York: Holt, Rinehart and Winston, 1971). This is not the place to summarize the sociobiological position, nor is it fair to attempt to do so in a few lines. And it is unfortunately not possible to attempt to show its irrelevance in the context of this book; those interested can consult Sahlins (1976), among others. Let me, though, ~tate that my bias is toward the culturalist view, while at the same time recognizing that we humans are of course also vertebrates, mammals, and primates—and that our evolutionary history has left its mark on our body and our behavior. But we are preeminently humans and our behavior must ultimately be explained in those terms.

Page 23 The number of cultural items in the North African landing comes from Steward (1955), p. 102.

Page 28 The statistic on the prevalence of incest was reported at the 1967 convention of the American Psychological Association by R. O. Olive.

Page 29 Kroeber (1948), section 167.

Page 30 Tylor (1888), p. 267.

Page 37 Powell and Ingalls (1874), pp. 3, 21.

III: ESKIMO

Basic sources for the Eskimo were Birket-Smith (1972), Balikci (1970), Oswalt (1967), Spencer (1959), Weyer (1932), Jenness (1922), and Boas (1888). For views of the modern life of the Eskimo, see Burch (1975), Briggs (1970), Chance (1966), and

VanStone (1962). For interesting insights rather than detailed information, Freuchen (1961) and Jenness (1929) are recommended. A nontechnical summary of Arctic archeology appears in Giddings (1967); more technical are Dumond (1974) and Bandi (1968).

Page 39	The quotation appears in Birket–Smith (1972).
Page 40	Estimates of Eskimo populations vary greatly. Recent Canadian and United States censuses place the population at about 46,000 (exclusive of the Greenland Eskimo), but it is possibly higher than that. For accounts of European explorers in contact with the Eskimo, see Morison (1971).
Page 43	Carpenter (1966), p. 206.
Page 46	The Netsilik are discussed in detail by Balikci (1970).
Page 51	Freuchen (1961), p. 154. An excellent volume on alliances, exchange, and ·gifts among the Eskimo is Guemple (1971).
Page 52	A brief discussion of communism in simple societies appears in Service (1966), pp. 21–25.
Page 53	Rasmussen (1927), p. 250.
Page 55	The scatological verse and the incident of the old woman appear in Birket–Smith (1972). An excellent discussion of legal mechanisms in Eskimo society appears in Hoebel (1968).
Page 60	Several psychological studies of the shaman have been made, among them Harner (1973) and Silverman (1967). Weyer (1932) describes several curing ceremonies in detail and also presents much excellent material on Eskimo religion. See also the indexed references to Eskimo religion in Norbeck (1961). A full discussion of shamanism in relation to American Indians is Park (1938).

IV: THE SUB-ARCTIC

General sources for the Sub-Arctic bands are VanStone (1974), Steward (1955, particularly chapter 8), Leacock (1954), Speck (1940), and Jenness (1935, 1932). The band's hunting adaptation is emphasized by Nelson (1973).

Page 66	For the Northern Ojibwa, see Bishop (1976, 1974, and 1970). Attempts to reconstruct the primeval social and political organization of the Sub-Arctic bands have also been made by VanStone (1974) and Hickerson (1976, 1970).

Page 66   The linguistic analysis is by Hockett and is mentioned in Service (1971), p. 75.

Page 67   The Tylor quote is from his *Anthropology* (Ann Arbor: University of Michigan Press, reprinted 1960), p. 249. For more on patrilocal bands, see Owen (1965).

Page 68   The LeJeune quotations are from Thwaites (1896–1901), vol. 6, pp. 243 and 165.

Page 70   The Champlain quotation is from *The Works of Samuel de Champlain*, edited by H. P. Bigger (Toronto, 1923), vol. 2, p. 171.

Page 70   LeJeune's observations are in Thwaites (1896–1901), vol. 5, p. 25.

Page 71   Quoted in Thwaites (1896–1901), vol. 8, p. 57.

Page 72   The quotation is from Knight (1965), p. 33.

Page 73   Much of the material on territories is drawn from Helm (1972, 1968), Bishop (1970), Snow (1968), and Leacock (1954).

Page 73   The quotation on anxiety is from Hippler (1973). A basic study of Sub-Arctic anxiety is Hallowell (1941); see also his 1960 and 1955 publications.

Page 76   Material on the Penobscot totems is mainly from Speck (1940), pp. 203–211.

Page 76   The study of the Rainbow Division is by Linton (1924).

Page 77   A critique of Freud's theory is Kroeber (1920).

Page 77   The Lévi–Strauss quotation is from his 1963 publication, p. 89.

V: ZUÑI

The Pueblo have probably inspired more anthropological studies than any other large group of American Indians. The publications listed here include only those directly concerned with the aspects of Pueblo life discussed in this chapter. For a good review of the Pueblo literature, see Dozier (1964). Scully (1975), Ortiz (1972), Underhill (1971), Dozier (1970), Eggan (1950), and Parsons (1939) are all of interest for general discussions. The archeology of the Pueblo, as well as of other southwestern Indians, is presented in McGregor (1965).

For theoretical aspects of tribal organization, see Service (1971), pp. 99–132, and Steward (1955), pp. 151–172.

Studies of the Zuñi in particular include Roberts (1956), Goldman (1937), Bunzel (1932), and Stevenson (1901). A good brief summary is in Spencer, Jennings, *et al.* (1977).

Page 80   An attempt to reconstruct ancient Pueblo society is Longacre (1970).

Page 84   For a wide-ranging discussion of clans, see Tooker (1971).

Page 87   The Mundurucú material is based on a study by Murphy (1956).

Page 88   Bunzel (1932), p. 480.

Page 92   Goldfrank (1945 A).

Page 92   Ellis (1951).

Page 93   Li An-che (1937).

Page 96   Norbeck (1961), p. 208, quotes portions of this account from *Scatologic Rites of All Nations* by J. G. Bourke, Washington, 1891.

Page 97   For the place of buffoonery in American Indian religions, see Steward (1930) and Parsons and Beals (1934).

VI: IROQUOIS

Morgan (1851) is essential for an understanding of the Iroquois, and Beauchamp (1905) also is valuable. Three more recent books are Wallace (1970), Noon (1949), and Hunt (1940). Several important papers have been published by Speck (among them, 1955 and 1944) and Fenton (1953, 1941).

Page 99   Quoted in Quain (1937), p. 240.

Page 103   The quotation is from Brown (1970), p. 156, as is the material that follows on the economic status of females.

Page 106   This discussion of great leaders owes a debt to the "Patterns" and "Cultural Processes" sections of Kroeber (1948) and to White (1969).

Page 107   The material on Iroquois dreams and psychotherapy comes from Wallace (1970, 1958).

Page 108   An excellent discussion of warfare is Harrison (1973).

Page 109   Quoted in Thwaites (1896–1901), vol. 13, pp. 59–79.

Page 111   As just one example, note Genesis 6:2. For commentary, see *The Anchor Bible: Genesis*, translated and edited by E. A. Speiser (Garden City, N.Y.: Doubleday, 1964), p. 44.

Page 111   These and numerous other fascinating facts can be found in *A Dictionary of Angels* by Gustav Davidson (Glencoe, Ill.: The Free Press, 1967).

Page 112   Fenton has published several papers on the False
            Face society, particularly 1940 A and 1940 B.
Page 112   *Observations on the Inhabitants, Climate, Soil* ...
            by John Bartram (London, 1751), pp. 43–44.
Page 114   Wallace (1969), p. 75.
Page 114   Morgan (1851), pp. 145–146.

VII: PLAINS

The literature on the Plains Indians is unusually rich, and only
highlights can be indicated here. The ethnological works listed
under Notes and Sources for Chapter I contain extensive bibliographies. The enthnology of particular tribes makes delightful
reading, and the choice of books and papers is tremendous. For
excellent brief discussions of Mandan, Teton Dakota, and Kiowa, see Spencer, Jennings, *et al.* (1977). The Mandan are
discussed in depth by Bowers (1950). Three particularly good
works on the Cheyenne are Hoebel (1960) and Grinnell (1956,
1923). For the Blackfoot, see Wissler (1911, 1910), Goldfrank
(1945 B), and Ewers (1958, 1955); for the Crow, Ewers (1953)
and Lowie (1935); for the Comanche, Wallace and Hoebel
(1952); for the Sioux, Hassrick (1964); for the Pawnee, Weltfish (1965). A classic on the Omaha is Fletcher and La Flesche
(1911). General works are, among others, Hyde (1959) and
Lowie (1954). Excerpts from Prince Maximilian's journal of
his explorations of the northern plains, together with reproduc-
tions of magnificent sketches and paintings of Mandan, Blackfoot, Cree, Sioux, and others can be found in Thomas and
Ronnefeldt (1976).

A pioneering work on the prehistory of the plains area is
Strong (1940). For more recent studies, see Wendorf and
Hester (1962), Wedel (1961), and Mulloy (1952).

Page 118   This quotation and subsequent ones from the
            Coronado expedition are from *Eyes of Discovery*
            by John Bakeless (New York: Dover, 1961), pp.
            92–93.
Page 121   Excellent summaries of the effect of the horse on
            many Indian cultures are Holder (1970) and Roe
            (1955). See also Ewers (1955).
Page 121   A recent volume on the sun dance is Jorgensen
            (1972).
Page 128   Hagan (1961), p. 15, is the source for the origin
            of White scalping.
Page 129   *On Aggression* by Konrad Lorenz (New York:
            Bantam, 1967).
Page 130   *The Study of Man* by Ralph Linton (New York:
            Appleton–Century, 1936), p. 463.

Page 130   Freud's letter on the causes of war is in *Character and Culture* (New York: Collier Books, 1963), p. 141.

Page 131   Two excellent papers on Plains warfare are by Newcomb (1960, 1950). See also Mishkin (1940) for the importance of economic factors. A general discussion of theories about causes of warfare is in Harrison (1973).

Page 135   The vision quest as a rationale for the differential distribution of wealth—and also its implications for cultural evolution—is discussed by Albers and Parker (1971).

Page 136   Information about the vision quest in several cultures is given by Underhill (1948).

Page 138   The Ghost Dance is described in much more detail in Chapter XV.

VIII: NORTHWEST COAST

A vast literature exists about the Northwest Coast chiefdoms. Drucker (1955) offers a brief but able summary and parts of this chapter are indebted to it. A valuable collection of papers, some of which are also cited below, can be found in McFeat (1966). A brief summary of several chiefdoms is in Spencer, Jennings, *et al.* (1977). General works on Northwest Coast art are Hawthorn (1967), Holm (1965), Inverarity (1950), and Davis *et al.* (1949). Excellent studies of particular chiefdoms are Drucker (1951) for the Nootka; Boas (1909), Drucker and Heizer (1967), and Rohner and Rohner (1970) for the Kwakiutl; Garfield (1939) for the Tsimshian; McIlwraith (1948) for the Bella Coola; Swanton (1909) for the Haida; Colson (1953) for the Makah; Oberg (1973) and de Laguna (1960) for the Tlingit; and Collins (1974) for the Skagit.

Page 143   For the theoretical aspects of chiefdoms in the preceding section and elsewhere in this chapter, see Service (1971), pp. 133–169.

Page 144   Material on the workings of the Tsimshian chiefdom and a fuller explanation of the system can be found in Garfield (1939), particularly pp. 182–184.

Page 146   Drucker (1939), p. 58.

Page 148   The source for the discussion of adultery and rank is Oberg (1934).

Page 153   The question of transoceanic and other influences on the totem pole is discussed by Quimby (1948).

Page 160   Anything so intriguing as the potlatch understandably has been the subject of a vast literature, with many differing points of view. Most of the books and papers listed for this chapter touch upon one aspect or another of it; it is discussed specifically by, among others, Suttles (1960), Codere (1956, 1951), and Barnett (1938). The comparison of the Tlingit and Kwakiutl potlatches is by Rosman and Rubel (1972). The ecological explanation is stated by Suttles (1968) and Piddocke (1965); a variation of this view—that the potlatch encouraged the migration of people from less productive to more productive villages—is put forth in Adams (1973). Drucker and Heizer (1967), however, take issue with an ecological interpretation.

IX: NATCHEZ

The basic source for the Natchez is Swanton (1911); everything published since on this group exists as footnotes to his major piece of scholarship. Swanton (1946) places the Natchez in the context of other southeastern cultures. Le Petit's account of the Natchez can be found in Thwaites (1896–1901), vol. 68.

Page 165   Le Petit and other primary sources are abundantly quoted in Swanton (1911). All quotations in this chapter are either from Swanton or from Thwaites (1896–1901), vol. 68.

Page 172   The problem of the replenishment of the Stinkards is discussed, along with other facts about the class system, in Hart (1943) and Quimby (1946). The re-evaluation mentioned here is by White *et al.* (1971); a different explanation for the Natchez paradox is offered by Brain (1971).

Page 173   The story of the two descendants of survivors is told in Swanton (1946), p. 160.

X: AZTEC

The definitive volume in English devoted exclusively to all aspects of Aztec life is Vaillant (1962). But it was published originally in 1944 and was only slightly revised posthumously in 1962; it should, for all its excellence in many ways, be read with caution because much of it is out of date. Another readable account is Soustelle (1964). Books that cover the Aztec from the larger perspective of other Mexican cultures are Bernal (1975), Weaver (1972), Coe (1962), and Wolf (1959). In addition, a voluminous literature exists in Spanish, German, and other languages; I have not listed these in my Bibliography, but many such works can be found in the bibliographies of the above volumes.

For specific information on Aztec art, see many of the above as well as Covarrubias (1957). For Aztec religion, see León–Portilla (1963), Séjourné (1960), and the attractive volume by Caso (1958). For the history of the conquest by Cortés, no better source exists than the eyewitness account by Bernal Díaz del Castillo (reprinted 1956). For the archeological background, see chapters in many of the general works already mentioned, plus Millon (1973) and Willey (1966).

Page 178   Estimates of the population of Tenochtitlán vary tremendously. The lowest estimate is somewhat less than 100,000; other estimates range up to 300,000. One specialist even estimates a total population for "metropolitan" Tenochtitlán (that is, for the capital city plus adjoining Tlaltelolco) of between 500,000 and 1,000,000. For the higher estimates, see Willey (1966) and Soustelle (1964).

Page 179   This quotation and the next are from Bernal Díaz (1956), pp. 190–191.

Page 180   Quoted by Wolf (1959), p. 161.

Page 181   Quoted in Séjourné (1960), p. 4.

Page 183   A discussion of sociopolitical organization at the level of the state can be found in Service (1975), which is highly recommended.

Page 187   Bernal Díaz (1956), p. 214.

Page 188   Quoted by Coe (1962), p. 168.

Page 190   Bernal Díaz (1956), p. 119.

Page 192   Harner (1977) maintains the position that Aztec sacrifice was practiced as an excuse for cannibalism, which was an ecological necessity. He is also the source for the estimate, given a few paragraphs ago, that the Aztec were sacrificing about 250,000 victims a year at the time Cortés arrived. His position is controversial.

XI: THE PEOPLING OF NORTH AMERICA

Basic sources about the peopling of North America are: Jennings (1974), Gorenstein (1974), Patterson (1973), Fitting (1973), Meggers (1972), Ceram (1971), Irwin–Williams (1968), Willey (1966), and Haynes (1966). Ceram is for the general reader; both Meggers and Gorenstein are valuable brief accounts; Jennings is recent and definitive; somewhat older but with a broad sweep is Willey. An important, but conservative, summary of the Eastern Woodlands is Griffin (1967).

A longer list appears in Wauchope (1962), p. 3.
For the Pleistocene, see Butzer (1971). A good
           recent account of what is known about the land
           bridge is Hopkins (1973).
Few people suspected even a part of the truth
           about the origins in Asia of the American Indians.
           Only several decades after Columbus discovered
           the New World, though, the Spanish priest José de
           Acosta speculated that somewhere in the northern
           part of North America would ultimately be found
           a portion of the continent that was "not altogether
           severed and disjointed" from the Old World. Two
           centuries after that, Thomas Jefferson, in his *Notes
           on the State of Virginia*, put forth the concept of
           an Asian cradle for the Indian and a crossing via
           Bering Strait. De Acosta and Jefferson, though,
           were exceptions. Until as recently as several dec-
           ades ago, anthropologists did not generally agree
           about the migration over the Bering land bridge.
Leakey (1972) supports the great antiquity of the
           Calico site. For the position that the supposed evi-
           dence is simply the result of natural processes, see
           Haynes (1973); a reply to Haynes appeared in
           Science, vol. 182 (1973), pp. 1371–1372.
The problem of archeological dating is both com-
           plex and technical. Two primary methods—the
           geological and the radioactive—have been used to
           date very ancient materials. The first of these relies
           upon the extensive knowledge that geologists have
           accumulated about the Pleistocene. As the ice ad-
           vanced and retreated, major climatic changes oc-
           curred that affected all life in the vicinity. So when
           geologists detect the bones of certain animals pre-
           dominating at one level of a site, they may be able
           to infer a particular climate and therefore a partic-
           ular glacial or interglacial period. Pollen grains
           preserved in the deposits also are valuable clues,
           for they reveal the character of the vegetation and
           hence the climate. Each plant species has a distinc-
           tive pollen grain, which is remarkably durable and
           may be preserved in lake sediments for many
           thousands of years. Because the kinds of trees and
           other plants in a given region vary with changes
           in climate, the variation from level to level in the
           ratio of different pollen grains in a dried lake bed
           reflects local climate changes. The approximate age
           of Indian artifacts found in or under certain pollen

series can in this way be estimated, but exact dating must be done by other methods.

The geological study of rivers has been of some use, since the terraces along the riverbanks were the result of high and low water at various times, and these changing volumes of water were due to glacial events. Lake beds also can be revealing, because wind, water, or glacial melt can cause annual deposits of sediments in distinct layers that vary in thickness and composition. Each layer is known as a varve, and some localities may have hundreds of varves, one atop the other. The position and depth of artifacts in the varve series can in this way indicate approximate age.

Geological methods, though, give only *relative* dates; these state that one thing is older or younger in relation to another. The statement that "the remains of a campfire are older than the nearby spear points" may be helpful, but it does not tell how old either is. For *absolute* dating, with considerable reliability back to about 40,000 years, the archeologist uses the radioactive methods discovered by Willard F. Libby in the late 1940's. Radioactive dating is based on the principle that several mildly radioactive substances have always been formed in the earth's atmosphere by the action of cosmic rays. Carbon-14, for instance, is present in all living matter, since every plant or animal absorbs it from its environment until it dies. Libby believed that, after death, the carbon-14 stored in plant or animal tissue decayed at the same very slow and fixed rate at every place in the world. Contrary to these early convictions, though, recent findings show that the carbon-14 is not unvarying at all times and places; in fact, at certain times in the past it may have varied by as much as twenty percent.

Generally speaking, an ounce of carbon-14 will decay to only half an ounce after 5,730 years (with a statistical probability of error of several hundred years); that half ounce will become a quarter of an ounce in 11,460 years; only a sixty-fourth of the original ounce of carbon-14 will be left after about 34,380 years. After about 40,000 to 50,000 years, too little carbon-14 remains for accurate measurement (although a very new technique promises to allow tiny samples to be dated by radiocarbon to 70,000, or even 100,000, years). So to arrive at a date for a given sample, all that was necessary was to develop laboratory techniques to determine the original store of carbon-14 absorbed by the plant or animal when it was alive. In this way, charcoal from a campfire found at an early site often can show with reasonable accuracy when the artifacts associated with it were used. An animal bone carved by Paleo-Indians might give the atomic laboratory the facts it needs to date when the animal died and therefore ceased absorbing carbon-14 from the atmosphere. The method is, though, limited in several ways. Certain parts of plants or animals often do not concentrate enough carbon-14 while alive to provide a reliable sample for the laboratory, or they may concentrate it in varying amounts. Second, a sample can become contaminated. Water trickling into a site may have leached out some of the carbon-14 and therefore made the sample appear older than it actually was; or the subsequent penetration of a root into the sample might have had the contrary effect. Such hazards to accuracy are being offset by more refined techniques and by using multiple samples. When several samples all give dates clustering around the same time, and nothing in the lay of the land disputes this, then the average of several radiocarbon dates can be accepted as a reasonably accurate pinpoint in time.

Page 206   The controversial new dating technique used for the San Diego skeletal materials is described in Bada *et al.* (1974). A very readable summary of present knowledge about early humans in the New World is MacNeish (1976); he makes a sound case for early arrival.

Page 209   Tolstoy (1975) has maintained that a continuing interchange of technologies and ideas took place across Alaska and Siberia. He has identified at least four kinds of archeological assemblages in the Alaskan area that show affinities to specific industries in Siberia and Japan.

Page 209   The lack of resemblance to Siberian artifacts during this period is stated by MacNeish (1976).

Page 210   Little of a scientific nature about Sandia has been published since the early discoveries. For a popular account by the archeologist involved, see Hibben (1960).

Page 212   A good review of Clovis appears in Haynes (1966).

Page 218   Paul S. Martin of the University of Arizona has upheld a theory of the Paleo-Indians as the cause for the North American extinction. Among his many publications, see particularly 1973 and 1967. A challenge to the overkill hypothesis has recently emerged. Approximately the same percentage of bird species (including ancestors of crows, jays, orioles, ducks, and storks), not hunted by humans and not directly associated with mammals, also disappeared at about the same time. Apparently some other cause, common to both birds and mammals, accounted for the extinctions; the most obvious cause is climate change. See Grayson (1977).

Page 220   For the important Danger Cave site, see Jennings (1957) and Irwin–Williams (1968).

Page 222   An excellent summary of Modoc is Fowler (1959).

Page 223   Caldwell's valuable study is his 1958 paper. For the variety of plants utilized around the Great Lakes, see Yarnell (1964).

Page 225   For the origins of corn and the Tehuacán caves, see MacNeish *et al.* (1967–1972).

Page 225   More information about the evolution of agriculture can be found in Flannery (1973).

Page 227   The report by Meggers, Evans, and Estrada (1965) contains numerous illustrations of Valdivia and Jomon pottery. Bischof and Viteri (1972) contradict their assertion of a connection between the two.

Page 228   An extensive list of apparent parallels found in both hemispheres is by Sorenson (1971).

Page 230   Numerous scholars have tackled the problem of the distribution of the sweet potato. For a dispassionate survey of the arguments, see Brand (1971). Other points of view can be found in *American Anthropologist,* vol. 74 (1972), pp. 342–366, and vol. 76 (1974), pp. 69–72.

Page 230   The question of transoceanic contacts is complex and in contention. A review article with a bias toward the influence of such contacts on the Olmec, the earliest civilization of Mesoamerica, is Meggers (1975). A less biased account—which does not support significant cultural contact between the Americas and Asia or Africa previous to the Norse—is the Society for American Archeology symposium volume edited by Riley *et al.* (1971).

Page 231   Some general sources on the Southwest are McGregor (1965) and Reed (1964).

Page 232   For Hohokam canals, see Woodbury (1960). The definitive work on the Hohokam is Haury (1976).

Page 233   Comparatively recent archeological dates in the Southwest can be given with exceeding accuracy because of a technique known as dendrochronology —that is, dating ruins by the study of the growth rings in their wood. Most trees that grow in areas of erratic rainfall, such as the Southwest, add rings of new growth in varying widths each year. For example, a period of three years of drought followed by one year of heavy rainfall shows a pattern of three very narrow rings and one wide ring outside of them. A two-hundred-year-old tree cut down today would reveal a pattern of two hundred wide and narrow rings going back to the tree's first sprouting. Also, the innermost (and therefore the oldest) rings in this tree would overlap the pattern of the outer rings of another log found in an adobe house that had been cut down, say, in 1790. And the inner rings of this 1790 log would similarly overlap the pattern on beams still older that had been used to construct Pueblo Indian dwellings. In this way, master charts of ring patterns that go back to 103 B.C. have been drawn up for various areas of the Southwest.

These charts allow samples of wood found in archeological sites to be dated accurately. When archeologists excavate a ruin in the Southwest, they are likely to find logs and pieces of wood incorporated into the construction. All they have to do is slide their sample along the master chart until they find the place where the patterns of wide and narrow rings match. Then they know that the outside ring of the sample will give them the exact year in which that tree was cut down, and presumably also the date when construction began. A side benefit of tree-ring dating is that it provides very precise information about the amounts of rainfall for each year; the study of tree rings has thus given archeologists a clear picture of the severe drought in the Southwest from 1276 to 1299. Dendrochronology is an exceedingly useful tool in this region, but attempts to apply it to other parts of North America have not been so successful—although some tree-ring studies in the Plains and Arctic are proving of use. The reason is that in these other areas the weather does not vary sufficiently from year to year to cause distinctive enough patterns in tree-ring widths.

The view that changes in the environment itself resulted in abandonment of the Anasazi villages has been stated by Schoenwetter (1962).

Page 237   For the Woodlands, see Struever (1968), Griffin (1967), and Caldwell (1962). Several points of view about Adena and Hopewell will be found in Caldwell and Hall (1970), Prufer (1964), Dragoo (1963), and Webb and Baby (1957).

Page 238   The classic study of the Mississippian culture is Phillips, Ford, and Griffin (1951).

XII: THE GENERATIONS OF ADAM

A good summary of physical anthropology in the Americas is T. D. Stewart (1973); also of interest is Newman (1962). Summaries of human evolution in general are Farb (1978), Campbell (1974), Pfeiffer (1972), and Hulse (1971). For general background information about linguistics and other fields of anthropology as well, consult Sapir (1963). Farb (1974) covers many aspects of general linguistics; the index of that volume will lead the reader to examples from American Indian languages.

Page 242   Information on genetic traits can be found in the basic sources on physical anthropology and evolution listed above and, in particular, in Bodmer and Cavalli–Sforza (1976).

Page 245   Facts on the number of languages, plus much else of interest, can be found in Voegelin and Voegelin (1964) and McQuown (1955).

Page 250   The quotation is from Sapir (1929). See also Whorf (1956). Various views of the Sapir–Whorf hypothesis are contained in the papers in Hoijer (1954).

XIII: THE END OF THE TRAIL

Excellent discussions of Indian–White relations, representing an assault upon a nation's conscience, are McNickle (1973), Oswalt (1973), Brown (1970), Jackson (1965), Hagan (1961), and Pearce (1953). Primary sources are documented in Washburn (1975, 1973, 1964) and in Forbes (1964).

Page 258   A fascinating volume about the attitude of sixteenth-century Spaniards toward the inhabitants of the New World is Hanke (1959). Readers who wish to

recapture the meeting of the two cultures—
explorers and natives—should read Morison's two
volumes (1974, 1971).

Page 259   The information and quotations in this paragraph
            are from Morison (1974).

Page 259   The full story of the Valladolid debates is told in
            Hanke (1959).

Page 260   The very high population estimates, which are
            controversial, are by Dobyns, Thompson, *et al.*
            (1966).

Page 261   For population statistics for United States and
            Canadian Indians and Eskimo, see McNickle (1973).

Page 262   This quotation is from Crosby (1972), p. 31, as
            are several other facts and quotations in the last
            two paragraphs.

Page 263   The World War II study was reported by Alex-
            ander Alland, Jr. of Columbia University at the
            1967 annual meeting of the American Anthro-
            pological Association.

Page 264   Montaigne's comments are from "On Cannibals,"
            chapter 31 of Book One of the *Essays* (Heritage
            Club edition).

Page 264   The Bressani quotation is from Thwaites (1896–
            1901), vol. 38, p. 257. The second Jesuit quotation
            is from the same source, vol. 29, p. 281. From here
            until the end of the chapter, it becomes impractical
            to cite sources for every quotation and fact. Most
            of them can be found in Spencer, Jennings, *et al.*
            (1977), McNickle (1973), Washburn (1964), and
            Hagan (1961).

Page 266   Quoted in Washburn (1964), p. 183.
Page 268   Quoted in Smith (1950), p. 219.
Page 269   An excellent recent history of the removals of the
            major eastern tribes is Jahoda (1975).

Page 271   The quotations from Tocqueville are from the
            Knopf edition (1945), vol. 1, pp. 339–341.

Page 275   Quoted in Hagan (1961), p. 121.
Page 276   Many well-intentioned Whites in the nineteenth
            century actually worked against the best interests
            of the Indians, believing that the Indians could—
            and indeed should—disappear into the great melt-
            ing pot. For statements by these reformers, see
            Prucha (1973).

Page 277   The present plight of the Indians has been docu-
            mented in detail in Steiner (1976), Leacock and
            Lurie (1971), and Levine and Lurie (1970),
            among others.

Page 277   Powhatan's speech is from Forbes (1964), p. 55.

XIV: BORROWED CULTURES

Two valuable symposium volumes on acculturation in several Indian societies are Spicer (1960) and Tax (1952 B). For a thorough documentation of the impact of Whites upon Indians in one specific area, the Southwest, see Spicer (1962). For the same sort of treatment about the Mexican Indians, see Tax (1952 A). Many of the ethnographic works listed as sources for previous chapters of this book contain sections on acculturation. For acculturation in general, see Bohannan and Plog (1967) and sections 162–182 of Kroeber (1948).

Page 281 Additional information on the debt of North American culture to the Indians can be found in Driver (1969), chapter 29, and Hallowell (1959, 1957).

Page 281 The Crèvecoeur quotation is from the Dutton edition (1957), p. 209.

Page 283 Swanton (1926).

Page 284 My dicussion of Indianization is based largely on Hallowell (1963). See his excellent bibliography for further sources.

Page 286 Considerable dispute exists about when the Navajo arrived in the Southwest. The earliest firm archeological date is A.D. 1491, but obviously their arrival was earlier. Ambiguous archeological evidence places them in the Southwest by A.D. 1300, and some perhaps arrived by A.D. 1000. A few bold archeologists place their arrival even earlier, but they lack support.

Page 290 Much of the material on the Navajo came from Vogt (1960). I am also indebted to several papers by Hill (1948, 1940 A, 1940 B). A brief review of Navajo life, emphasizing ecological relations, is Downs (1972). See also Underhill (1956) and Kluckhohn and Leighton (1946).

Page 290 The potlatch example is from Drucker and Heizer (1967), pp. 27–34.

Page 293 The example of the Navajo and Zuñi veterans is based on the study by Adair and Vogt (1949); see also Goldfrank (1952).

XV: THE HOPES OF THE OPPRESSED

This chapter owes a primary debt to Mooney (1896), a work that discusses many Indian revitalization movements in addition to the Ghost Dance of 1890. See also Wilson (1973), and for general information about millennial movements around the world, Thrupp (1970) and Lanternari (1963). Other important basic sources appear in the notes below.

Page 299   For more on the Ghost Dance and its origins, see
              La Barre (1972), DuBois (1939), and Spier (1927).
Page 301   This explanation has been suggested by Hill (1944).
Page 303   For a full study of the Handsome Lake religion,
              see Wallace (1970).
Page 305   The statement on peyote is from La Barre *et al.*
              (1951).
Page 306   An extensive literature exists on peyotism, in par-
              ticular Aberle (1966), La Barre (1960, 1938), and
              Slotkin (1956). An excellent volume about the use
              of hallucinogens is Harner (1973).
Page 306   Much of the analysis that follows is based on
              Wallace (1956).
Page 309   Quoted in Astrov (1962), p. 142.
Page 311   The story of Ishi has been told by Kroeber (1961).
              Ishi slept in the museum and worked as a helper
              for the custodian while anthropologists studied his
              language and recollections of his culture. Possess-
              ing no immunity to tuberculosis, he died within a
              year of contracting it.
Page 312   The Black Elk quotation is from *Black Elk Speaks*
              edited by John Neihardt (Lincoln, Nebr.: Univer-
              sity of Nebraska Press, 1961), p. 221.

Bibliography

ABERLE, D. F. 1966. *The Peyote Religion Among the Navaho.* New York: Viking Fund Publications in Anthropology.

ADAIR, J. and E. VOGT. 1949. "Navaho and Zuñi Veterans: A Study in Contrasting Modes of Culture Change." *American Anthropologist*, vol. 51, pp. 547–561.

ADAMS, J. W. 1973. *The Gitksan Potlatch: Population Flux, Resource Ownership and Reciprocity.* New York: Holt, Rinehart and Winston.

ALBERS, P. and S. PARKER. 1971. "The Plains Vision Experience: A Study of Power and Privilege." *Southwestern Journal of Anthropology*, vol. 27, pp. 203–233.

ASTROV, M., editor. 1962. *American Indian Prose and Poetry (The Winged Serpent).* New York: Capricorn.

BADA, J. F., *et al.* 1974. "New Evidence for the Antiquity of Man in North America." *Science*, vol. 184, pp. 791–793.

BALIKCI, A. 1970. *The Netsilik Eskimo.* Garden City, N.Y.: Natural History Press.

BANDI, H. G. 1968. *Eskimo Prehistory.* Seattle: University of Washington Press.

BANK, T. P. 1958. "The Aleuts." *Scientific American*, vol. 199 (November), pp. 112–120.

BARNETT, H. G. 1938. "The Nature of the Potlatch." *American Anthropologist*, vol. 40, pp. 349–358.

BEAUCHAMP, W. M. 1905. *History of the New York Iroquois.* Albany: N.Y. State Museum Bulletin.

BENEDICT, R. 1934. *Patterns of Culture.* Boston: Houghton Mifflin.

BERNAL, I. 1975. *Mexico Before Cortez.* Garden City, N.Y.: Anchor.

BINFORD, S. R. and L. R. BINFORD, editors. 1968. *New Perspectives in Archaeology.* Chicago: Aldine.

BIRKET-SMITH, K. 1972. *The Eskimos.* New York: Crown.

BISCHOF, H. and G. VITERI. 1972. "Pre-Valdivia Occupation on the South Coast of Ecuador." *American Antiquity*, vol. 37, pp. 548–551.

BISHOP, C. A. 1976. "The Emergence of the Northern Ojibwa: Social and Economic Consequences." *American Ethnologist*, vol. 3, pp. 39–54.

————. 1974. *The Northern Ojibwa and the Fur Trade: An Historical and Ecological Study*. New York: Holt, Rinehart and Winston.

————. 1970. "The Emergence of Hunting Territories Among the Northern Ojibwa." *Ethnology*, vol. 9, pp. 1–15.

BOAS, F. 1909. "Kwakiutl of Vancouver Island." *American Museum of Natural History Memoir*.

————. 1888. "The Central Eskimo." *Smithsonian Annual Report*. (Reprinted Lincoln: University of Nebraska Press, 1964.)

BODMER, W. F. and L. L. CAVALLI-SFORZA. 1976. *Genetics, Evolution, and Man*. San Francisco: Freeman.

BOHANNAN, P. and F. PLOG, editors. 1967. *Beyond the Frontier: Social Process and Cultural Change*. Garden City, N.Y.: Natural History Press.

BOWERS, A. W. 1950. *Mandan Social and Ceremonial Organization*. Chicago: University of Chicago Press.

BRAIN, J. P. 1971. "The Natchez 'Paradox.' " *Ethnology*, vol. 10, pp. 215–222.

BRAND, D. D. 1971. "The Sweet Potato: An Exercise in Methodology." In Riley *et al.* (1971), pp. 343–365.

BRANDON, W. 1974. *The Last Americans*. New York: McGraw–Hill.

BRIGGS, J. L. 1970. *Never in Anger: Portrait of an Eskimo Family*. Cambridge, Mass.: Harvard University Press.

BROWN, D. 1970. *Bury My Heart at Wounded Knee*. New York: Holt, Rinehart and Winston.

BROWN, J. K. 1970. "Economic Organization and the Position of Women Among the Iroquois." *Ethnohistory*, vol. 17, pp. 151–167.

BUNZEL, R. L. 1932. "Introduction to Zuñi Ceremonialism." *Bureau of American Ethnology Annual Report*.

BURCH, E. S., JR. 1975. *Eskimo Kinsmen*. St. Paul, Minn.: West.

BUTZER, K. W. 1971. *Environment and Archaeology: An Introduction to Pleistocene Geography*. Chicago: Aldine–Atherton.

CALDWELL, J. R. 1962. "Eastern North America." In Willey and Braidwood (1962).

———— and R. L. HALL. 1970. *Hopewellian Studies*. Springfield: Illinois State Museum.

CAMPBELL, B. G. 1974. *Human Evolution*. Chicago: Aldine.

CARPENTER, E. 1966. "Image Making in Arctic Art." In *Sign, Image, and Symbol*, edited by G. Kepes (New York: Braziller, 1966), pp. 206–225.

CASO, A. 1958. *The Aztecs, People of the Sun.* Norman: University of Oklahoma Press.

CERAM, C. W. 1971. *The First American: A Story of North American Archeology.* New York: Harcourt Brace Jovanovich.

CHANCE, N. A. 1966. *The Eskimo of North Alaska.* New York: Holt, Rinehart and Winston.

CODERE, H. 1956. "The Amiable Side of Kwakiutl Life." *American Anthropologist,* vol. 58, pp. 334–351.

———. 1951. "Fighting with Property." *American Ethnological Society Monograph.*

COE, M. 1964. "The Chinampas of Mexico." *Scientific American,* vol. 211 (July), pp. 90–98.

———. 1962. *Mexico.* New York: Praeger.

COLLINS, J. 1974. *The Valley of the Spirits: The Upper Skagit Indians of Western Washington.* Seattle, Wash.: *American Ethnological Society Monograph.*

COLSON, E. 1953. *The Makah Indians.* Minneapolis: University of Minnesota Press.

COVARRUBIAS, M. 1957. *Indian Art of Mexico and Central America.* New York: Knopf.

———. 1954. *The Eagle, the Jaguar, and the Serpent: Indian Art of the Americas.* New York: Knopf.

CROSBY, A. W., JR. 1972. *The Columbian Exchange: Biological and Cultural Consequences of 1492.* Westport, Conn.: Greenwood.

DAVIS, R. T., *et al.* 1949. *Native Arts of the Pacific Northwest.* Stanford, Cal.: Stanford University Press.

DE LAGUNA, F. 1960. "The Story of a Tlingit Community." *Bureau of American Ethnology Bulletin.*

DÍAZ DEL CASTILLO, B. 1956. *The Discovery and Conquest of Mexico, 1519–21.* New York: Farrar, Straus.

DOBYNS, H. F., H. P. THOMPSON, *et al.* 1966. "Estimating Aboriginal American Population." *Current Anthropology,* vol. 7, pp. 395–449.

DOLE, G. L. and R. L. CARNEIRO, editors. 1960. *Essays in the Science of Culture in Honor of Leslie A. White.* New York: Crowell.

DOWNS, J. F. 1972. *The Navajo.* New York: Holt, Rinehart and Winston.

DOZIER, E. P. 1970. *The Pueblo Indians of North America.* New York: Holt, Rinehart and Winston.

———. 1964. "Pueblo Indians of the Southwest." *Current Anthropology,* vol. 5, pp. 79–97.

DRAGOO, D. W. 1963. *Mounds for the Dead.* Pittsburgh: Carnegie Museum.

DRIVER, H. 1969. *Indians of North America.* Chicago: University of Chicago Press.

DRUCKER, P. 1955. *Indians of the Northwest Coast.* New York: McGraw–Hill. (Reprinted Garden City, N.Y.: Natural History Press, 1963.)

———. 1951. "The Northern and Central Nootkan Tribes." *Bureau of American Ethnology Bulletin.*

———. 1939. "Rank, Wealth, and Kinship in Northwest Coast Society." *American Anthropologist,* vol. 41, pp. 55–65.

——— and R. F. HEIZER. 1967. *To Make My Name Good: A Reexamination of the Southern Kwakiutl Potlatch.* Berkeley: University of California Press.

DU BOIS, C. 1939. "The 1870 Ghost Dance." *University of California Anthropological Records.*

DUMOND, D. E. 1974. *Archaeology and Prehistory in Alaska.* Andover, Mass.: Warner Modular Publications.

EGGAN, F. 1950. *Social Organization of the Western Pueblos.* Chicago: University of Chicago Press.

———, editor. 1955. *Social Anthropology of the North American Tribes.* Chicago: University of Chicago Press.

ELLIS, F. H. 1951. "Patterns of Aggression and the War Cult in Southwestern Pueblos." *Southwestern Journal of Anthropology,* vol. 7, pp. 177–201.

EWERS, J. C. 1958. *The Blackfoot.* Norman: University of Oklahoma Press.

———. 1955. "The Horse in Blackfoot Indian Culture." *Bureau of American Ethnology Bulletin.*

———. 1953. "Of the Crow Nation." *Bureau of American Ethnology Bulletin.*

FARB, P. 1978. *Humankind.* Boston: Houghton Mifflin.

———. 1974. *Word Play: What Happens When People Talk.* New York: Knopf.

———. 1963. *Face of North America: The Natural History of a Continent.* New York: Harper & Row.

FENTON, W. N. 1953. "The Iroquois Eagle Dance." *Bureau of American Ethnology Bulletin.*

———. 1941. "Towanda Longhouse Ceremonies." *Smithsonian Institution Bulletin.*

———. 1940 A. "Museum and Field Studies of Iroquois Masks and Ritualism." *Smithsonian Report.*

———. 1940 B. "Masked Medicine Societies of the Iroquois." *Smithsonian Report.*

FITTING, J. E., editor. 1973. *The Development of North American Archeology.* Garden City, N.Y.: Doubleday.

FLANNERY, K. V. 1973. "The Origins of Agriculture." *Annual Review of Anthropology,* vol. 2, pp. 271–310.

———, et al. 1967. "Farming Systems and Political Growth in Ancient Oaxaca." *Science,* vol. 158, pp. 445–454.

FLETCHER, A. C. and F. LA FLESCHE. 1911. "The Omaha Tribe." *Bureau of American Ethnology Report.*

FORBES, J. D., editor. 1964. *The Indian in America's Past*. Englewood Cliffs, N.J.: Prentice–Hall.

FOWLER, M. L. 1959. "Modoc Rock Shelter: An Early Archaic Site in Southern Illinois." *American Antiquity*, vol. 24, pp. 257–270.

FREUCHEN, P. 1961. *Book of the Eskimo*. Cleveland: World.

FREUD, S. 1918. *Totem and Taboo*. (Reprinted in new translation, New York: Norton, 1962.)

GARBARINO, M. S. 1976. *Native American Heritage*. Boston: Little, Brown.

GARFIELD, V. E. 1939. "Tsimshian Clan and Society." *University of Washington Publications in Anthropology*, vol. 7, pp. 167–349.

GIDDINGS, J. L. 1967. *Ancient Men of the Arctic*. New York: Knopf.

GOLDFRANK, E. S. 1952. "The Different Patterns of Blackfoot and Pueblo Adaptation to White Authority." In Tax (1952 B).

———. 1945 A. "Socialization, Personality, and the Structure of Pueblo Society (with particular reference to the Hopi and Zuñi)." *American Anthropologist*, vol. 47, pp. 516–539.

———. 1945 B. "Changing Configurations in the Social Organization of the Blackfoot Tribe During the Reserve Period." *American Ethnological Society Monograph*.

———. 1943. "Historic Change and Social Character, a Study of the Teton Dakota." *American Anthropologist*, vol. 45, pp. 67–83.

GOLDMAN, I. 1937. "The Zuñi of New Mexico." In Mead (1937).

GOODE, W. J. 1951. *Religion Among the Primitives*. New York: Crowell–Collier.

GORENSTEIN, S., *et al.* 1975. *North America*. New York: St. Martin's.

GRAYSON, D. K. 1977. "Pleistocene Avifaunas and the Overkill Hypothesis." *Science*, vol. 195, pp. 691–693.

GRIFFIN, J. B. 1967. "Eastern North American Archaeology: A Summary." *Science*, vol. 156, pp. 175–191.

GRINNELL, G. B. 1956. *The Fighting Cheyennes*. Norman: University of Oklahoma Press.

———. 1923. *The Cheyenne Indians*. New Haven, Conn.: Yale University Press. (Reprinted New York: Cooper Square, 1962.)

GUEMPLE, L., editor. 1972. *Alliance in Eskimo Society*. Seattle: University of Washington Press.

HAGAN, W. T. 1961. *American Indians*. Chicago: University of Chicago Press.

HALLOWELL, A. I. 1967. *Culture and Experience*. New York: Schocken.

———. 1963. "American Indians, White and Black: The Phenomenon of Transculturalization." *Current Anthropology*, vol. 4, pp. 519–531.

———. 1960. "Ojibwa Ontology, Behavior, and World View." In *Culture in History*, edited by S. Diamond (New York: Columbia University Press, 1960), pp. 19–52.

———. 1959. "Backwash of the Frontier." *Smithsonian Report*, pp. 447–472.

———. 1957. "The Impact of the American Indian on American Culture." *American Anthropologist*, vol. 59, pp. 201–217.

———. 1941. "The Social Function of Anxiety in Primitive Society." *American Sociological Review*, vol. 6, pp. 869–881.

HANKE, L. 1959. *Aristotle and the American Indian*. Bloomington: Indiana University Press.

HARNER, M. 1977. "The Ecological Basis for Aztec Sacrifice." *American Ethnologist*, vol. 4, pp. 117–135.

———. 1973. *Hallucinogens and Shamanism*. New York: Oxford University Press.

HARRISON, R. 1973. *Warfare*. Minneapolis, Minn.: Burgess.

HART, C. W. 1943. "A Reconsideration of the Natchez Social Structure." *American Anthropologist*, vol. 45, pp. 374–386.

HASSRICK, R. B. 1964. *The Sioux*. Norman: University of Oklahoma Press.

HAURY, E. W. 1976. *The Hohokam: Desert Farmers and Craftsmen*. Tucson: University of Arizona Press.

HAWTHORN, A. 1967. *Art of the Kwakiutl Indians and Other Northwest Coast Indian Tribes*. Seattle: University of Washington Press.

HAYNES, C. V. 1973. "The Calico Site: Artifacts or Geofacts?" *Science*, vol. 181, pp. 305–310.

———. 1966. "Elephant Hunting in North America." *Scientific American*, vol. 214 (June), pp. 104–112.

HELM, J. 1972. "The Dogrib Indians." In *Hunter and Gatherers Today*, edited by M. G. Bicchieri (New York: Holt, Rinehart and Winston, 1972), pp. 51–83.

———. 1968. "The Nature of the Dogrib Socioterritorial Groups." In *Man the Hunter*, edited by R. B. Lee and I. DeVore (Chicago: Aldine, 1968), pp. 118–125.

HIBBEN, F. C. 1960. *Digging Up America*. New York: Hill and Wang.

HICKERSON, H. 1970. *The Chippewa and Their Neighbors: A Study in Ethnohistory*. New York: Holt, Rinehart and Winston.

———. 1967. "Some Implications of the Theory of the Particularity, or 'Atomism,' of Northern Algonkians." *Current Anthropology*, vol. 8, pp. 313–343.

HILL, W. W. 1948. "Navaho Trading and Trading Ritual." *Southwestern Journal of Anthropology*, vol. 4, pp. 371–396.

———. 1944. "The Navaho Indians and the Ghost Dance of 1890." *American Anthropologist*, vol. 46, pp. 523–527.

———. 1940 A. "Some Navaho Culture Changes During Two Centuries." *Smithsonian Miscellaneous Collections*, pp. 395–415.

———. 1940 B. "Some Aspects of Navaho Political Structure." *Plateau*, vol. 13, pp. 23–28.

HIPPLER, A. E. 1973. "The Athabascans of Interior Alaska: A Culture and Personality Perspective." *American Anthropologist*, vol. 75 (1973), pp. 1529–1541.

HODGE, F. W. 1906. "Handbook of American Indians North of Mexico." *Bureau of American Ethnology Bulletin*. (Reprinted New York: Pageant, 1960.)

HOEBEL, E. A. 1968. *The Law of Primitive Man*. New York: Schocken.

———. 1960. *The Cheyennes: Indians of the Great Plains*. New York: Holt, Rinehart and Winston.

HOIJER, H., editor. 1954. *Language in Culture*. Washington, D.C.: American Anthropological Association Memoir.

———, *et al*. 1946. *Linguistic Structures of Native America*. New York: Viking Fund Publications in Anthropology.

HOLDER, P. 1970. *The Hoe and the Horse on the Plains*. Lincoln: University of Nebraska Press.

HOLM, B. 1965. *Northwest Coast Indian Art*. Seattle: University of Washington Press.

HOPKINS, D. M. 1973. "Sea Level History in Beringia During the Past 250,000 Years." *Quaternary Research*, vol. 3, pp. 520–540.

———. 1967. *The Bering Land Bridge*. Stanford, Cal.: Stanford University Press.

HULSE, F. S. 1971. *The Human Species*. New York: Random House.

HUNT, G. T. 1940. *The Wars of the Iroquois*. Madison: University of Wisconsin Press.

HYDE, G. E. 1959. *Indians of the High Plains*. Norman: University of Oklahoma Press.

INVERARITY, R. B. 1950. *Art of the Northwest Coast Indians*. Berkeley: University of California Press.

IRWIN–WILLIAMS, C., editor. 1968. *Early Man in Western North America*. Portales, N.M.: Eastern New Mexico University Press.

JACKSON, H. H. 1965. *A Century of Dishonor*. New York: Harper & Row. (Originally published in 1881.)

JAHODA, G. 1975. *The Trail of Tears: The Story of the American Indian Removals, 1813–1855*. New York: Holt, Rinehart and Winston.

JENNESS, D. 1935. "The Ojibwa Indians of Parry Island, Their Social and Religious Life." *National Museum of Canada Bulletin.*

————. 1932. *The Indians of Canada.* Ottawa: National Museum of Canada.

————. 1929. *People of the Twilight.* New York: Macmillan. (Reprinted Chicago: University of Chicago Press, 1959.)

————. 1922. "Life of the Copper Eskimos." *Canadian Arctic Expedition Report. Vol. 12.*

JENNINGS, J. D. 1974. *Prehistory of North America.* New York: McGraw–Hill.

————. 1957. *Danger Cave.* Salt Lake City: University of Utah Anthropological Papers Number 27.

————, editor. 1956. "The American Southwest: A Problem in Cultural Isolation." In Wauchope (1956), pp. 59–128.

JORGENSEN, J. G. 1972. *The Sun Dance Religion.* Chicago: University of Chicago Press.

JOSEPHY, A. M. 1968. *The Indian Heritage of America.* New York: Knopf.

JUDD, N. M. 1954. "The Material Culture of Pueblo Bonito." *Smithsonian Miscellaneous Collections.*

KELLY, I. T. 1964. *Southern Paiute Ethnography.* Salt Lake City: University of Utah Anthropological Papers.

KLUCKHOHN, C. and D. LEIGHTON, 1946. *The Navaho.* Cambridge, Mass.: Harvard University Press. (Reprinted Garden City, N.Y.: Natural History Press, 1962.)

KNIGHT, R. 1965. "A Re-examination of Hunting, Trapping, and Territoriality Among the Northeastern Algonkian Indians." In Leeds and Vayda (1965), pp. 27–42.

KROEBER, A. L. 1948. *Anthropology.* New York: Harcourt, Brace.

————. 1939. "Cultural and Natural Areas of Native North America." *University of California Publications in American Archaeology and Ethnology.* (Reprinted Berkeley: University of California Press, 1963.)

————. 1920. "Totemism and Taboo: An Ethnological Psychoanalysis." *American Anthropologist*, vol. 22, pp. 48–55.

————, editor. 1953. *Anthropology Today.* Chicago: University of Chicago Press.

KROEBER, T. 1961. *Ishi.* Berkeley: University of California Press.

LA BARRE, W. 1975. *The Peyote Cult.* Hamden, Conn.: Archon.

————. 1970. *The Ghost Dance: The Origins of Religion.* New York: Dell.

————. 1960. "Twenty Years of Peyote Studies." *Current Anthropology*, vol. 1, pp. 45–60.

————, et al. 1951. "Statement on Peyote." *Science*, vol. 114, pp. 582–583.

LANTERNARI, V. 1963. *The Religions of the Oppressed*. New York: Knopf.

LEACOCK, E. 1954. "The Montagnais 'Hunting Territory' and the Fur Trade." *American Anthropological Association Memoir*.

────── and N. O. LURIE, editors. 1971. *North American Indians in Historical Perspective*. New York: Random House.

LEAKEY, L. S. B., *et al*. 1972. *Pleistocene Man at Calico*. San Bernadino, Cal.: County Museum Association.

LEEDS, A. and A. P. VAYDA. 1965. *Man, Culture, and Animals*. Washington, D.C.: American Association for the Advancement of Science.

LÉON–PORTILLA, M. 1963. *Aztec Thought and Culture*. Norman: University of Oklahoma Press.

LÉVI–STRAUSS, C. 1963. *Totemism*. Boston: Beacon Press.

LEVINE, S. and N. O. LURIE, editors. 1970. *The American Indian Today*. Baltimore: Penguin.

LI AN-CHE. 1937. "Zuñi: Some Observations and Queries." *American Anthropologist*, vol. 39, pp. 62–76.

LINTON, R. 1924. "Totemism and the A.E.F." *American Anthropologist*, vol. 26, pp. 296–300.

LONGACRE, W. A., editor. 1970. *Reconstructing Prehistoric Pueblo Societies*. Albuquerque: University of New Mexico Press.

LOWIE, R. H. 1954. *Indians of the Plains*. New York: McGraw-Hill. (Reprinted Garden City, N.Y.: Natural History Press, 1963.)

──────. 1935. *The Crow Indians*. New York: Farrar & Rinehart. (Reprinted New York: Holt, Rinehart and Winston, 1956).

──────. 1924. "Notes on Shoshonean Ethnography." *American Museum of Natural History Anthropological Papers*, pp. 185–314.

MC FEAT, T., editor. 1966. *Indians of the North Pacific Coast*. Seattle: University of Washington Press.

MC GREGOR, J. C. 1965. *Southwestern Archaeology*. Urbana: University of Illinois Press.

MC ILWRAITH, T. F. 1948. *The Bella Coola Indians*. Toronto, Ontario: University of Toronto Press.

MAC NEISH, R. S. 1976. "Early Man in the New World." *American Scientist*, vol. 64, pp. 316–327.

──────, *et al*., editors. 1967–1972. *The Prehistory of the Tehuacan Valley* (5 volumes). Austin: University of Texas Press.

MC NICKLE, D. 1973. *Native American Tribalism*. New York: Oxford University Press.

MC QUOWN, N. 1955. "Indigenous Languages of Native America." *American Anthropologist*, pp. 501–570.

MARTIN, P. S. 1973. "The Discovery of America." *Science*, vol. 179, pp. 969–974.

———— and H. F. WRIGHT, editors. 1967. *Pleistocene Extinctions: Search for a Cause.* New Haven, Conn.: Yale University Press.

MEAD, M., editor. 1937. *Cooperation and Competition Among Primitive Peoples.* New York: McGraw–Hill. (Reprinted Boston: Beacon Press, 1961.)

MEGGERS, B. J. 1975. "Transpacific Origins of Mesoamerican Civilization." *American Anthropologist,* vol. 77, pp. 1–27.

————. 1972. *Prehistoric America.* Chicago: Aldine–Atherton.

————. 1960. "The Law of Cultural Evolution as a Practical Research Tool." In Dole and Carneiro (1960), pp. 302–316.

————. 1954. "Environmental Limitations on the Development of Culture." *American Anthropologist,* vol. 56, pp. 801–823.

————, C. EVANS, and E. ESTRADA. 1965. "Early Formative Period of Coastal Ecuador. The Valdivia and Machalilla Phases." *Smithsonian Contributions to Anthropology.*

MEIGS, P. 1939. "The Kiliwa Indians." *Ibero-Americana,* pp. 1–114.

MILLON, R. 1973. "The Study of Urbanism at Teotihuacan, Mexico." In *Mesoamerican Archaeology: New Approaches,* edited by N. Hammond (Austin: University of Texas Press, 1973), pp. 335–362.

MISHKIN, B. 1940. "Rank and Warfare Among Plains Indians." *American Ethnological Society Monograph.*

MOONEY, J. 1896. "The Ghost Dance Religion and the Sioux Outbreak of 1890." *Bureau of American Ethnology Annual Report.* (Reprinted Chicago: University of Chicago Press, 1964.)

MORGAN, L. H. 1877. *Ancient Society.* (Reprinted New York: Meridian, 1963.)

————. 1851. *League of the Ho-De-No-Sau-Nee or Iroquois.* (Reprinted New York: Corinth, 1962.)

MORISON, S. E. 1974. *The European Discovery of America: The Southern Voyages.* New York: Oxford University Press.

————. 1971. *The European Discovery of America: The Northern Voyages.* New York: Oxford University Press.

MURPHY, R. F. 1956. "Matrilocality and Patrilineality in Mundurucú Society." *American Anthropologist,* vol. 58, pp. 414–434.

NELSON, R. K. 1973. *Hunters of the Northern Forest.* Chicago: University of Chicago Press.

NEWCOMB, W. W. 1974. *North American Indians: An Anthropological Perspective.* Pacific Palisades, Cal.: Goodyear.

————. 1960. "Toward an Understanding of War." In Dole and Carneiro (1960), pp. 317–336.

————. 1950. "A Re-examination of the Causes of Plains Warfare." *American Anthropologist*, vol. 52, pp. 317–329.

NEWMAN, M. T. 1962. "Evolutionary Changes in Body Size and Head Form in American Indians." *American Anthropologist*, vol. 64, pp. 237–256.

NOON, J. A. 1949. *Law and Government of the Grand River Iroquois*. New York: Viking Fund Publications in Anthropology.

NORBECK, E. 1961. *Religion in Primitive Society*. New York: Harper & Row.

OBERG, K. 1973. *The Social Economy of the Tlingit Indians*. Seattle, Wash.: American Ethnological Society Monograph.

————. 1934. "Crime and Punishment in Tlingit Society." *American Anthropologist*, vol. 36, pp. 145–156.

ORTIZ, A., editor. 1972. *New Perspectives on the Pueblos*. Albuquerque: University of New Mexico Press.

OSWALT, W. H. 1973. *This Land Was Theirs*. New York: Wiley.

————. 1967. *Alaskan Eskimos*. San Francisco: Chandler.

OWEN, R. C. 1965. "The Patrilocal Band: A Linguistically and Culturally Hybrid Social Unit." *American Anthropologist*, vol. 67, pp. 675–690.

PARK, W. Z. 1938. *Shamanism in Western North America*. Evanston, Ill.: Northwestern University Press.

PARSONS, E. C. 1939. *Pueblo Indian Religion*. Chicago: University of Chicago Press.

———— and R. L. BEALS. 1934. "The Sacred Clowns of the Pueblo and Mayo–Yaqui Indians." *American Anthropologist*, vol. 36, pp. 491–516.

PATTERSON, T. C. 1973. *America's Past*. Glenview, Ill.: Scott, Foresman.

PEARCE, R. H. 1965. *Savagism and Civilization*. Baltimore: Johns Hopkins University Press.

PFEIFFER, J. E. 1972. *The Emergence of Man*. New York: Harper & Row.

PHILLIPS, P. J., J. A. FORD, and J. B. GRIFFIN. 1951. *Archaeological Survey in the Lower Mississippi Alluvial Valley*. Cambridge, Mass.: Peabody Museum of Archaeology and Ethnology, Harvard University.

PIDDOCKE, S. 1965. "The Potlatch System of the Southern Kwakiutl: A New Perspective." *Southwestern Journal of Anthropology*, vol. 21 (1965), pp. 244–264.

POWELL, J. W. and G. W. INGALLS. 1874. "Report on the Conditions of the Ute Indians." *Smithsonian Institution*.

PRUCHA, F. P., editor. 1973. *Americanizing the American Indians*. Cambridge, Mass.: Harvard University Press.

PRUFER, O. H. 1964. "The Hopewell Cult." *Scientific American*, vol. 211 (December), pp. 90–102.

QUAIN, B. H. 1937. "The Iroquois." In Mead (1937), pp. 240–312.

QUIMBY, G. I. 1960. *Indian Life in the Upper Lakes.* Chicago: University of Chicago Press.

———. 1948. "Culture Contact on the Northwest Coast Between 1785 and 1795." *American Anthropologist,* vol. 50, pp. 247–255.

———. 1946. "Natchez Social Structure as an Instrument of Assimilation." *American Anthropologist,* vol. 48, pp. 134–137.

RASMUSSEN, K. 1932. "Intellectual Culture of the Copper Eskimo." *Canadian Arctic Expedition Report.*

———. 1927. *Across Arctic America.* New York: Putnam.

RIBIERO, D. 1968. *The Civilization Process.* Washington, D.C.: Smithsonian Institution Press.

RILEY, C. L., *et al.,* editors. 1971. *Man Across the Sea.* Austin: University of Texas Press.

ROBERTS, J. M. 1956. "Zuñi Daily Life." *Notebook of Laboratory of Anthropology of University of Nebraska.*

ROE, F. G. 1955. *The Indian and the Horse.* Norman: University of Oklahoma Press.

ROHNER, R. P. and E. C. ROHNER. 1970. *The Kwakiutl Indians of British Columbia.* New York: Holt, Rinehart and Winston.

ROSMAN, A. and P. G. RUBEL. 1972. "The Potlatch: A Structural Analysis." *American Anthropologist,* vol. 74, pp. 658–671.

SAHLINS, M. D. 1976. *The Use and Abuse of Biology: An Anthropological Critique of Sociobiology.* Ann Arbor: University of Michigan Press.

———. 1967. *Tribesmen.* Englewood Cliffs, N.J.: Prentice–Hall.

SANDERS, T. E. and W. W. PEEK, editors. 1973. *Literature of the American Indian.* New York: Glencoe Press.

SAPIR, E. 1963. *Selected Writings in Language, Culture, and Personality.* Berkeley: University of California Press.

———. 1929. "The Status of Linguistics as a Science." *Language,* vol. 5, pp. 207–214.

SCHOENWETTER, J. 1962. "Pollen Analysis of Eighteen Archaeological Sites in Arizona and New Mexico." In *Chapters in Prehistory of Arizona,* edited by P. S. Martin (Chicago: Chicago Museum of Natural History, 1962).

SCULLY, V. 1975. *Pueblo: Mountain, Village, Dance.* New York: Viking.

SÉJOURNÉ, L. 1960. *Burning Water: Thought and Religion in Ancient Mexico.* New York: Grove Press.

SERVICE, E. R. 1975. *Origins of the State and Civilization: The Process of Cultural Evolution.* New York: Norton.

———. 1971. *Primitive Social Organization.* New York: Random House.

————. 1966. *The Hunters*. Englewood Cliffs, N.J.: Prentice–Hall.

SILVERMAN, J. 1967. "Shamans and Acute Schizophrenia." *American Anthropologist*, vol. 69, pp. 21–31.

SLOTKIN, J. S. 1956. *The Peyote Religion*. Glencoe, Ill.: The Free Press.

SMITH, H. N. 1950. *Virgin Land: The American West as Symbol and Myth*. Cambridge, Mass.: Harvard University Press.

SMITH, W. and J. M. ROBERTS. 1954. *Zuñi Law: A Field of Values*. Cambridge, Mass.: Peabody Museum of Archaeology and Ethnology, Harvard University.

SNOW, D. R. 1968. "Wabanaki Family Hunting Territories." *American Anthropologist*, vol. 70, pp. 1143–1151.

SORENSON, J. L. 1971. "The Significance of an Apparent Relationship Between the Ancient Near East and Mesoamerica." In Riley *et al.* (1971), pp. 219–241.

SOUSTELLE, J. 1964. *The Daily Life of the Aztecs*. Baltimore: Penguin.

SPECK, F. G. 1955. *The Iroquois*. Bloomfield Hills, Mich.: Cranbrook Institute.

————. 1944. *Midwinter Rites of the Cayuga Longhouse*. Philadelphia: University of Pennsylvania Press.

————. 1940. *Penobscot Man*. Philadelphia: University of Pennsylvania Press.

SPENCER, R. F. 1959. "The North Alaskan Eskimo: A Study in Ecology and Society." *Bureau of American Ethnology Bulletin*.

————, J. D. JENNINGS, *et al.* 1977. *The Native Americans*. New York: Harper & Row.

SPICER, E. H. 1962. *Cycles of Conquest*. Tucson: University of Arizona Press.

————. 1960. *Perspectives in American Indian Culture Change*. Chicago: University of Chicago Press.

SPIER, L. 1927. "The Ghost Dance of 1870 Among the Klamath of Oregon." *University of Washington Publications in Anthropology*.

STEINER, S. 1976. *The Vanishing White Man*. New York: Harper & Row.

STEVENSON, M. C. 1901. "The Zuñi Indians." *Bureau of American Ethnology Bulletin*.

STEWARD, J. H. 1956. "Cultural Evolution." *Scientific American*, vol. 194 (May), pp. 69–80.

————. 1955. *Theory of Culture Change*. Urbana: University of Illinois Press.

————. 1938. "Basin–Plateau Sociopolitical Groups." *Bureau of American Ethnology Bulletin*.

————. 1930. "The Ceremonial Buffoons of the American Indian." *Michigan Academy of Sciences*, pp. 187–207.

STEWART, O. C. 1939. *Northern Paiute Bands*. Berkeley: Univer-versity of California Press.

STEWART, T. D. 1973. *The People of America*. New York: Scribner.

STRONG, W. D. 1940. "From History to Prehistory in the Northern Great Plains." *Smithsonian Miscellaneous Collections*, pp. 353–394.

STRUEVER, S. 1968. "Woodland Subsistence–Settlement Systems in the Lower Illinois Valley." In Binford and Binford (1968), pp. 285–312.

SUTTLES, W. 1968. "Coping with Abundance: Subsistence on the Northwest Coast." In *Man the Hunter*, edited by R. B. Lee and I. DeVore (Chicago: Aldine, 1968), pp. 56–68.

SWANTON, J. R. 1952. "The Indian Tribes of North America." *Bureau of American Ethnology Bulletin*.

———. 1946. "The Indians of the Southeastern United States." *Bureau of American Ethnology Bulletin*.

———. 1926. "Notes on the Mental Assimilation of Races." *Journal of Washington Academy of Sciences*, pp. 493–502.

———. 1911. "Indian Tribes of the Lower Mississippi Valley and Adjacent Coast of the Gulf of Mexico." *Bureau of American Ethnology Bulletin*.

———. 1909. "Contributions to the Ethnology of the Haida." *The American Museum of Natural History Memoir*.

TAX, S., editor. 1952 A. *Heritage of Conquest*. Glencoe, Ill.: The Free Press.

———, editor. 1952 B. *Acculturation in the Americas*. Chicago: University of Chicago Press.

THOMAS, D. and K. RONNEFELDT, editors. 1976. *People of the First Man*. New York: Dutton.

THRUPP, S. L., editor. 1970. *Millennial Dreams in Action*. New York: Schocken.

THWAITES, R. G., editor. 1896–1901. *The Jesuit Relations and Allied Documents* (73 volumes). Cleveland: Burrows Brothers.

TOLSTOY, P. 1975. "From the Old World to the New World via Bering Strait." In Gorenstein *et al.* (1975), pp. 165–185.

TOOKER, E. 1971. "Clans and Moieties in North America." *Current Anthropology*, vol. 12, pp. 357–376.

TRENHOLM, V. C. and M. CARLEY, 1964. *The Shoshonis*. Norman: University of Oklahoma Press.

TURNER, F., editor. 1974. *The Portable North American Indian Reader*. New York: Viking.

TYLOR, E. B. 1888. "On a Method of Investigating the Development of Institutions; Applied to Laws of Marriage and Descent." *Journal of the Royal Anthropological Institute*, pp. 245–267.

———. 1871. *Primitive Culture*. (Reprinted New York: Harper & Row, 1958, as *The Origins of Culture and Religion in Primitive Culture*.)

UNDERHILL, R. 1971. *Red Man's America*. Chicago: University of Chicago Press.

———. 1956. *The Navahos*. Norman: University of Oklahoma Press.

———. 1948. "Ceremonial Patterns in the Greater Southwest." *American Ethnological Society Memoir*.

VAILLANT, G. C. 1962. *The Aztecs of Mexico*. Garden City, N.Y.: Doubleday.

VAN STONE, J. 1974. *Athapaskan Adaptations: Hunters and Fishermen of the Subarctic Forests*. Chicago: Aldine.

———. 1962. *Point Hope, An Eskimo Village in Transition*. Seattle: University of Washington Press.

VOEGELIN, C. F. and E. W. VOEGELIN. 1964. "Languages of the World: Native America." *Anthropological Linguistics*, vol. 6, pp. 1–149.

VOGT, E. Z. 1960. "Navaho." In Spicer (1960), pp. 278–336.

WALLACE, A. F. C. 1970. *The Death and Rebirth of the Seneca*. New York: Knopf.

———. 1958. "Dreams and Wishes of the Soul: A Type of Psychoanalytic Theory Among the Seventeenth Century Iroquois." *American Anthropologist*, vol. 60, pp. 234–248.

———. 1956. "Revitalization Movements." *American Anthropologist*, vol. 58, pp. 264–280.

WALLACE, E. and E. A. HOEBEL. 1952. *The Comanches*. Norman: University of Oklahoma Press.

WASHBURN, W. 1975. *The Indian in America*. New York: Harper & Row.

———, editor. 1973. *The American Indian and the United States* (4 volumes). New York: Random House.

———, editor. 1964. *The Indian and the White Man*. Garden City, N.Y.: Doubleday.

WAUCHOPE, R. 1962. *Lost Tribes and Sunken Continents*. Chicago: University of Chicago Press.

WEAVER, M. P. 1972. *The Aztecs, Maya, and Their Predecessors*. New York: Seminar Press.

WEBB, W. S. and R. S. BABY. 1957. *The Adena People*. Columbus: Ohio Historical Society.

WEDEL, W. R. 1963. "The Plains and Their Utilization." *American Antiquity*, vol. 28, pp. 1–16.

———. 1961. *Prehistoric Man on the Great Plains*. Norman: University of Oklahoma Press.

———. 1941. "Environment and Native Subsistence Economies in the Central Great Plains." *Smithsonian Miscellaneous Collections*, pp. 1–29.

WELTFISH, G. 1965. *The Lost Universe.* New York: Basic Books.

WENDORF, F. and J. J. HESTER. 1962. "Early Man's Utilization of the Great Plains." *American Antiquity,* vol. 28, pp. 159–171.

WEYER, E. M. 1932. *The Eskimos.* New Haven, Conn.: Yale University Press.

WHITE, D. R., *et al.* 1971. "Natchez Class and Rank Reconsidered." *Ethnology,* vol. 10, pp. 369–388.

WHITE, L. A. 1975. *The Concept of Cultural Systems.* New York: Columbia University Press.

———. 1969. *The Science of Culture.* New York: Farrar, Straus.

———. 1959. *The Evolution of Culture.* New York: McGraw-Hill.

WHORF, B. L. 1956. *Language, Thought and Reality.* Cambridge, Mass.: MIT Press.

WILLEY, G. R. 1966. *An Introduction to American Archaeology: North and Middle America.* Englewood Cliffs, N.J.: Prentice–Hall.

———, editor. 1956. *Prehistoric Settlement Patterns in the New World.* New York: Viking Fund Publications in Anthropology.

——— and R. BRAIDWOOD, editors. 1962. *Courses Toward Urban Life.* New York: Viking Fund Publications in Anthropology.

WILSON, B. R. 1973. *Magic and the Millennium.* New York: Harper & Row.

WISSLER, C. 1911. "The Social Life of the Blackfoot Indians." *American Museum of Natural History Anthropological Papers,* pp. 1–64.

———. 1910. "Material Culture of the Blackfoot Indians." *American Museum of Natural History Anthropological Papers,* pp. 1–175.

WITTFOGEL, K. A. 1957. *Oriental Despotism.* New Haven, Conn.: Yale University Press.

WOLF, E. 1966. *Peasants.* Englewood Cliffs, N.J.: Prentice–Hall.

———. 1959. *Sons of the Shaking Earth.* Chicago: University of Chicago Press.

WOODBURY, R. 1960. "The Hohokam Canal at Pueblo Grande, Arizona." *American Antiquity,* vol. 26, pp. 267–270.

YARNELL, R. A. 1964. "Aboriginal Relationships Between Culture and Plant Life in the Upper Great Lakes Region." *University of Michigan Anthropological Papers.*

Index

Acculturation: accommodation movements, 302–304; Americanization of Indians, 276–277; antagonistic, 292; without assimilation, 284–286; borrowing and, 286–288, 289, 292; defined, 279; social organization and, 37–38. *See also* Assimilation

Adaptation: accommodation movements, 302–306; convergence and, 226; culture and, 15–16, 218–219; to environment, 40–42, 43–45, 226; preadaptation and, 218–219

Adena culture, 234–235

Adoption of captives, 110, 282

Adultery: Eskimo, 47–49, 52–53; Northwest Coast Indian, 147–148

Agriculture: Aztec chinampa farming, 177–178; calorie balance and, 33; female role in, 209–210; Iroquois, 99; irrigation and, 44, 86, 176–178, 224, 231, 232, 233; Natchez, 163; Old World vs. New World, 229–230; origin of, 222–225; Plains Indians and, 118

Alcohol, Indians and, 93, 137

Aleut, 203, 241–242, 260–261

Algonkians, 62–79, 99, 108, 110, 121; art, 42; language family, 247–248; primitive Northern, 62–63, 122; wampum belts and language, 245–246. *See also* Ojibwa (Chippewa); Penobscot; Sub-Arctic Indians

Amherst, Lord Jeffrey, 266

Anasazi culture, 232–233, 286–287

Animal(s): associated with Paleo-Indians, 207; ecological laws and, 218; extinction of, 203, 214–219, 274

Anne, Queen of England, insert

Anxiety, social function of, 73–74

Apache, 80, 118, 121, 233, 242, 274, 286–287, 305

Arapaho, 125, 131, 301

Arawak Indians, 258

Archaic cultures, 218–223, 231. *See also* Desert culture; Eastern Archaic culture

Arikara, 121

Art: Algonkian, 42; culture and, 152; earliest Eskimo, 42; Haida, insert; Mississippian, 237–238; Navajo sand-painting, 252, 288, insert; Northwest Coast Indians, 150–153, insert; Plains Indians, insert; Pueblo Indians, insert; status and, 150–151; totem poles, 152–153. *See also* Masks

Artifacts: carbon-14 dating, 323–324; Clovis, 211; in dating humans, 205–206, 240; Desert, 220; Eastern Archaic, 221; Folsom, 212, 240; geologic dating, 322–323; Plainview, 212–213; Sandia, 210; theories on similarities in, 225–230

Assimilation: acculturation without, 279, 284–286; chiefdoms and, 161–162; degrees, 279; Indian culture by Whites, 279–283; voluntary, 289–290

Athapaskans, Northern, 42, 62–63, 121, 242, 247. *See also* Sub-Arctic Indians

Athapaskans, Southern. *See* Apache; Navajo

Aztecs, 121, 154, 174–196, insert; calendar, 179, insert; cannibalism, 192; chinampa farming, 177–178; cities, 174, 176, 177, 178–180; clans, 184–185; class system, 146, 182, 184–187; Cortés and, 174–175, 178, 179–181, 183; cultural evolution, 176–177; fall of Empire, 180, 193–196; gods, 175, 179, 191; maps, insert; nobility, 184, 185, 186; occupational classes, 185–186; power of ruler, 182, 186–187, 195; priests, 187, 189–190, 191; religion, 189–193; rites, 189–193; socio-political

347

ABOUT THE AUTHOR

PETER FARB, when he wrote the first edition of *Man's Rise*, had already demonstrated a deep knowledge of the American land and the American Indian. His continued involvement in anthropology and the other social sciences —as shown, for example, by *Humankind* (1978) and by the publication in recent years of his widely acclaimed *Word Play: What Happens When People Talk*—has made this revised edition even more authoritative and readable. Mr. Farb, in addition to membership in many anthropological societies, is a Fellow of both the American Association for the Advancement of Science and the Society of American Historians. He has taught classes about the Indian in American culture at Yale and lectured at many colleges and universities.

READ THE BOOKS THAT MAKE A DIFFERENCE

Fiction and non-fiction, here are the books that tell the stories of America's minority groups—personal stories, documented accounts, past and present experiences. They affect us all—don't miss them!

☐	2609	**STRANGERS AT THE DOOR** Ann Novotny	$1.95
☐	12101	**AUTOBIOGRAPHY OF MISS JANE PITTMAN** Ernest J. Gaines	$1.75
☐	11516	**SOUL CATCHER** Frank Herbert	$1.50
☐	8095	**MACHO!** Edmund Villasenor	$ .95
☐	T10619	**FAREWELL TO MANZANAR** Jeanne Wakatsuki Houston & James D. Houston	$1.50
☐	11979	**BURY MY HEART AT WOUNDED KNEE** Dee Brown	$2.75
☐	10371	**THE INDIAN HERITAGE OF AMERICA** Alvin M. Josephy, Jr.	$2.25
☐	10617	**THE BLACK POETS** Dudley Randall, ed.	$1.95
☐	10621	**BLACK RAGE** William H. Grier & Price M. Cobbs, M.D.'s	$1.95
☐	10747	**ISHI, LAST OF HIS TRIBE** Theodora Kroeber	$1.50
☐	12252	**I KNOW WHY THE CAGED BIRD SINGS** Maya Angelou	$1.95
☐	11520	**UP FROM SLAVERY** Booker T. Washington	$1.50

Buy them at your local bookstore or use this handy coupon for ordering:

The world at your fingertips

Leading historians, sociologists, political scientists, economists, and anthropologists offer personal and political analyses of the world's developing lands.

Bantam Book Catalog

Here's your up-to-the-minute listing of over 1,400 titles by your favorite authors.

This illustrated, large format catalog gives a description of each title. For your convenience, it is divided into categories in fiction and non-fiction—gothics, science fiction, westerns, mysteries, cookbooks, mysticism and occult, biographies, history, family living, health, psychology, art.

So don't delay—take advantage of this special opportunity to increase your reading pleasure.

Just send us your name and address and 50¢ (to help defray postage and handling costs).